Immortal Highway

Immortal Highway

A Memoir

Jon Magidsohn

IGUANA

Copyright © 2015 Jon Magidsohn
Published by Iguana Books
720 Bathurst Street, Suite 303
Toronto, Ontario, Canada
M5V 2R4

Publisher: Greg Ioannou
Editor: Kate Unrau
Front cover image: Léonie Cronin
Front cover design: Meghan Behse
Book layout design: Kathryn Willms

Library and Archives Canada Cataloguing in Publication

Magidsohn, Jon, 1968-, author
    Immortal highway : a memoir / Jon Magidsohn.

Issued in print and electronic formats.
ISBN 978-1-77180-142-3 (paperback).--ISBN 978-1-77180-143-0
(epub).--ISBN 978-1-77180-144-7 (kindle)

    1. Magidsohn, Jon, 1968-. 2. Magidsohn, Jon, 1968- --
Family. 3. Father and infant--Biography. 4. Bereavement--
Psychological aspects. 5. Authors, Canadian (English)--21st
century--Biography. I. Title.

PS8626.A373Z53 2015   C813'.6   C2015-906693-X
                                              C2015-906694-8

This is an original print edition of *Immortal Highway: A Memoir*.

For Myles

Prologue

To find the beautiful

"What are you going to do now?"

That was the question of the day at the Celebration of Sue's Life. Though I'd never asked it of myself, everyone else seemed to want to know what I'd do next. But it wasn't asked as if the bottom had just fallen out of the box containing my life — *Oh no, what could you possibly do now that your life is over?* It wasn't like that. And it wasn't like wanting to know what I was going to do immediately after leaving this place — *So, are you going to catch that band at the El Mocambo tonight?* It wasn't like that. They had recognized that this day marked the beginning of the rest of my life; that I was about to undertake the most arduous transformation.

What do you think you'll need to do to help you through the next bit? It was like that.

So what was next for me? I was focused on the Celebration of Life; the world hadn't existed beyond Saturday. Sue had been dead only six days. I was sad, that's all I knew. But as soon as the first person asked me that question, the answer spontaneously fluttered out of my mouth.

"I'm going to take a trip." *Huh? Where did that come from? I'm going to what?*

Then the next person asked me the question and more of the answer came out.

"I'm going to take a trip. Yeah, Myles and me."

Then the next person.

"Sue and I were planning a holiday to celebrate the end of her life as a cancer patient. So we're still going to do that, Myles and me."

"What are you going to do now?"

"We're going on a road trip. I've never been to the American Southwest. I've always wanted to see Monument Valley. I've got family I can visit along the way. Maybe I'll make it out to the west coast."

By the time the sun began to set I had the whole itinerary planned. The summer would be a good time to travel. I could use the intervening three months to settle into a routine with Myles, who was barely six months old. I would also have time to sort out Sue's loose ends and some of my own. But on this memorable day I figured out what would propel me into the next phase of my life: moving forward. I would pack Myles into the car and just drive.

I had a plan.

At the end of July, three months later, after all the emotional preparations were done and there were no urgent tasks to complete, we were ready to go on the Road Trip of Undetermined Duration. Myles was now nine months old. The dog, Mika, and two cats, Sydney and Seattle — Sue had named one after the character from *Melrose Place*, the other after the film *Sleepless In ...* — were sent off to their respective minders, the goodbyes unceremoniously broadcast, and advance emails sent to the people I'd planned to see along the way. I couldn't wait to hit the road — "*Frapper la rue*," as Sue used to say.

The night before we left I read Myles a story, sitting in the antique rocking chair Sue had insisted on putting in the corner of his bedroom, and lay him in his cot, where he fell asleep in an instant. I walked out to the front porch, sat down, and put my bare feet up on the smooth banister. In the humid night air I cracked open the blank journal I'd just brought home and turned to page one.

July 30, 2003 - Toronto

Dear Myles,

Instinctively I spoke to Myles; my pen simply wrote his name just as my voice and thoughts had so recently become most accustomed. I smiled. I will tell him my story, I thought. Our story.

We start this book at the beginning of an adventure of sorts. Tomorrow you and I are heading out on the road. You won't remember it but hopefully it's just the first of many road trips we will take together. I hope you will read this one day and gain some understanding about me ... and yourself. Much the same way I hope to gain some understanding about your mom and what I'm supposed to do without her.

So we begin.

Part I

The Great Affair

"He did not expect an answer and yet wept because there was no answer and could be none."

— *Leo Tolstoy,* The Death of Ivan Ilych

1

Our family grew faster than we'd anticipated. No sooner had we learned we were to be parents than we were nursing the nascent breast cancer. It was like having twins.

From the beginning, like some biblical tale, Sue's pregnancy was enigmatic, almost mythical. For forty weeks she nurtured another life while barely clinging to the reins of her own. With complete faith, conjured out of desire for a long life, she kept the spectre of sickness in check just long enough to sustain the lifeblood of the person growing inside her. Pregnant, she appeared chosen, as the original woman herself. Our son within that mystical pool of fluid — floating among the bulrushes, eyes closed tightly in a kind of prayer — was the only obstacle preventing a guarantee of killing the cancer. Sue glowed, as expectant new mothers do, with joy in a future of which she may have had no vision.

Those forty hallowed weeks of gestation began, by Canadian standards, normally enough. Sue and I had both started new jobs and had just moved into our new house in Toronto's west end. We shared the news of the pregnancy with our respective families, brought together so that neither side would feel slighted to hear it second. Our delight was tempered only slightly by the memory of Sue's first pregnancy, which ended in a spontaneous miscarriage on a long, hot night during a camping trip the previous summer. But now, only one whirlwind spring later, we had won the middle-class trifecta — house, career, baby. Our lives were moving along as planned and everything seemed, at least so far, normal.

By the time Sue's pregnancy had gone to term, the enemies of normal surrounded us. For forty weeks our son, we feared, had been swimming in a pool of cancer. For twelve of those weeks, anti-cancer concoctions were thrown into the pool. Our efforts to neutralize seemed to be going strong, but we were on the outside. Inside the warm, swirling incubation fluid — infused, we worried, with cancer and anti-cancer alike — he was alone. Throughout the countless hospital visits, we believed that our son would hold his own and that everything would end up, if not normal then, as normal as possible.

* * *

Summer crept closer like a crippled kitten. Each day lasted a week; every week a month. My daily tasks generally revolved around Myles's needs, which I'd become quite adept at satisfying. Somehow I'd take care of my own needs along the way. I was anxious to set out on our road trip, but in the meantime I had to settle Sue's estate, such as it was. She hadn't left a will. She wasn't supposed to die.

If I'd had the energy and focus to commit to it, I could have completed everything in a day or two. But it took weeks, ten or fifteen minutes at a time. It was tedious work that involved explaining my situation to a series of generic customer service representatives from banks, insurance firms, credit card companies, and anyone else who had Sue's name on a mailing list. There was always a perfunctory expression of condolence followed by a more sincere gasp as they looked at their files and realized they weren't talking to an octogenarian. For some reason, probably self-pity, I'd imagined credit card balances would be struck after someone's death. But I was obligated to pay off all debts in Sue's name, not that there were many. First I had to wait for the life insurance benefit, which could only be paid after they determined, through Sue's medical records, that we hadn't taken out the policy after she was diagnosed with cancer. It wasn't enough that my wife had died, now I had to prove it. To the minute.

Months later I was still getting unsolicited phone calls for Sue from any number of enterprises. It was a mistake they only made once.

With the paperwork wrapped up, I could put more effort into preparing for our road trip. I had most of June and July to make sure I had everything we would need, a shopping list that mostly included bulk quantities of mental preparation. As much as I looked forward to being on the road, I wondered if I would have the wherewithal to ensure that Myles and I would be safe. Moreover, would that much time out of my comfort zone — away from the sanctuary of my home and the steadfast support of loved ones — provide the kind of solace I was looking for?

Summer in Toronto, as any Torontonian will concede, means hot, humid days followed by long, restless nights. Unless you subscribe to the local code of air conditioning, which is "if you can't store meat in your living room, it's not cold enough." Some days the newspapers run articles outlining the dangers of spending more than a few minutes outside unless you constantly hydrate. People complain about the relentless heat, praying for a respite as the sun burns the grass on their manicured lawns, all the while forgetting that in six months they'll be damning the dry, sub-zero air that crystallizes their nostril hair within seconds of stepping outside, and the ice storms that make their commutes to work treacherous and stressful. As the annual cycle repeats, they seem once again caught off guard by the return of the sticky summer heat.

This particular summer, when I had more than enough time to sit inside my refrigerated house pondering my life without Sue, I spent as much time outside as possible, hydration be damned. Often, while Myles was with a grandparent, I went for long, early-afternoon runs through High Park, the sun at its peak. Breathing was akin to drinking hot soup, and my sweat-soaked shirt weighed me down. But I didn't care. Could I have had a small sense of immortality? *Other people died. I just live on to suffer without them.* The searing heat was responsible for countless deaths every summer, just as the petrifying cold was in winter. But I never saw a weather forecast I didn't ignore. The summer sun always drew me outside. Besides, I couldn't just sit around feeling sorry for myself. There was work to be done.

With three more weeks before Myles and I were to leave on our road trip, I decided to rebuild the front porch. The tired structure had seen better days and, beyond being an eyesore, it needed some essential improvements. I always feared that one day the mailman would fall through the rickety porch floor, landing on his tailbone amid the broken glass and mouse nests on the dusty ground below. It was a project I'd wanted to tackle since Sue and I had moved in over a year earlier.

It started with a solid *thwack* from the crowbar into one of the decaying banister supports. Steel on soft wood like a paring knife into an apple; like flesh, I imagined. The banister came down easily. Too easily, I thought, from a construction perspective, but it felt good to render something useless. I had been drifting in my shadowy realm, rotting from the inside like the banister. Now I had found a way to turn the tables. *Take that, you piece of crap — you see how it feels for a change.* The fragments of timber accumulated on the front lawn. I moved on to the floor planks, grey and weathered with an unlimited supply of toe splinters for anyone brave enough to walk barefoot over them. One by one they cracked like ribs under the heavy blows of my crowbar. With each swing another bead of sweat wept from my forehead, my chest, my armpits, until I was drenched and gasping for breath in the humidity, standing on the porch's skeleton under the summer sun.

Sue was constantly on my mind as I worked. The house — our house — still rang with the echoes of her footsteps and her clear voice. I imagined her inside, talking on the phone or making the decor "just so" while she made faces and waved to me through the living room window. Then she'd put some music on, loud enough for me to hear, and sing along at the top of her lungs as she fluttered around the house. Occasionally she would come outside to see how it was going ("Wow, look how much you've done!"), tolerating my sweaty moans with typical mockery: "*Pauvre petite crotte*," she'd say with perfect French intonation. It was her favourite saying she'd picked up from her time in Aix-en-Provence. "Poor little turd." Then she'd bring me a cold drink, kiss me, and thank me for doing the hard labour.

Among the ruins, panting and taking stock of the budding blisters on my hands, I paused for thought. For the first time in over a year, I was in control of my world. I was solely responsible for the destruction in my life. Only I would destroy the house's feeble appendage, and only I would be responsible for rebuilding it. I accepted being sad. I cried at the thought of my new-found control. I cried at the exhilaration. I just cried. I was in the process of reducing myself, like the porch, down to my basic components: wooden joists, brick, dust — *body, mind, spirit*. I had my tools: crowbar, saw, hammer — *grief, time, Myles*. And once I had gone down as far as I could go, only then would I be ready to build myself up again into a stronger, bolder, shiny new me: timber, nails, paint — *health, hope, happiness*.

Aside from playing with Myles, constructing the new porch was easily the most fun I'd had since Sue died: the smell of freshly cut timber, the satisfying feel of deck screws penetrating a new board. It was like piecing together a monumental jigsaw puzzle that would stand forever as a testament to my struggle and progress. By the time it was finished, it looked exactly as I'd hoped, given my skills: not perfect but strong and orderly. The new porch stood where the old one had been, and that was all it needed to do.

The following week I rebuilt the back deck.

* * *

The night before the Celebration of Life, I'd left Sue's parents' house and gone home to search for the ideal picture and poem to print in the program. I pored over every page of every photo album, starting at our year one. There was the picture taken on the ferry to Prince Edward Island; another in our backyard picking raspberries; I liked the one with our two cats; there she was pregnant. I finally settled on a picture from Sue's journalism school graduation. In it she's wearing her navy-blue Ryerson University gown with its white-and-gold sash, looking coyly back over her shoulder at the camera — at me — bestowing her inimitable smile. The sun is brilliant, lighting up her golden hair and the deciduous backdrop. She looks beautiful, proud, happy. And very much alive.

One of Sue's favourite poets was P. K. Page, by whose words, Sue often told me, she'd been moved when she'd studied poetry in university. I sat on the floor in front of the bookcase in our tiny spare room upstairs and read every page in two of the poet's collections, finally settling on an excerpt from a poem called "Sleeper" in which Page beautifully elicits the pleasure of getting ready for bed, fluffing pillows, welcoming the heaviness of head and eyes, and rising from the body in a transformative dream state, leaving the dreamer "alone upon a bed."

As I read it, I could see Sue getting ready for bed, her nightly ritual: washing, preening, making sure the bedsheets lay flat. Or was the poem about me? The final stanza uses *his* not *her*, as if I had chosen the poem as some sort of bodiless declaration. Because while I thought of Sue as a "gentle dreamer … softly in eiderdown" in some fantastical hereafter, I was the one who was "alone upon a bed."

Outside my window the street was quiet and I thought I heard birds. It was nearly sunrise by the time I'd finished my mission with the photos and books. Sitting on the floor amid the debris of my research, a heavier weight bore down on me than when I'd started. All around me were photographs, books, furniture, clothing, pets, scattered files, and other paraphernalia that had been Sue's or ours. Everywhere in the clutter, Sue was there, but she wasn't there. I wanted to hoard it all. Or throw it away. I was now the curator of all things Sue.

This was the first time I realized the task in front of me. Not the emotional task — nobody can plan for that — but the laborious task of sorting through Sue's precious belongings. Sue kept everything. In our basement, for example, were two jumbo-sized storage containers jam-packed with every greeting card Sue had ever received. Ever. Congratulations-on-being-born cards from 1963. Baby's-first-Christmas cards. Baby's-first-birthday cards. Baby's-second-birthday cards, and every subsequent birthday card from the past thirty-nine years. Christmases, Easters, graduations, Halloweens, Thursdays, and every wish-you-were-here postcard from anyone Sue had ever known who'd gone on a holiday. Thousands of cards stored collectively but sorted chronologically and by occasion, should the need ever arise to access any of these historical documents. The only cards I wanted to keep were the cards I had given to her, which she'd kept in her dresser drawer tied together in a red ribbon.

I managed a couple of hours sleep and then drove back to Sue's parents' house. Sue's mother, Joyce, and I went to the funeral home to offer payment and submit the poem and photograph for printing.

"That's a pretty picture," the woman said.

"It's a spectacular picture," I said. Nothing short of the most unreserved adjective would do. Sue was the most beautiful woman in the world.

Later when I collected the programs I was also given several copies of a document, on which an official-looking round stamp had been embossed. At the top of the page was written "Proof of Death."

"Why do I need proof?" I asked. "I was there."

* * *

"What do you want after you die?"

Sue and I lay in her bed during one of our frequent afternoon trysts, looking up through the skylight at the leafless maple silhouetted against the pale blue. We were still in the no-holds-barred stage early in our courtship. Learning about each other was like digging for gold. Her question wasn't my idea of pillow talk, but Sue had five years on me so I was convinced that being in a mature relationship meant talking about grown-up things like mortgages and death.

"I want to be cremated," I said.

"Yes, me too. But I mean what do you want to happen? Do you want there to be a funeral?"

"Something like a funeral, I suppose."

"Like a party?"

"A party? A party might be nice."

"I want a party. Definitely. A big party for all my friends and family. I can't stand the solemn funeral thing and I don't want anyone standing around moping. Just have a big party for me, okay? There can be music and everything."

We never spoke about it again. Her willingness to discuss funeral arrangements and reincarnation disappeared the moment she was diagnosed with breast cancer. The fear embedded in her reality quelled the fantasies of parties and music. But since dying wasn't part of her blueprint, there was no need to plan a funeral. We focused instead on making plans for a healthy future. It had been ten years since she'd made that request, but here I was, about to throw this party in her honour. Still, I didn't think I would be able to select any adequately suitable music. Adhering to her wishes it couldn't be solemn ruled out most music that initially came to mind. Anything more upbeat might seem inappropriate and I doubted anyone would be in the mood for dancing. Either way, I wanted it to feel less like a memorial and more like a party so we rented a hall and phoned the caterers.

And she thought I never remembered anything she said.

Pulling into the parking lot of the Burlington Arts Centre, where the Celebration of Life was to be held, the blinding sun reflected off the chrome and glass of the parked cars and the pale tarmac. If I'd believed in the afterlife, like Sue did, I'd have said she was trying to make my world a little brighter. But the sun only made the shadows bolder. I was met by a group of my work colleagues, other sales reps from the designer-textiles company I'd worked at for the past year. The five of them walked along the line of parallel cars to offer their condolences and blinked with the cringing anxiety of having to face me. I looked away from the pain reflected back at me in the mirrors of their eyes.

Inside the arts centre, an unassuming, hand-lettered sign welcomed us into the concrete building with an arrow pointing the way, as ceremonious as if it were announcing a meeting of the local chapter of one-legged toothpick repairmen. But at least we knew we were in the right place. The L-shaped room that we'd rented was not pretty, but it didn't need to be. Nobody would be looking at the room. There was a giant collage of pictures Sue's sister, Nancy, had put together the night before. We hung it on the wall opposite the floor-to-ceiling windows that let in the midday sun and lit a hundred Sues: pictures with her family, with me, and with the numerous friends she'd collected. There were Sue's baby pictures and pictures of Sue with her baby. I knew then, as I looked at her life in pictures, why this would be a celebration and not a funeral.

As I stepped up to the small podium and switched on the microphone, I was greeted by 200 sets of eyes — more mirrors.

"Welcome everyone. I'm so glad you're all here today," I said, pausing as people scuffled around, inching closer to the front. "This is a great day."

I believed that, and I paused to let the guests consider what I meant. As sad as I was, I still revelled in the ability of human beings to gather out of love, out of joy in celebration of having known another human being, and in sharing their happiness in spite of the occasion.

"This is a great day because we are celebrating Sue … and it's very clear to me that we have a lot to celebrate. Not the least of which is all of you. Wherever Sue went she made good friends; people whose friendships she nurtured even after she moved on to other places… There are friends here today who have come from as far as Vancouver and Washington, DC. And you've proven that her life is worth celebrating."

The room was silent but for a few sniffles, including my own. I could have dissolved right there and would have been happy to do so — crying made me feel like I was shielded by an armour of solace — but I kept hearing Sue saying, "A party … not solemn." I took a deep breath.

"Look over there, at all those pictures of Sue with her beautiful smile … She hated her picture being taken without her knowing; she never wanted to be caught candidly … with food in her mouth or something. So she always insisted that she be allowed to smile. In every picture she's smiling for eternity.

"And if there could ever be any doubt about what Sue's legacy is, all we have to do is look over there at Myles." Two hundred people turned their heads to watch Myles in his buggy wearing his blue OshKosh overalls and bare feet. He was smiling up at both of his grandmothers, who each held one of his little hands. "He embodies everything I'll ever need to remember about his mother. Nobody can ever take that away from me … that much I know. And that's why this is a great day."

I looked down at my hands resting on the podium. I folded them together forming a finger-lined cordon around my wedding ring.

"Please stay and talk about Sue," I said. "Enjoy her memory."

For the rest of the morning we did talk about Sue. It wasn't at all solemn. My broken happiness was slowly restored by the hugs and smiles and laughter. For a short while I didn't want it to end. I would have been delighted to stay and talk about Sue until the Burlington Arts Centre kicked us out. I would talk about Sue with anyone who knew her. I'd talk about her until there was nothing left to say and then find someone who didn't know her and talk about her some more. Everybody should know about her, I thought. That way she would live forever.

It didn't seem so absurd to me that Sue would request music at her party. If she'd been there, she would have danced in death as she did in life.

There were more people at the Celebration than there were at our wedding. Sue would have loved that. People laughed, and children ran around. The sun continued to shine. The gathering left me with the comforting realization that Sue would go off in all directions — to

Vancouver, to Washington, DC, and to points in between — and would live on in the people who loved her.

Myles and I would go off in all directions too. In response to the steady 'What are you going to do now?' inquiries, I had a slightly more comprehensible vision of what came next. It really was a great day.

2

Myles sat on the lawn, bare toes tickling the grass, sunhat firmly on his head. He was nearly camouflaged in his green-and-blue striped outfit. If it wasn't for the ever-present smile, his four teeth glistening in the sunlight, I might have lost him in the expanse of the backyard. My big boy, nine months old and growing by the minute, looked like a tiny toy out there.

He crawled over to the raspberry bushes that poked through the fence from our neighbour's garden and secured a morning snack. Thankfully the brambles didn't prick him. Neither did the rough grass, which scratched his knees but left no mark. Myles's pain threshold, it seemed to me, was extremely high. I'd seen him crawl on pavement and even gravel, but as I gritted my teeth in anticipation of the scabs I'd be nursing, he always continued unscathed. Too often, while carrying him on my hip through the house, I'd carelessly knocked his head on a door frame, but he never cried. I wondered if his exposure to anti-cancer chemicals in utero — the chemotherapy Sue underwent while she was pregnant — had zapped him with invulnerability to a superhuman degree. I half-expected to see him throw a rogue berry over the house at turbo speed.

Occasionally Myles turned to watch me trudge between the house and the car, the back doors of each remaining wide open as I shuttled back and forth — one way with my arms full, the other way empty. The Toyota RAV4 slowly filled like a jar of jelly beans. From floor to ceiling, front to back, everything we would need for a month on the road. Or two months, who knew?

The contents were basic essentials: a bag with a week's worth of my clothes; a larger bag of Myles's clothes; a bag of toys; his stroller complete with detachable canopy and transparent rain shield; a folding cot sheathed tidily in its navy-blue nylon case with white racing stripes; another bag of toys; a case and a half of his favourite formula; two bags of diapers; maps; snacks; our brand new baby backpack; all the other necessary baby paraphernalia including bottles and bibs; and, of course, Doggy Dog, Myles's constant companion.

In the glove box I stored our passports, our birth certificates, my cellphone (which never worked outside Ontario), and Sue's death certificate for placating any suspicious border guards. Driving into Canada is rarely a problem, but damned be he who tries to enter the US of A without proper identification, documentation of provenance, and proof of shoe size.

Of prime importance was my CD wallet, filled with forty-eight discs carefully selected during a two-hour collection-filtering session the night before. If I was going to be on the road for who-knows-how-long, I was going to need an ample and varied supply of music to satisfy my discriminating taste. Actually, forty-eight seemed inadequate to me. If only I'd found a CD wallet with more than twelve pages. Better still, if only someone could have invented a small, portable, digital machine onto which I could have loaded all of my favourite music without prejudice. But since I was a pre-mp3 music lover, I had whittled my extensive collection down to a meagre but significant forty-eight discs, many of which I simply couldn't have lived without.

There were Joe Jackson, Elvis Costello, and the Police, the meat in my musical sandwich. Ninety degrees from that spectrum were John Mayer, Stevie Wonder, and some old-school Jethro Tull, at once melodic and driving. For those more meditative moments we had Paul Simon and Bruce Cockburn, with welcome additions from Miles Davis and Mozart. There was a discernible lack of despondent music: no acoustic, twanging, singer-songwriter, folky introspection. No Joni Mitchell or Leonard Cohen. Neither of the Nicks: Cave nor Drake. There was music I could scream along with, music that could transport me to other worlds, and music from people I'd been lucky enough to have as friends. My playlist — "Songs from the Healing Tour," I called it — was upbeat and roadworthy. If I had been stranded on an actual desert island, this collection would have been sufficient. The CDs sat at arm's-length in the front seat, along with the snacks, maps, and baby formula. I was ready to go. It was July 31st, just over three months since Sue had died.

I locked the back door of the house, picked Myles up off the grass, and strapped him into his rear-facing baby seat in the back seat of the car.

"Ready, Superman?" I asked. Myles's jovial eyes told me he trusted me unconditionally and was ready for anything. I loved that look. "Good. Me too," I said.

Any whiff of diaper doody emanating from the back seat would immediately be masked by the RAV4's still-potent new-car smell. I'd driven it home for the first time just a few weeks earlier after trading in the old purple Ford minivan. The van had served me well when I had my upholstery business, and it had also sufficed as a family vehicle, but by the time I'd committed to the road trip I realized I needed a new ride. With over

200,000 kilometres on the odometer and visits to the
dealership every three months for various mechanical
problems (FORD: Fixed or Repaired Daily), I knew she
wouldn't be too reliable on a long expedition. I was the
only person I knew who'd traded in a minivan for a
smaller car *after* having a baby.

That first day's drive was essentially a warm-up, a
rehearsal for the rest of the trip. It would be no longer than
the four and a half hours it would take to get to Windsor,
Ontario, where Sue and I had lived for three years as she
began her career in broadcast journalism. Almost all of the
driving was due west on Highway 401, the scourge of
Ontario motorists that stretches between the Quebec border
and Windsor. It's as straight as a pencil but not nearly as
interesting. The boredom factor that sets in on long drives
(the only thing to look at is the next exit sign, which you
regard with fervent delight as the exit numbers shrink) is
responsible for countless car accidents every year. Along
the way the 401 passes through rural towns with such
borrowed names as Cambridge, Chatham, and London, but
offers nothing of the rolling countryside of England's green
and pleasant land.

If a map of Southern Ontario is shaped like the petrified
skull of a cow, we were heading for the snout.

In Windsor I knew I would see some old friends and
Sue's former colleagues at the television station where
she'd worked, so it felt less like the beginning of our tour
and more like a trek down the road. Also I knew that if any
wildly impossible intricacies of travelling with Myles
became evident, Windsor would be an easy distance to
manage. Not that I was worried. Myles was as compliant in
the car as he was everywhere else.

At last I was moving forward. And that was the goal.

I put Joe Jackson's *Big World*, an album about global travel, into the car's CD player. The first song was "Wild West," a throwback to the acoustic guitar twangs of rail-riding vagabonds who sang about the days when America's western frontier was being explored and populated; about being far from home, missing loved ones, and wondering what awe-inspiring sights will greet them around the next corner.

"This is Joe," I said to Myles. He was less interested in the music and more concerned with the steady stream of Cheerios I handed back to him one at a time. "You're going to be hearing a lot of him. He's, like, the greatest musician ever, so you'd better get used to him. Listen. Are you listening?"

I tried making eye contact with Myles in the back seat as I spoke to him. Although he was facing backwards, there was a small, round mirror attached to the headrest in front of him, so I could see his face in my rear-view mirror. Occasionally he met my gaze, but mostly he looked out the window, squinting from the sun as fields and trees skidded by him. The long furrowed rows of farmland sped past us like the animated green legs of a giant running man. As the white lines strobed past me with meditative regularity, and I watched the approaching west, Myles's world retreated out the rear window to the east. We were always somewhere right in the middle of two endless horizons, about halfway between coming and going.

We stopped for a break, pulling into a truck stop near Woodstock. They had done their best to blend it into its leafy surroundings next to the Massey Ferguson tractor retailer, but it was just a truck stop. Once inside, three large fast-food outlets merged into one enormous grease pit. I changed Myles's diaper on a patch of grass beside the parking lot and then took the first photo of our trip: Myles sitting on the grass smiling in front of our jelly-bean-jar vehicle. He always seemed to know what the camera was for. *If you point that thing at me, I'm going to smile at it.* He smiled like one of those hairy, red-hatted gnomes that people sometimes pose in front of famous landmarks. *Click ... look where we are now.*

Sue and I had encountered one of those gnome fanatics when we visited Greece on our honeymoon. The ruins of Akrotiri on the island of Santorini had been buried by a volcanic eruption some time during the Bronze Age. While touring the ancient village of meticulously excavated buildings and relics, we witnessed a security guard running over to the couple next to us. He waved his finger at them and shouted *"Oki! Oki!"* — *No! No!* The woman reluctantly removed her precious plastic gnome from the crumbling five-thousand-year-old stone wall before her husband could snap the picture. We chuckled and for the rest of the trip we played "Spot the Gnome" when we found ourselves among a group of tourists.

Back in the car, Joe Jackson continued to sing about Monument Valley and the Rio Grande. I was sure I'd get there in a few weeks, but first I'd have to negotiate the monotony of the 401 and my troublesome tears, which made driving difficult. But then again, so did the blinding sun and the dependent nine-month-old behind me. I shouldn't have been allowed behind the wheel for all the distractions.

What lay beyond Windsor, Ontario, was mostly a mystery to me. My senses propelled me toward places I'd never seen but had always wanted to: Colorado, New Mexico, the Grand Canyon, the Painted Desert, California. It didn't matter to me how long it took to get there. Speed was not the object of this exercise. The maps only showed me the roads, but I would have to avoid the potholes, oil slicks, and hazardous forks. And for direction, I was on my own.

* * *

I scoured Myles's face for anything that looked familiar: a dimple, a glance, the shape of an earlobe, or any pore that held the genetic information to prove he was Sue's son. I craved evidence of that tenuous link to the past, to Sue, to "us." The string running through my life, tying one moment to the next, was severed when Sue died. It wasn't cut cleanly though because Myles, still whole, remained the tiny thread maintaining the fragile connection. The longer Myles and I spent together, the more he felt like "mine" and less like "ours." I didn't want him to be just mine, but the connection to Sue was growing ever more feeble even only three months after she'd gone.

He did have Sue's hands, which admittedly lacked the lithe charm of some women's hands. A few of her fingers were bent, a subtle dogleg at the top joint leaning toward the thumbs. Myles had these fingers too.

"Look, Jon," Sue said moments after Myles was placed in her arms for the first time. She was still panting and sweating on the delivery table. "He's got my crazy fingers."

We both laughed while we surveyed the rest of him.

"At least he has your eyes," she said.

"Every baby is born with blue eyes."

"I hope they stay blue," she said, gushing. "I hope he keeps those beautiful blue eyes."

He didn't. His eyes turned hazel and his fingers straightened out too. He just looked more and more like Myles, which was who I recognized in my rear-view mirror as we flew down the 401 at 100 kilometres per hour. But I found it awkward talking to him, which surprised me because at home I talked to him all the time. Whenever I dressed him, changed his diaper, fed him, went for a walk, or just looked at him, infantile chatter flew spontaneously from my lips like pee-pee from an infant's bladder. But there, locked together inside a moving vehicle, driving for the sake of driving, I was suddenly at a loss for what to say. He was a good listener, but the conversations were a bit one-sided. So I decided to tell him about the music coming through the car speakers.

"This is the Beatles, Myles ... like the insect, only spelled differently." No reaction. "Um ... John, Paul, George, and Ringo..." *Why are they always listed in that order? Myles doesn't care. Keep talking.* "Listen closely. These guys are at the top of the musical pyramid. Every popular musician today owes a debt to them." I may have exaggerated, but I was trying to make an impression on my oblivious back-seat prodigy. "Paul McCartney is one of the greatest rock singers of all time, Myles. And his bass playing is what made their sound unique on so many songs."

I finally caught his eye in my mirror and he smiled at me. He may not have made any sense of what I was saying, but I'm sure the music was getting in. He paid closer attention when I started to sing "Two of Us" along with John and Paul. I wondered if Myles sensed that we too were riding in the direction of nowhere. Or if, like me, it even mattered to him.

"You can check out the words later, Myles. But for now just listen to the melody. It's all about the melody. If you don't have a decent one you may as well not have a song."

Even though many of my favourite musicians happened to be excellent lyricists, I rarely paid close attention to the words. I'd always been grabbed by catchy melodies and interesting arrangements. But Sue said she'd always heard the lyrics first and then decided whether or not she liked the song. So I started to listen more closely to the poetry behind the melodies, and suddenly there was more for me to enjoy in the songs I thought I already knew.

At home, Sue always sang along with her favourite songs, her voice resounding in various degrees of dissonance, bouncing off our parquet floors. But now my voice — only mine — thudded against the car upholstery and plastic dashboard. The Beatles sang as my memories stretched out longer than the road ahead.

As Myles and I drove into Windsor, I kept singing and talking and passing on my invaluable musical knowledge. But I'd stopped checking to see if he was listening.

The anticipation of returning to the place where Sue and I had set up temporary roots was tempered by the obvious changes in my life in the year and a half since I'd last set foot there. Though we'd settled in well with the community in Windsor and with Sue's colleagues from the television station, few of our friends there had made it to Toronto for the Celebration of Life, and they'd never met Myles. When Sue and I moved to Windsor, the town was undergoing a regeneration of sorts: the auto industry was thriving, the new casino had just opened, and the local economy was strong. We watched the long waterfront along the Detroit River evolve from a neglected eyesore with boarded-up buildings and wasted land into around five kilometres of pedestrian-friendly parkland. As Windsor flourished, so did we; we'd been married nearly four years. Initially we only had ourselves to rely on, which brought us closer together. Before long we felt like Windsorites, and occasionally I even found myself entertaining the idea of staying there forever.

However, I'd wager most Torontonians would have difficulty locating it on a map. Windsor is like Toronto's neglected younger brother who always gets into trouble, never grows up, and misbehaves for fear of being ignored. The fact that Sue and I managed to live there for three relatively happy years has continued to baffle me. Having grown up in Canada's cultural capital, I suppose we found it quaint to live in a town with only two movie theatres and one concert hall, a place where you could easily drive across town in less than ten minutes and where people actually said hello to you on the sidewalk. Despite its proximity to Detroit, Michigan — or perhaps because of it — Windsor was proudly Canadian, and Sue and I became staunch advocates of our new home. At least until we outgrew it.

The lingering sense of fondness I had for Windsor was strictly due to the experiences Sue and I had shared there. My memories of the place were intertwined with those of my wife. But now, here I was going in without her.

The 401 was about to end, swinging up toward its terminus in central Windsor before the road continues toward the tunnel to the USA. Instinctively I got off the highway at Walker Road — the second to last exit — and continued north into town, past the airport, the Silver City megaplex, the pet shop with the misspelled sign ("Kitten's For Sale") and the Chrysler plant. Without thinking I turned left onto Ottawa Street and then another quick left onto Windermere Road. I parked the car across the street from where Sue and I had lived and turned off the engine.

"There it is, Myles," I said. He was looking the other way. "That's the first house your mom and I bought together."

The house looked smaller than I'd remembered, the brown brick darker, the vanilla paint paler. The wide detached facade didn't seem so wide. The fire hydrant had been painted. In the front yard stood the young maple tree, the top branches of which were just tall enough to be seen from our bedroom window. We used to pretend we were sleeping in a tree house.

"We worked hard to get that house. Houses are expensive, Myles, and require the services of lawyers and banks ... but you don't need to worry about that. The day we moved in was a beautiful, sunny spring day. But by the evening it had started to rain. Quite hard. Your mom and I went outside and gazed at the rain from the shelter of the front porch. We had always wanted a house with a porch like this one. She grabbed my hand in the dark as we both stared out into the rainy street. And she quietly said to me, 'We did it.'"

The entire street seemed older, as if our leaving had relegated this area to a forgotten, sepia-toned ghost town. I was a visitor to my own past.

Just around the corner was the train station where friends and family from Toronto used to arrive when they visited. Some of the train tracks continued along the river to the Hiram Walker distillery, home of Canadian Club rye, its iconic C.C. logo visible from the Detroit side of the river. We'd spend weekends down at the river — the Festival Terrace — where we'd sit and listen to live music or watch the fireworks during the Freedom Festival every summer. We saw concerts by Leon Russell, Ashley MacIsaac, Jeff Healey, and others.

The sun rapped at my side window and awakened me from my daydream. I got out of the car, stretched, and walked around to get Myles from the back. I carried him in my left arm, his right arm around my neck, baby bag over my right shoulder. Myles carried Doggy Dog. Slowly I walked toward our house, then glided past it and rang the bell next door. Bonnie was expecting us.

Myles and I spent two hours with our old neighbour. Husky-voiced, silver-tressed Bonnie, who first greeted Sue and me with a tin full of freshly baked cookies the day we moved in, and who fed the cats when we were away. She had just retired from a long career in the offices of "Chrysler's," as they say in Windsor, and she lived with her elderly mother.

"Jon, he looks just like Sue," Bonnie said as Myles crawled around her nicotine-stained carpet, Doggy Dog in tow.

"Do you think so?"

"Just look at his smile," she said. "That's Sue's smile."

She was right. He did have her smile. I'd never noticed because everyone said he looked like me. But Sue's distinctive smile was clearly visible on Myles's little face — the same lips, the same gentle arc, the dimples. Was Bonnie's memory of Sue clearer than mine?

"Do you remember Lucy and Allen's son from two doors down?" she asked.

"Of course," I said. Actually I had almost no memory of them at all. Was it the family with three kids or the one with the only child?

"Yes, Darryl. He's gone off to the University of Waterloo on a full science scholarship. And their other kids are doing well too."

She continued to update me on who the new mayor was and about such-and-such shop on Ottawa Street that had closed. I didn't feel like Bonnie's neighbour anymore and not just because we'd moved away. She, like all of Windsor, had been relegated to a history I no longer felt attached to. My life had bounded over a pothole-infested road, tossed me about like an infant without a seatbelt, and landed on a completely different road heading in a different direction. It wasn't Bonnie's fault, but I didn't belong there.

Despite it feeling like centuries long gone, Windsor was as familiar as the feeling of holding Sue's hand. It represented a block of time in our lives as memorable as every other. More than anything, it was something we had shared. The big moments with Sue in my life stand tall and proud whether they were happy or sad, brazen or subtle. And every moment with Sue was big. Or at least it seemed so.

The moment we met, an innocent happenstance in the late summer of 1992, was one of the biggest. One Sunday evening I made my way through the Toronto sunset to the Bathurst Street Theatre, where a bartender-actor friend of mine was performing in a play that was closing that night. It was a small, forsaken church turned into an even smaller theatre, so when I took my seat in the second row just off to the left of the thrust stage I was nearly at the back. As the lights dimmed and the actors took the stage, a man and woman came in and sat directly in front of me. I tried to ignore their uncharitable sounds drowning out the first lines of dialogue and shuffled in my seat so I could see the action between the heads of the two latecomers. I enjoyed the play and praised my friend MaryPat — always known as MP — when she came out into the lobby afterwards. I chatted with some other friends whom I'd met there, including MP's boyfriend, Terry, before being introduced to some strangers.

"Jon, this is my friend Susan and … sorry, Simon is it?" MP had clearly never met the tall, lanky ginger-haired fellow before.

I shook hands with this Susan and Sorry Simon, politely trying to bury my annoyance in recognizing them as the pair who stumbled in late for the performance. We exchanged how-do-you-dos and went together for an *après*-theatre drink in the closest bar. I spent most of the time talking and laughing with Terry, a fellow musician with whom I'd always gotten on well. We most likely criticized the crappy music playing in the bar. I feared our boisterous guffaws didn't impress MP and her friends, who sat nursing their cranberry juices while they quietly talked about acting and travel. They rarely looked in our direction.

But I noticed Susan even though most of the night she was in profile. She wore a white blouse with a frilly collar buttoned to the top, and sat with her back straight, her hands folded on her lap. Her shoulder-length chestnut hair was swept off her face and held in place by a thin band. She was without a doubt more mature than me, though I hadn't guessed on an age, and Sorry Simon was clearly older still. What struck me most, though, was something I wasn't sure I could identify. What was it? Grace? No, she was too flat-footed to be graceful. Harmony? Gravitas? I thought she was shy but quietly confident, composed, and articulate. Poise. That's what it was. She seemed to have that in abundance.

At the end of the night I congratulated MP again on her performance as she went off with Terry, said goodbye to Susan and Sorry Simon, and stumbled home to my ground-floor apartment on Euclid Avenue. I slept alone, as I had nearly every night for the previous two years. It was a despondent spell of singlehood in which I'd been languishing, the only benefit of which — and a dubious one at that — was that I never bothered washing my sheets. Who knows what I dreamt of that night on my bedraggled futon, but I'm certain it wasn't about marrying the woman I'd just met.

For more than two years, MP and I had worked together at a restaurant on the Danforth in Toronto's east end. We commiserated over the discontentment of being struggling actors; although, I'd struggled significantly more than her, which is why I quit acting to focus on music — same struggles, different angst. After her play closed, she was back working at the restaurant, and a few months later we were the only two remaining Friday-night staff when a man and a woman entered. MP greeted them affectionately and sat them in a booth near the front. I barely noticed and went about my work until I was back at the bar.

"Jon, will you take these drinks over to my friends at table two?"

I recognized the woman by her smile and her hair as the poised one I'd ignored a few months before. She was striking, dressed all in black from her shoes to her hair band. I had to be reminded of her name.

"Hi, Susan," I said, dropping off the drinks. "Nice to see you again."

"Hi, Jon," she said with a smile that pasted bright red lip prints over my entire body. Like a wonderfully contagious yawn, her smile made me smile back. I wondered if she had to be reminded of my name too.

She introduced me to her friend — just a friend, not Sorry Simon — and I went off to do some work elsewhere. But I kept thinking about the smile at table two. I went back to chat, and not just because the restaurant was nearly empty. Susan wasn't as shy as she had been when we first met. She was looser, more relaxed. Infinitely more appealing. There was plenty of eye contact, familiarity, and banter.

"How long have you worked here?" she asked.

"Seems like forever."

"That bad, eh?"

"I shouldn't complain. It's not so bad … if you like going home every night smelling like old shoes that have been fried in grease."

Her friend faded into the walnut wainscotting as I forced myself to find more things to talk to her about. I had to have another fix of that smile.

"Where have you been tonight, then?" *Really? Is that the best you can do?*

"We went to see a film ... *Glengarry Glen Ross.*" She sang when she spoke.

"I hear that's good."

"Yeah."

Her brown eyes sparkled as she tucked her hair behind her ear. I'd always interpreted a well-choreographed hair-tuck as a crafty flirtation, a gesture equally coy and wholesome. And in this case, entirely welcome.

"You're a musician, aren't you?"

"Yes. I sing in a band. In fact," — *Oh, what a brilliant opportunity we've just been presented with!* — "we're playing tomorrow night at C'est What. Why don't you come out?"

"I'd love to," she said without hesitation, without pretense, and without checking with her friend. I knew she'd be there.

C'est What is a popular basement bar on Front Street near the lake, known throughout the city for its own microbrews as well as hosting a wide and often eclectic variety of live music. My band, Still Life, had managed to play fairly regular Saturday nights there, typically filling up the long and too-narrow room with people we could loosely describe as fans. The view from the stage had the best vantage point from which to scan the whole place, and my position on the stage, front and centre, was the best of the best. I spotted Susan as soon as she poked her head around the corner of the doorway. We were in the middle of a song, but I made a mental note to talk to her after the set. I didn't need much reminding.

"You guys are great," she shouted over the din. Everyone says that when they speak to a musician at a gig, whether they mean it or not.

"Thanks for coming."

"No problem. I'm really glad I came."

I bathed privately in her smile for a moment. Her face was warmly shadowed under the diffuse yellow lights in the dim basement. She looked me in the eyes when we spoke. I started to get that awkward nervous feeling I hadn't felt in a long time. The feeling you get when you start to think the other person might be thinking the same thing you are. I wanted to spend the time finding out for sure, but the band was expected back on stage. Sue came up to me afterwards.

"Thanks for inviting me tonight. I really enjoyed it."

"You're not leaving, are you? We've got one more set."

"Yeah, I need to catch the last subway home."

Somehow I remembered from our first meeting at the Bathurst Street Theatre that she lived in my neighbourhood. I even remembered what street it was: Madison Avenue. So when I offered to drive her home if she stayed to the end, she was impressed enough to accept.

After the gig we sat in a quiet corner finishing our drinks. My ears were still ringing from the hours of unnecessarily loud music, and my vocal chords grated with the rasping of overuse. But I wanted to stay up all night talking to Susan. She sheepishly began apologizing for her behaviour the night we met at the Bathurst Street Theatre.

"I wasn't myself that night," she said.

"Who were you?"

She smiled. "No, I mean that was a difficult night for me. That guy I was with was my boyfriend."

I'd completely forgotten about Sorry Simon.

"We'd had a big fight in the car and had actually broken up on the way to the theatre. He wanted to turn around and go home, but I was determined to see MP's play. Simon stubbornly said he was coming with me. So that's why we were late, and that's why I was so quiet that night."

"I thought you were just shy."

"No, I'm not a shy person." She was adamant about that. "Do you still think I am?"

"Not at all."

So it wasn't poise I noticed that night — not that she was entirely without poise. It was an intense display of restraint; a proud woman trying to keep it together, which, to me, was not an altogether unattractive quality. While people around the table that night were laughing and carousing, she could only just manage to speak above a whisper, anxiously keeping her hands folded in her lap for fear of them shaking. My first impression was completely wrong. Fortunately my second impression was perfectly sound. Susan was vivacious, honest, articulate, and lighthearted. There was an inviting buoyancy about her. And by this time I was fairly certain she dug me as much as I dug her.

The short drive from C'est What to Madison Avenue was electric, at least from my point of view: locked together like willing prisoners, elbows nearly bumping up against each other, trying to look at her in my peripheral vision while I drove, her breath fogging up the window, every sound she made amplified within the hermetically sealed vehicle. We came to our destination far too quickly.

"How old are you?" she asked.

Funny, I was the one wondering about her age. Strange how it seemed relevant all of a sudden now that I was getting ready to ask her out on a proper date.

"Twenty-four."

She chewed on that for a moment before saying, "I'm twenty-nine."

We both paused to do the quick arithmetic. Five years in your twenties, I thought, was nothing. We were both mature adults — well, we were both adults anyway — and it wasn't as if we were teenagers where five years is enough to qualify as strangers. *Just ask her out. Go on. You like her. You're attracted to her. But wait ... don't seem too eager. Be cool. Be cool.* I waited until I thought we'd paused enough.

"We live so close to each other ... we should get together for lunch some time." *Lunch? Really?*

"Um, yeah ... that would be nice."

We said good night in a courteous fashion, like two people who had just met. When I was left alone in the car I couldn't shake the sensation that she had been let down by my proposition. Lunch. Shit. I'd have been let down too.

* * *

The visit with Sue's colleagues at her old Windsor newsroom could not have lasted longer than twenty minutes. As with my old neighbours, I didn't feel very close to them either, but they, too, were happy to meet Myles as he crawled under the desks. I took a photo of him posed in front of a sign with the station's call letters. I used to love being in Sue's workplace; the buzz of news-gathering, editing suites, countless television screens, and broadcast apparatus were exciting to be around. And most of our local friends worked there too. But since we'd left, so had many others. Sue was gone and so was the buzz. It was time for me to leave Windsor forever.

My grandmother's oldest surviving friend, Melba, lived across the river in one of Detroit's leafy suburbs, long after most of her contemporaries had permanently relocated to Florida. Nearly ninety years old, she lived alone, still drove her Cadillac, and directed plays at her local synagogue. She made up for her stature — barely five feet in heels — by commanding a room with her bombastic voice and unmatched charisma. She was the closest thing to a grandmother I had left and had insisted we stay with her. You didn't say no to Melba.

I paid my toll and drove through the tunnel that wormed its way under the Detroit River. From the Windsor side, Detroit looks as inviting as any American city, all shiny skyscrapers and metropolitan flair. But arriving in downtown Detroit after the provinciality of Canada never ceases to shock. It's little more than a kilometre away on the map, but it feels like a different world. Since Henry Ford turned it into the Motor City in the early twentieth century, Detroit has experienced spells of boom and bust with dizzying frequency. To me, the city core, with Woodward Avenue splicing through the middle of it, never felt anything other than post-apocalyptic. Neglect and suburban development have left downtown Detroit in a constant state of tension, part ennui, part high alert. I know this city better than any other in the United States, due to my father and grandparents having grown up there. When I was a kid, my family drove down from Toronto to visit my grandparents and cousins a few times a year. So even while hit by the innate anxiety that dwells downtown, I knew how to quickly access the roads leading to the more savoury parts.

But first I had to face US Customs, which was like answering to the crafty Bridgekeeper in *Monty Python and the Holy Grail*. One wrong response and you'd be catapulted into the next realm.

"Citizenship?"

Not even a "Hello." The border guard stared at me as if trying to read my mind, stiff-necked in his starched pale blue button-down shirt with inexplicably military-looking epaulets. He'd just finished typing my license-plate number into his computer to see what kind of terrorist I was.

"Canadian," I said.

He bent at the waist to investigate the back seat. "Both of you?"

"Yes."

"Where do you live?"

"Toronto."

"Where are you going?"

Oh crap. Where am I going? And for how long? If I tell him I'm heading generally in a westerly direction until I reach the Pacific Ocean, staying at various cheap motels along the way with no clear idea of my itinerary, he may get slightly suspicious. There is, after all, a baby in the back seat. I don't really feel like going into all the details of my grieving process with a border guard in a tiny Detroit customs booth.

"I'm going to see a friend in Southfield." It wasn't a lie.

He continued to examine his computer screen then asked, as if it had just occurred to him, "Where is the boy's mother?"

"She's deceased," I said quickly. *Deceased? I've never used that word before.*

"Okay," he said.

He just waved me through and waited for the next car to pull up. Off I drove, merging onto Jefferson Avenue with equal parts relief and surprise. From downtown Detroit, the roads fan out in all directions. I went up the Lodge Freeway, a sunken highway that slithers its way northwest past 7 Mile Road, 8 Mile Road, 9 Mile Road … disappearing into the suburbs. A man and a baby had just entered a foreign country and didn't even need to show proof of the "deceased."

3

"Fronting a band," I told Sue, "is like being the lead dog in a team of huskies. When we're on stage, I feel like I have a big fat rope tied around my waist, and I'm pulling the rest of the band along behind me."

Still Life was started by some York University music students who wanted to play pop music with worldly influences. I wasn't the original singer, in fact I was the band's third, and by the time I joined the group it was an omnipresent voice on the Toronto music scene. For a while in the early nineties, its logo — an eyeball with a map of the earth for an iris, and long lashes that made it look like an angel fish — was almost as recognizable on posters around the city as Tim Hortons signs. I loved the band before I was given the opportunity to sing with them, so I jumped at the chance when Norm, Still Life's creative leader, called and asked me to join them. His songs were flavoured with rhythmic influences and time signatures from around the world: reggae, Afro-Cuban, ska, Creole, raga. "Ethnoclectic," we called it. My musical education blossomed during the seven years I sang with those musicians, and Norm, a guitar virtuoso with distinctive Mediterranean features and hair almost to his waist, became one of my closest friends.

Most of the time we performed like a well-oiled machine, shifting effortlessly and organically from one song to the next. But some nights, when perhaps the stars weren't aligned or the great god of live music wasn't smiling down on us, that rope around my waist was tied to five other smaller ropes, each attached to a different musician: two guitarists, bassist, drummer, and saxophonist. There I was, the budding rock star with my nose pointed into the wind, mushing and barking orders to my team as I pulled them through the blinding snow. It was empowering, if sometimes exhausting. Each set of songs we played was a voyage, and it was my job to take us from point A to point B. If we got lost along the way, I felt it was my fault. And I still had to hit all the high notes.

This voyage that Myles and I were on, however, was quite different. I still had the big fat rope tied around my waist, but this time I was the one being pulled. After a day and a half in the Windsor–Detroit area, I felt a mysterious tug and I knew I had to move on.

August 2, 2003 — Detroit

Dear Myles,

It's time to go. Sue always said to leave a party before it "turns." We should get out of here before I change my mind about Windsor. I think that this adventure you and I are on, Myles, is supposed to help me put my life into perspective. But I won't get any perspective by hanging around this place. You see today, for example, I realized that the Windsor part of my life, as special as it was, is long in the past. Sometimes that's where special things have to stay.

I'm looking forward to spending more time
alone with you on the road, just moving forward.
Then we will get into a real travel rhythm. That's
when you know you're in the groove.

The next morning Melba made us breakfast with scrambled eggs and bacon, which Myles and I ate while she shuffled around the kitchen in fuzzy slippers with three-inch heels. The place seemed clean to me but she still tidied, sorted, and stowed while she spoke. She had a play rehearsal to get to.

"Take your time," she said. "Make sure you get enough to eat before your long drive."

"Thanks. It's delicious," I said, still chewing. "Not sure how far we'll get today."

"Which way are you heading?"

"South. I think."

"Take some of these," she said as she plunked down a brand new box of Ritz Crackers, juice boxes, and some yogurt pots. "Myles likes them too."

"Thank you." I smiled at Melba.

"Your gramma would have done the same."

"I was just thinking that."

Melba and my Gramma Esther were alike in as many ways as they were different. They'd met at their local synagogue, studied Yiddish together, and loved the sun. They both looked after their husbands, who, it seemed, never quite appreciated the lengths their wives went to. But Melba was in a different tax bracket. She travelled more, went out more, and spoiled her grandchildren more. She also had a self-assurance, the type rarely seen in a nearly-ninety year old, that Esther could never quite aspire to.

After breakfast I packed up the car and Myles and I said goodbye. Melba craned her neck up at me, grabbed my cheeks, and kissed me like any grandmother would have as I hunched over to hug her.

"Thanks for coming to see me," she said with a lovely smile. "Now hurry up. I gotta go."

We left the familiar surroundings via Interstate 75. Once you get outside the "Mile" roads of Detroit and into the verdant back roads, southeast Michigan has legitimate beauty. Numerous lakes, small enough to swim across, surrounded by spruce and oak trees — archives of their own history — flank the roads. It could be some faraway wilderness. An hour later I'd left Michigan and entered Ohio. A hard morning rain had passed and the sun climbed to my left as I eagerly drove south. I rolled down the window and stuck my elbow out, the wind rushing across my face and through what was left of my hair.

There wasn't anything to look at on the interstate, just the grey guardrails meandering over the flat ground, trees scorched by the midsummer sun mingling with ubiquitous billboards. I became hypnotized by the steady reminders of the next approaching Walmart or Dairy Queen. Each town had the same stores in the same suburban strip malls with easy access from the same interstate. All that corporate America had succeeded in doing was to assure me that in an emergency I was never more than fifteen kilometres from a Home Depot.

I curled up deep inside my head and let my body do the driving. One thing I couldn't drive away from was the void Sue left in my life. What became painfully obvious was that losing her also meant I'd lost the future I was supposed to have with her. Both of our lives, our shared past and our anticipated future, had come to an end.

Sometimes people describe their moods using expressions of altitude. In elation they walk "on cloud nine" or are "high as a kite." In sorrow they are "down in the dumps" or in "the depths of despair." My experience would be more accurately defined by degrees of density. Thick or thin. Opaque or transparent. Murky or lucid.

My head was heavy with the thick rubble of grief. The walls around me solidified and became impenetrable from the inside. I walked around with a pickaxe in my hand, swinging hysterically at the thick stone walls like a claustrophobic miner hundreds of metres underground. But the more I struck, the worse it got: the walls grew thicker with each blow and my dark chamber only grew tighter around me. With each chop of my axe I envisioned a tiny ray of light shining through a newly opened pore in the rock. But instead it just got darker, the stone walls expanding like the universe. So thick.

Even my body felt thick. Physically I had the sensation of being overfull, sated with a melancholy whose volume never ebbed. Like a balloon ready to burst. In fact it did burst, frequently, but instead of the balloon rupturing beyond repair, it just filled back up again instantly. My legs felt heavy on my slight frame. When I ran, it was as though I were pulling myself along by sheer will, by the simple desire to never stand still. I even put on weight, a first-time phenomenon in my life; I had been the same size and weight since I was 16 years old. But suddenly I was eating alone, hastily preparing frozen ready-meals with too few vegetables, following them with ice cream right out of the tub. My thick mood also held the weight. With everything I was trying to rid my body of — tears, sadness, hopelessness — my body found something it could hang on to.

Thick, too, was the path to progress. Looking to the future was like walking through waist-deep mud in the pouring rain wearing a rusty suit of steel. I was thick with grief and I couldn't wait until my body felt less pulled and more able to push.

The first step in thinning all this thickness was to leave Michigan. Almost everything from here on was going to be new territory for me. Surely, I thought, the exploration, the adventure, and the acceptance of the unknown could only help.

Sue was curled up with me as I drove, all soft skin and smiles. She just looked at me and held my hand. Images started to take the form of television news clips with Sue staring directly into the camera, microphone in hand, reporting in her favourite silver jacket. Memories spun like psychedelic slide shows with swirling melodies in the key of Sue.

At the centre of this kaleidoscope — it was as vivid as if I'd been watching it projected onto the road in front of me — was the moment I walked up Sue's front steps on Madison Avenue to take her out for the first time. I'd been looking forward to that moment all week. In my anticipation, the week passed in super slow motion with dreamy schemes of perfectly choreographed romance. I wanted this to be the best first date in history.

I had long harboured an unfulfilled quixotic teenage notion about first dates, mainly based on never having been out on one. To this point, I'd met all of my girlfriends at school or at a job. First dates never came into play; we'd just hit it off and became a couple. But this was different. With Sue I imagined long-winded conversations about movies, animals, and philosophy. I imagined subtextual glances across a table of fine French food and clinking wine glasses. I imagined sweeping her off her feet with my wit, charm, and general "desirable-ness."

"Just be yourself and don't blow it," I kept telling myself as I showered, shaved, and looked for something cool to wear. Based on the questionable fashion of 1992, I had few options, but I settled on black corduroy pants with a black-and-white patterned button-down shirt. On my feet I wore my still new-smelling leather cowboy boots, which I'd purchased a couple years earlier in Calgary, Canada's home of cowboy culture. I convinced myself I was hip, handsome, and hunky.

I slipped on my leather jacket and headed out the door into the November dusk to collect Sue at six o'clock, as promised. I drove the dozen or so blocks to her place and parked a few houses away. She rented a third-floor apartment in a grand, red brick house in the trendy and youthful Annex area of Toronto. I pressed the button triggering the buzzer in her apartment and I waited, expecting to hear another buzz signalling me to enter. But she caught me by surprise, appearing at the door with a smile.

"Hi," she said, swinging the door wide open.

"Oh … hi. I was … I mean…"

"What?"

"No. Ummm… I thought…"

"Come in."

"Right. Okay."

Still trying to find enough words to form complete sentences, I tripped into the entrance of her building. Sue was slick and refined as she led me up the stairs to give me a tour of her cozy shoebox apartment. She was dressed all in black — long-sleeved tunic, slightly Madonna-ish frilly skirt over black leggings, pointy-toed low-rise boots that were *de rigueur* — and freshly swathed in the jasmine and

sage of Miss Dior. She walked a bit heavy-footedly but
with purpose, not clumsily.

"Well, this is it," she said, welcoming me into her snug
apartment. I could have almost touched opposite walls if
I'd stretched out my arms.

"It's … cute…"

"Small."

"No. Well, yeah. I mean…"

"I had to find it quickly in one weekend when I came
down from Ottawa to get a place. The rent is good, but it's
so much smaller than my Ottawa apartment. I even had a
balcony there."

"Yeah. Toronto prices…" Like I knew anything about
real estate.

"I'll just get my coat," she said, disappearing into
the bedroom.

I looked around again at the colourful furniture and
decor. She had two tub chairs upholstered in lemon-yellow
vinyl that barely had the leg room to be occupied across
from the two-seater sofa that took up one entire wall. There
was no distinct colour scheme, and yet everything seemed
to match. I heard a clock ticking from the kitchen. From
where I stood, I also spied a clock in the bedroom, one
beside the tiny television, and through the open door to the
bathroom, one in there too. I noted we still had time before
our dinner reservation.

I stopped at a photograph hanging on the wall near
the kitchen.

"That's my sister, Nancy," Sue said, coming out of the
bedroom with her black wool coat on.

"She's very attractive," I said.

"Mm-hmm," she hummed as she opened the door for
us to leave.

I had complimented the wrong sister. This was not intended to be a feature of my long-anticipated ideal first date.

We went back down the stairs, exited the building by the side door, walked down to the sidewalk, and turned left. A few seconds later I pointed to my blue Corolla, parked comfortably at the curb.

"That's my car."

"Oh," she said, slowing her pace.

"I figured we should take the bus down to the restaurant since we're likely to have wine with dinner. I don't want to drink and drive."

"Okay." Then an awkward silence as she walked past the car and caught up with me, looking down at her feet.

I could tell immediately that taking the bus was not her idea of how to be taken out. But I was proud of myself for proving how responsible I was. Besides, as Sue reluctantly pointed out, she had her own bus tokens.

Fortunately the wait for the Spadina bus, in front of the Jewish Community Centre at the corner of Bloor Street, was a short one. During that brief time, however, a friendly but pungent homeless man approached Sue to ask her for some change. He already had a bottle in a brown paper bag in his hand, so she figured he was set for the night and courteously rebuffed him. All I could think was, *This guy is making me look bad.*

The bus ride down to Queen Street was noticeably short on conversation. Over the din of my thumping heart, I hoped that Sue, being new to Toronto, assumed this was the way things were done in the big city. According to the rules of my romantic first date, it was. But according to the expression on Sue's face — serious, dour, embarrassed (for me?) — big-city ways were seriously lacking. It was about this time that I considered I might have made an error in judgment regarding our transportation.

The interminable bus journey ended at Queen Street and, after a short walk, we arrived at Le Sélect Bistro in time for our seven o'clock reservation. I knew this restaurant well, with its grotto-like ambience and snooty French owner — *Le patron mange ici* — and was convinced it would help me impress Sue. When we sat down and were finally able to talk face to face, the conversation began to flow with a bit more ease. I ordered wine with as much flair as I could rally — I think it was Chardonnay because that was the only wine I knew — and I could tell Sue, in contrast to me, began to loosen up.

Le Sélect was famous for the bread baskets that hung from the ceiling over each table. The customers could lower the basket to the table on a simple pulley and then raise it again when the plates of food came, freeing up table space. I'd had practice at this manoeuvre so I was prepared to dazzle Sue with my basket-lowering proficiency. But on the first attempt, my elbow knocked against the table, jostling the thin rope, which upended the basket and spilled slices of warm sourdough everywhere including Sue's lap and the floor.

She yelped like a tickled puppy and then tittered as the patrons at neighbouring tables looked over at us. *What a great laugh. Sorry about the crumbs.* Our food arrived. Neither of us had any more bread.

"I'm really nervous," Sue said about halfway through our meal.

"Really? Me too," I said.

That should have put an end to my wretchedness. *She feels the same way I do, thank goodness.* We looked at each other as our smiles turned into nervous chuckles.

Then, unexpectedly, there was another awkward silence, as if voicing our nervousness to each other had merely aggravated the elephant in the bistro.

We spoke guardedly about our families, places we'd travelled, and, as anticipated, animals.

"I grew up with a husky," I said. "She lived to be fourteen."

"My dog lived to be fourteen too."

"Wow. What a coincidence." I was piling on the charm now. "I prefer big dogs. They seem like proper dogs to me. I don't get off on tiny toy dogs with names like Frisky."

Sue's face went blank, a silent pause inside a vacuum.

"My dog was a chihuahua named Frisky," she said.

In the history of awkward moments, this one couldn't have been more perfect. Sue laughed it off, like she'd done all evening, but I thought she was going to drop huge puppy-dog tears into her barely touched glass of Chardonnay. My peppercorn-encrusted swordfish didn't taste quite as nice with my foot planted in my mouth.

I spent a long time just staring at Sue's face from the other side of the table. I wanted to memorize it, swallow it up, sip by sip, until it was a part of my built-in lexicon of images. Her heart-shaped face caressed my glance like a warm hug. It drew me in with sponge-like efficiency, simultaneously emitting a confidence and maturity so bold as to nearly intimidate. Her eyes, deep brown and almond shaped, enormous and passionate, stared at me with relentless focus. Her graceful nose — the feature that Sue hated the most about her own face — pointed directly at me as if to say, "Hey! I'm talking to you." Cheekbones like pink marshmallows. Her shoulder-length chestnut hair was swept off her face and held by a headband, reminiscent of Audrey Hepburn in *Sabrina*.

But before all else it was her bright, beaming smile that made me tingle in all the right places. The curve of her upper lip, flawless and precise, sloped tenuously to each side until it reached the immaculate resolution of a precise point at each corner of her mouth. Her bottom lip, its right side drooping slightly lower than the left, was soft and voluptuous. The sideways chevron dimples on either side of her mouth, conducting infinity, accentuated her perfect smile. It arose with such ease and stood out from her face as if it had been embossed there. It was the smile of forever.

I was smitten. But my poor show in wooing had left me with a dreary sense of disappointment. My wit and charm had abandoned me in my hour of need. We never even discussed philosophy.

* * *

We went Dutch. It's difficult to justify now, but that evening it fit in with my desire to impress without being heavy-handed. *Here is an intelligent, independent nineties woman who surely doesn't expect me to pay for her meal just because I invited her out.* She pulled out a crisp fifty-dollar bill as I scrambled to gather enough money to cover my half of the tab. The look on her face was resigned with a hint of irritation. In the ensuing years, I would become quite familiar with this look.

We left the restaurant and entered the biting Queen Street night just as it was beginning to snow, silvery flakes twinkling in the streetlights. Despite being underdressed for the weather, I suggested that we go for a walk, mostly out of shame for the earlier Spadina bus ignominy. She agreed and we slowly sauntered east along one of the trendiest blocks in Toronto, acknowledging people not too much younger than us in their urban best: black clothing, hair of every conceivable colour, piercings, and lots of leather. We got to Yonge Street, the longest street in the world, and headed north.

"In the olden days," Sue said, "men always walked on the curb side. It was deemed more chivalrous."

"Yes, I've heard that," I said, realizing I was not, in fact, walking on the curb side. Then I added with way too much enthusiasm, "It was because people used to toss their chamber pots out of their windows into the gutter. Men didn't want the ladies to get splashed with … stuff."

Sue giggled. "I didn't know that fascinating detail," she said, and I quickly switched sides with her.

The wind picked up and I dug my hands deeper and deeper into my corduroy pockets for warmth. Before we knew it, we had walked more than three kilometres to Bloor Street and we were beyond the halfway point back to her home. We decided to keep walking, but we'd picked up our pace. For me it was to keep warm; for Sue, I feared, it was to get home, say good night, and close the door on the evening.

As we passed by the University of Toronto, one of the faculty buildings abutted the sidewalk enclosed by a two-metre-high red brick wall. The second homeless man of the evening was pissing against the wall, his runoff snaking onto the sidewalk. Sue, who was walking nearest to him — not on the curb side — nearly got her shoes polished before making a last-second sidestep to evade the rogue urine. I couldn't have been more uncomfortable if I were pissing on her shoes myself.

Sue invited me up for tea when we arrived back at her place on Madison Avenue. I accepted her invitation and followed her up the three flights of stairs, curious as to why she'd want to continue our date. As we sat in her tiny living room I made sure to avert my eyes from the photo of her sister.

By half past midnight I figured I'd pushed my luck far enough and stood up to leave. Sue walked me to the door, which was only three steps away from where we'd been sitting.

"Thanks, Jon," she said. "I had a good time."

Really? Is that what you call a good time? I made you take the bus and pay your own way and freeze all the way home. You'd have had a better time if you'd stayed at home watching reruns of Dynasty *and eating Chinese food with a plastic fork with clothes pegs stuck on your face.*

"Me too," I lied, looking into her eyes for instructions of what to do next. I opted for trying to leave with my so-called dignity and quickly bent down to kiss her on the cheek. I didn't think I'd earned more.

Slowly walking down the stairs I finally felt the full force of self-pity. I'd shown her a horrible time, and I expected never to hear from her again. But halfway down I heard a door open.

"Jon," Sue hollered from just outside her apartment.

I heard her heavy footsteps frantically racing down the stairs above me. I halted.

"Yes?"

"I, um … I have to let you out."

I looked down at the door with its traditional handle and remembered using it earlier in the evening. Grab, twist, push. I could do that myself. But if she wants to help me…

"Okay," I said meekly.

We took a few more steps down the stairs when she stopped me again.

"Jon."

"Yes?" I said, turning to face her on the stair above me.

"Let's try that kiss again."

With that she put her hands around my neck and gently pulled my face toward hers. I finally got to kiss those flawless lips I had been staring at all night. We stood there on the stairs, lip to lip, for ten minutes or more. I discovered I was exactly one step taller than her.

Somehow despite the misdirected compliments, bus ride, spilled bread, awkward conversation, random encounters with homeless men, and my escalating self-loathing, she had still wanted to kiss me. She'd saved the evening and set us off on a roller-coaster ride that would last ten years.

4

It was time to put some music on. I wanted momentum, enthusiasm, and vitality. I wanted road music. I wanted U2. Flipping through the CD wallet, I found what I was looking for.

"Listen to that guitar, Myles. Let it wash over you. Hear how the harmonics dance around the pulsing bass and drums. And right up front is the voice. Sincere, passionate, earnest. Can you hear the singing, Myles? That's the melody."

Myles was asleep. But the songs continued to take me places the interstate couldn't, their melodies drawing maps in my mind with a paintbrush flourish. One melody took me back to where I was when I first heard the song. The next one brought an image of twelve-year-old me with my ear pressed up against the small radio speaker on which I first listened to music. More than one song painted pictures of Sue, her peerless smile, dancing to the music, her eyes focused on mine as she took my hand. The music achieved what I'd hoped it would when I so carefully chose the CDs days before. It provided a much-needed dialogue with myself — every song a conversation — to counter the relentless, oppressive, self-pitying inner monologue.

By late afternoon we had reached Cincinnati at the bottom of Ohio, and I decided to stop for the night, checking into the first suburban Travelodge I came to. I had no intention of going into the city, which was, as far as

I knew, the home of Colonel Sanders, Les Nessman, and a baseball team that wore red. Across the road from the hotel was a Perkins restaurant where Myles and I went for some chicken and potatoes. Myles always ate with an epicurean smile on his face, and he never shoved food into his mouth without regard for table manners. Although he ate with his hands, he was tidy and he savoured every bite.

Sue never got to feed Myles anything other than formula from a bottle; he only started eating solid food after she died. The joy of watching Myles discover the myriad flavours and textures of what he was offered was reserved for me alone. He took two or three bottles a day, but when I had my meals, he enjoyed them right along with me. When I fed him pieces of chicken and watched him licking his lips, I couldn't help acknowledging that this was one more thing Sue was missing out on.

On the wall above our table hung a familiar-looking piece of tacky chain-restaurant commercial "art." White flowers, lilies maybe, atop long reedy stems in front of a shopping-bag-brown background. *Where have I seen this before?* It wasn't pretty hanging over the crimson-striped wallpaper, but when I got back to the hotel room I saw the same lilies on the cover of my journal. The painting that some anonymous artist had been commissioned to produce suddenly didn't look so bad.

So this is where the rope is pulling me. A Perkins in Cincinnati.

It was the first time I felt like I was meant to be on this trip. I'd been shown a sign — the painting matched my journal — and I chose to see it as one. Some might have called it fate or coincidence. I called it a Harmony Moment.

In our hotel room I spread Myles's toys out and let him crawl among them on the heavily trampled navy-blue carpet with its curious stains as I unfolded his cot under the window. The walls, painted hospital grey, were festooned with the type of paintings no gallery would clamour to buy. It wasn't a palace, but it was cheap and clean, characteristics matching the brief for this trip. Myles chose to throw a ball around with his Superman strength and chased after it, stopping every so often to chew on the corner of *Each Peach Pear Plum*, his book of choice that week. His omnipresent smile told me that he could play ball all night. He was teething, but aside from the soggy, masticated storybooks, you wouldn't have known. He never cried, never complained, once again proving his Marvel Comics qualities.

His cries were more nudges than commands, even as an infant when he woke up for feedings. "Pardon me," his noises said. "Sorry to wake you at this uncommon hour, but if it's not too much trouble, would you very much mind fetching something for me to eat? Thank you so much."

His temperament made tending to his needs a relative pleasure during those 2 a.m. meals. We'd leave a small light on all night so that none of us would have to wake in complete darkness. I'd scoop Myles up from the bed where he lay between us and carry him downstairs to fix his bottle. Then back upstairs to feed him in our bed so Sue could watch. She said she wanted to participate in the feeding since she couldn't nurse Myles. In the soft light we sat, propped up by pillows, watching our son eat.

At three months old, Myles was happily sleeping twelve hours a night. I would have too if Sue hadn't been waking up several times for other reasons.

"He's so good to us," Sue said.

"What do you mean?"

"I mean, can you imagine if we had one of those babies that cries all night? I think he knows."

"Knows what?"

"He knows what we need. He knows that I need to sleep at night and that you need to help me sometimes, so he'll have to wait. He's so good."

"He's the best." I smiled at both of them. My family. The best.

"I think you're given what you can handle," she said. "You're definitely given what you can handle."

Myles fell asleep just as easily in the unfamiliar cot in a corner of this strange hotel room. I was, as usual, grateful for his consideration, listening to his breathing as I sat in the quiet, dim room. I hadn't gone very far from home, but I already felt a world away from Toronto's claustrophobia. This was all different: the room, colours, sounds. The burden of grief, though far from vanished, was lighter on my shoulders.

August 3, 2003 — Cincinnati, Ohio

Dear Myles,

Today would have been your mom's 40th birthday. In honour of this day I am writing this instalment while sitting in the bathtub. I'll try not to let the water smudge the ink.

A hot bath was one of her three favourite indulgences. The other two were a cup of tea with lots of milk and sugar (I never could make it right) and a peanut butter sandwich. I used to sit on the bathroom floor and keep her company while she soaked in the tub. That's where we'd catch up. When she was sick with cancer, a bath was the only thing that could ease her pain. She would sometimes take three or four a day.

The only feeling stronger than the sadness I have for missing your mom is the feeling of sheer joy I have for you, Myles. You are only 9½ months old right now but I already know that you're a great guy. I am proud and thrilled to be your dad. I can't wait to see how you turn out, but I promise to enjoy every step of the way.

Sue used to say, "It's all about the journey." We're on a wild one, my boy.

* * *

The countryside got greener as I continued west and south. Hills began to tumble and multiply like kilometres of rolled-up carpet. It looked fresh compared to the parts of America I'd seen before. Through my blurry eyes, however, every cookie-cutter town, every exit ramp, and the strip of grey road stretching out in front of me remained hypnotically familiar.

I'd always been comfortable on my own. As a child I used to spend countless hours in my room listening to music and doing jigsaw puzzles. I never felt bored and I couldn't understand why my mother always encouraged me to call on friends or go outside. I liked it in my room. It was comfortable, and all of my things were where I had put them. The original MySpace. It wasn't very different when I'd grown up and worked in my upholstery shop on Pape

Avenue. I was on my own, all my tools at my fingertips, listening to music while doing what amounted to little more than assembling an elaborate jigsaw puzzle. I liked it there too, and I got paid for it.

The thought of travelling without a base for several weeks, despite my inherent laziness, was not intimidating. It gave me, among other things, permission to be alone at a time when I really needed it. And yet I wasn't alone. My son was with me. Myles and I were two-thirds of a family, but we were a whole one. I had everything I needed packed into my car and I was, for lack of a more suitable word, fine. I had music and Myles, my little puzzle, mysterious in his infancy.

But all this justification for being alone was no match for loneliness. I was so busy dealing with the Sue-shaped void in front of me that I failed to manage the debilitating seclusion hidden behind it.

I didn't know where I belonged. I was no longer part of the two-headed, two-hearted organism who laughed at dinner parties with our other couple-friends. Within our circle, my identity had long been merged with Sue's. From the outside I was, if nothing else, the husband of that pretty journalist lady. But what's half of a couple? You can't be half of something when the other half is missing. The half-ness slowly loses sight of what once completed it. It must eventually turn itself into something else that is, in a different way, entirely whole. Eventually the new me would swallow the old me. But I wanted the old me back.

I was a single dad, too, and not by choice. I was new — unfamiliar even to myself. Initially I thought that being a single father was probably no different, at least in practice, than being any other type of parent. We experienced the same emotions, the same challenges, and the same joys. But somehow we remained on the outside looking in.

Back in Toronto I searched for evidence that I could feel like every other parent, especially fathers. I read articles revealing the mysterious and secret pleasures of fatherhood, eagerly poring over them in search of anything I might be missing out on. But I found no answers. Their experiences were not mine. Just outside my house, hastily taped to a telephone pole, was a flier advertising the "Mom and Baby Café," a place for mothers and their children to go for snacks, music, and conversation. I was not invited.

I frequently found evidence that the sight of a father and his child was still exceptional to some people. I received comments that a mother would never get when she is out with her child. I'd get one of those "Isn't that sweet" looks from somebody — usually a woman. She might ask, "Is it Dad's day?" or even worse, "Babysitting?" Though I knew she meant no disrespect, I typically responded with a forced smile or some kind of noncommittal grunt, too indifferent to try to explain the truth. But once in a while, and with more frequency, I'd have the balls to say, "Actually, every day is my day." And it was.

I was a wandering member of a unique species, nameless and unclassified, and I wasn't getting any closer to understanding who I was.

A few months earlier I'd made an appointment to see my doctor. He was a kind, thoughtful man whom I trusted, even though I rarely saw him — my "annual" checkups typically being four or five years apart. But I had to start somewhere. I dropped Myles off at my sister's house and drove to his office not knowing what I'd say.

We sat opposite each other. He slouched in his chair and looked at me with his dark, narrow eyes. "What brings you in?" he asked, his voice chewing on what was left of his South African accent. And there it was: the question; the call to arms signalling the beginning of the march toward conquering grief. Let the real work begin, I thought.

"Three weeks ago my wife died ... and I'm really sad all the time."

He winced. "Oh boy. I'm so sorry. How did she die?"

"Breast cancer."

He winced again. "How old was she? Susan, right?"

"Yes. She was thirty-nine."

A hat trick of winces. "Of course you're sad," he said. "It's only been three weeks." It felt like three years.

I was already crying. When I told him about Myles, his wincing really got out of hand. I'm not sure what I expected from him, but his reaction prompted me to realize that my story — Sue's story — could profoundly affect people, not just me or my family and friends. That was enough to give me solace; I already felt less lonely. I hoped every step would be that easy.

He referred me to a psychiatrist colleague of his, who in turn referred me to a grief counsellor. The psychiatrist asked me if I minded that the grief counsellor worked out of a senior citizens' home. I thought about all the older people who need access to counselling, about those couples, lovers of forty, fifty, sixty years who'd never spent a day apart. I was thirty-five years old playing in an elderly arena. I told him the environment was irrelevant to me, I just wanted to get to work. This was my job now.

A few days later I had my first meeting with Dr. Cindy Grief: grief counsellor. I ignored the simmering absurdity. I also ignored the hospital-like starkness of the Baycrest Centre, in the heart of Toronto's Jewish neighbourhood, as I found my way up to her fourth-floor office. She was a quiet, thoughtful woman with a slight build and dark eyes that didn't smile. She looked as though she'd heard enough sad stories to last a lifetime, but she was still young — younger than me, certainly — and most likely fresh out of grief-doctoring school.

"So, why are you here?" was her first question.

Why the hell did she think I was there? To discuss ironically named mental health professionals?

"I'd like to try and make sense of my wife's death," I said after a deep breath. "Because right now it doesn't make any sense to me at all. I can't see any reason why she had to die. I'd like to try and understand my sadness and figure out how I'm going to get through it."

The cold fluorescent lights highlighted the paleness of Dr. Grief's face, which was framed by a shell of dark, straight hair. She sat perfectly still, her eyes hardly blinking as she stared at me.

"I want to put this period of my life into some kind of perspective; to figure out how this fits in with everything that has led up to this point and where I'm going from here. I need to feel like I'm healing."

The truth lay somewhere in that last sentence. It wasn't enough just to get through each day. There had to be a reason for going on. If I was going to be strong enough to raise my son on my own, I couldn't wallow in sadness. Grieving was an affliction that I had to remedy, otherwise it would simply trample me into submission. So I found myself prepared to engage in war with it. I just didn't have the ammunition.

"If I were a religious man," I told the blank stare across from me. "If I believed that everything was a part of some god's plan, then this might be easier for me. I wouldn't have to take responsibility for my sorrow because that would be a part of the plan too. But I can't imagine the kind of disease and suffering I saw could have been created — or allowed — by any merciful god."

Dr. Grief remained silent. She sat with her legs crossed, staring at me over her dark-rimmed glasses. The top of her chrome and plastic desk was bare except for one piece of paper (my "file"?), a pencil, and something I couldn't identify, like a flowery paperweight or snow globe.

"I don't know where to go from here and that frightens me," I said. "I'm completely paralyzed by sadness."

Occasionally Dr. Grief looked past my shoulder to the clock that was facing her. I wasn't allowed to watch the time.

"There are so many other things I'm sad — even angry — about, other than just Sue dying. I mean, we had long-term plans, you know, things we were going to do together. So now, as much as I miss her I also miss me." *Hmmm. That sounded good.* "I cry for her and I cry for the life we were supposed to have together."

Dr. Grief nodded. From my hard seat I looked out over the grey carpet, through the window at the building's air-conditioning units that loomed outside, blocking whatever light may have been inclined to enter. I learned one important lesson that first day: my sorrow was as much for losing a part of me as it was for losing Sue. I carried that with me all week, hoping to explore that topic the next time I saw Dr. Grief.

* * *

Maybe it was the endless stretch of grey road winding through the boring Midwestern landscape that inspired the questions. Because even though I'd told myself this tour was all about forward momentum, it began to feel like I wasn't going anywhere. The one-sided conversations with Myles in the back seat certainly magnified the fact that the seat next to me was empty. I'd spent so much time with myself, I was beginning to forget what it was like to have a partner. Reluctant as I was to admit it, my grip on Sue was slipping.

Loneliness crept up on me like a fiend. I thought I was coping well; I thought I was doing everything right. But the loneliness made me feel sadder and, even worse, full of self-pity. The reverberating blows of death would eventually dissipate, but I wasn't sure I'd ever cope with the loneliness. I knew that even so-called successful people could be some of the loneliest: movie stars with entourages at their disposal, the embarrassingly rich, princesses. I had considered myself a success simply because I'd chosen to marry Sue. I had neither fame nor wealth nor royal blood, but I did have intimacy, companionship, and true love. When Sue died, she took all the fruits of my success with her.

So this was where the strange contradiction started. Deep down at the bottom of that dark empty hole that Sue left sat jolly young Myles stretching his little arms out as wide as he could and saying to me in his own wordless way, "Here I am, Daddy, and I love you, and I'll hold your hand when you're feeling lonely, and I'll listen to your secrets, and I'll let you cry on my shoulder, and we can be a family." And if that hole wasn't in the process of growing persistently larger, he might just have been able to fill it up.

Myles was the ever-present counterbalance to the weight of sadness. He'd served that function for us even before he was born. The anticipation of his birth gave Sue and me something to look forward to during the long, wearying months of cancer management. We almost certainly talked more about our pending parenthood than of her illness. He saved us from the constant burden of fear and doubt.

After Sue died, he kept fulfilling his duty as my protector. The grief was manageable because of Myles, whether we were at home or driving through the middle of Middle America. I had to look after him so that he'd still be able to look after me. We trusted each other. I needed those moments when he'd wrap his arms around my neck and offer me intimacy. And those moments talking to him about music when he'd smile like a faithful companion. And when he'd look at me with the same bright eyes his mother had, and I knew there was love in my life.

August 5, 2003 — Marion, Illinois

Dear Myles,

It just hits me sometimes right out of the blue and the tears will start to flow. Today it was feeding you at a quiet rest stop, sitting under a tree for some shade. We had just taken a tour of a cave, and I reminded myself of how Sue was afraid of the dark and confined spaces. She would have hated that cave. I missed the feeling of her needing me to comfort her when it got too dark — like in a movie theatre or the planetarium or 200 metres underground in the Paris Catacombs. It gets harder as time goes on, yet it feels good when I cry for her. It makes me feel close to her. I need to miss her in order to feel her.

Driving through the Mark Twain National Forest in southern Missouri, I was testing out the four-wheel drive on my youthful RAV4. The tires hugged the undulating roads like they were on rails. I shifted into fifth gear, too high, I realized, for these winding country roads, but the power it gave me was irresistible. I drove faster than I knew I ought to, especially with my family in the car with me. The turns were tight and there was no paved shoulder. The scenery stretched into a blur as my vision narrowed, and my breathing grew shallow and quick. The trees stood up on their tiptoes like prickly, distended ghouls and raised their arms, joining hands over the road to form a tunnel. If there were any other cars on the road, I didn't notice them. All I saw was the next turn up ahead as I drove into it without slowing down. Then the next turn, and the next. The whooshing wind through the open window formed a helmet around my head. Time and distance became incalculable. My mouth went dry. Then my stomach lurched — the family curse. The old motion-sickness gurgle started inching its way up my esophagus, and I was forced to slow down. Normally if I'm in control of the vehicle, I can withstand the curves and blind crests. But I had driven perilously close to roller-coaster territory. The trees drew back into focus. I caught my breath. Myles was still asleep, none the wiser to my reckless interlude in rural Missouri.

* * *

The approach to Oklahoma City was, in a word, flat. There was no doubt we were in the prairies now. With no visible landmarks, it looked the same in every direction. Yet I wouldn't have called it featureless. The tall grass prairie rippled in the wind — the "amber waves" of song — and if we were lucky, we'd see bison grazing in the distance, somewhere in the blank landscape under the hovering sky. It was the perfect antidote to the crowded streets back home. I had room to breathe and a seemingly endless road on which to survey the possibilities of my future.

Oklahoma City appeared to rise out of the earth in the distance, sprouting like an enormous antler from the otherwise unblemished horizon. It approached with cartoon-like intensity, growing larger with every kilometre, and ultimately overwhelmed the swaying fields of grass and wheat. I'd heard radio reports that this had been a particularly warm and dry summer west of the Mississippi River, with drought and forest fires making headlines. Farmers struggled with the heat and with water shortages. The Oklahoma vegetation, in every direction, was baked in several shades of neutral, and the sky was stark white reflecting off it. But as we drove into the suburbs, things transformed before my eyes: front lawns were thriving, the flourishing trees providing generous shade. The barren, matchstick-straight highway had splintered off into winding, flora-lined rivulets of subdivided communities filled with skipping children and tinkling ice-cream vans. Ivy climbed up the brick of the two-car garages while water sprinklers danced their *pas de bourrées* over the verdant grass.

In this bucolic enclave lived my cousin Amy, her husband, Jason, and their daughter, Joelle. My extended family is small, Amy being one of only two first cousins, so we'd always tried to stay close even though we lived far apart. Joelle was born within a few months of Myles, so we had even more reason now. We hadn't seen each other for about three years and had spoken only occasionally, but I had no trouble inviting myself to stay.

Amy and Joelle met us at the top of their driveway. My cousin still had her baby face, but her black hair was cropped short and showed hints of grey. She wore a long cotton skirt, the same style I'd always remembered her wearing. Joelle, although fairer in complexion, was a mini-Amy, right down to the matching sandals.

"Hello, Cuz," Amy said with a smile as I got out of the car. I retrieved Myles from the back and Amy came over to coo. "Hi, Myles," she said and kissed him on the cheek. We hugged and then I returned the cooing to Joelle.

"How are you?" she asked.

"Okay." My default answer. It was the only response I could always say convincingly.

"How was the drive?"

"Fine. Nice."

"Where did you come from today?"

"West Plains, Missouri."

"Where's that?"

"I don't know," I said. Any small talk was welcome after the recent lack of adult conversation though it was clear I was out of practice. We'd only been on the road for a week, but being among family and enjoying some home-cooked meals was a welcome comfort. Myles had a playmate more his size for a change, and I was happy not to be sleeping in a motel.

We filled the days catching up on lost time, each getting to know the other's child. I talked about where I'd been travelling and where I'd like to go. She didn't assail me with questions about life as a widower, and I was grateful. We saw some local sights: the Oklahoma City Memorial, a moving park-side monument to the deaths of 168 innocent people, which left me cold — I wasn't in the mood to mourn anyone else's death — and the National Cowboy Museum (with one impressive room dedicated to its vast collection of barbed wire). As usual, Myles fell asleep in his buggy while touring the museum. He was still asleep when I loaded him into the car and started driving home. His cousin Joelle sat next to him, hoping he would stir. Finally she could take no more of his idleness and let us all know.

"Baby sleeping," she peeped.

Amy swung her head around from my passenger seat glowing with the largest maternal smile. "Oh my goodness, Joelle. Yes, the baby *is* sleeping." She kept smiling at her daughter as we drove on. I wondered why all the fuss over a sleeping baby. Then Amy said to me in a more grown-up voice, "That was Joelle's first complete sentence."

I was happy to have witnessed the grand moment, even though the complete sentence was only two words long. It was one of those moments parents remember like baby's first steps, baby's first poop in the toilet, baby's first time shaving. I shared Amy's excitement and quietly wondered when Myles would speak his first full-length, two-word sentence. I couldn't wait to talk with him. I wished we could discuss what he and I were seeing together out on the road. Instead I had to rely solely on my thoughts and trying to interpret Myles's facial expressions. I'd love to have known what his opinions were about the changing landscape, the driving, his dad. And the music. I wanted to talk to him about music and have him actually pay attention; we could listen to our favourite artists and go to concerts. We'd play music together too, singing and enjoying each other's voices. Maybe we'd form a father-and-son band, get interviewed by *Rolling Stone*, and tour the world, knowing that it had all started with this one little road trip.

But for now, baby sleeping.

On our last night in the suburbs of Oklahoma City, after putting the kids to bed, Amy and I sat facing each other in the dimly lit living room.

"So, you off to Santa Fe tomorrow?" She curled her bare feet under herself in the armchair and leaned on her elbow.

"No. I don't think I'll go straight there."

"My dad's looking forward to seeing you."

"Yes, me too," I said. I wanted to see my Uncle Jack, but I needed to see the open road first. After this brief reprieve, I craved our old driving routine again. "I think I'll take a more rambling route. Maybe go up to Colorado and then drive down from there."

Amy gave a pursed smile. She'd always been strong on empathy but occasionally, like everyone else I encountered, she clearly had no idea how to react to me. I'd become perplexing even to myself.

"Are you enjoying the driving?" she said.

"It's serving a purpose."

"Moving forward."

"Exactly." I stared at my feet and picked at my fingernails. If I were in a hotel now, I thought, I'd be writing in my journal.

"How are you feeling … generally?"

Generally? How could I define *generally* when every moment was different, moving from loneliness to fear to anger to love to adventure to misery, each moment diffused through a filter of grief. Generally wherever I was, I'd rather have been somewhere else.

"I'm sad."

"Of course you are. I can't imagine … I mean…"

"I hope you never have to."

Amy brought up examples of her own grief after losing her mother, my aunt Julie, who'd died just a few years earlier. But I discounted it. *Mother/daughter versus husband/wife — I don't think so.* Nobody's pain was like mine. It wasn't simply thinking that everybody's grief is different, which is true. I actually believed that I was the saddest person alive and I wouldn't be swayed. I didn't want to read anyone's books or hear about death on the news. I was convinced that in all of history's examples of lost loves through war, sickness, and misfortune, I had surpassed them all. I was the King of Pain, and I would reign over my kingdom of sadness with all the authority I had at my disposal.

My least favourite expression of condolence was "I know how you're feeling." *No, you don't. You have no idea how I'm feeling. Even if you've been sad before, that's your sadness, your loss. This is mine and I'd be quite grateful if you'd keep yours to yourself, thank you very much.* I hoped my cousin wouldn't use that phrase with me.

But I wasn't belligerent, not to Amy at least. I told her about the way we'd coped with cancer, about Myles's birth, and about Sue's last quiet moments. Amy only spoke when my long, wistful pauses invited her to.

"Do you think Sue's pregnancy affected the tumour?" she asked.

"It certainly affected how we treated it," I said, staring at the yellow carpet in front of my chair, avoiding the mirrors of her eyes. "But it was clear that it exacerbated the cancer. All those crazy hormones ... they accelerated the whole process. She was diagnosed just two months after we knew she was pregnant."

"You might not have even detected it that early."

"That's right. Sue gave Myles credit for allowing her to find the lump in the first place. He wasn't even born yet and she'd created this whole mythology about him." I smiled.

"She was so brave," Amy said.

"Yes." I considered this, figuring anybody faced with cancer would need a significant amount of courage. Was Sue any different just because I witnessed her bravery up close? "People have suggested to me that she basically gave up her life to save her son."

"Exactly. I'm not sure I would have had the selflessness to do that."

I thought there were fine lines separating courage from selflessness from foolishness. Sue certainly walked those lines and no matter how much I wanted to, I could never have cajoled her to land squarely in any of the zones. She thought she could please everyone, including her baby.

"Maybe it was selflessness, maybe not … I mean, look at all the contributing factors: her age, the miscarriage, new house, new jobs — the time was right to have a baby. To her it was, like, now or never. She didn't want to have an abortion just so that she could deal with the cancer because by then, if she'd even beaten the thing, she might be too old anyway. It wasn't going to get in her way. She wanted her child right then. So in a way … she was kind of selfish."

I replayed what I'd just heard myself say. Did I really believe Sue was acting selfishly or was I just playing down the heroics? And is there anything wrong with being selfish? Especially under those circumstances. Why shouldn't Sue want to do it all her way, regardless of whether or not she thought she was going to die?

I looked to see if Amy got my drift. She raised her eyebrows slightly and gave another pursed smile. I looked back at the floor.

"We talked about all our options," I said. "But ultimately it was her choice. Everything was always her choice. Big and small, from life-changing decisions to the most minor things. And nothing I ever said was going to change her mind." I heard Amy sniffle as I thought of Sue's iron-willed decisiveness and — sometimes — stubbornness. "I loved that about her."

"There was a lot to love about her," Amy added.

5

Inside the oncology wing of Toronto's Princess Margaret Hospital, it is forever dusk. The dim fluorescent bulbs always glow at half power, keeping the ward in a constant gloaming. It suggests there are things the hospital doesn't want its patients to see. Why shine a light on cancer? Sitting in a small, grey room off a long, grey corridor with grey doors leading to other small, grey rooms, the scenario is obvious. It's all about setting the right mood. Who wants to be submersed in all the colours of the rainbow when you've just received bad news?

Sue and I had walked that corridor once before, the previous week. It hadn't seemed so off-putting then, only slightly inconvenient. The small lump she'd found in her left breast definitely needed to be checked out, but we had been assured by Sue's GP that cancer was "way down the list" of possible diagnoses. It was most likely due to her hormones going crazy. Sue was four months pregnant.

"It's probably just a cyst," Sue said to her parents over the phone. "But we have an appointment to see an oncologist so we can rule out cancer."

She sounded confident and undaunted. I followed her lead.

Dr. Callaghan, the oncologist, was a withered, elfin woman wearing Birkenstocks below her white lab coat. She affirmed the lump was benign, also chalking it up to the pregnancy. But she performed a biopsy anyway. "Just to be sure," she said. Before we left, she showed us how to dress the biopsy incision, which she'd left open in order for the excess fluid to drain. I'd have to change the dressing three or four times a day — Sue was too squeamish to even look at it. I didn't mind the task of dealing with the wound on Sue's breast. I felt necessary. A husband, I thought, must be a part of his wife's languishing (besides occasionally being responsible for it). Between the pregnancy and the possible cancer, everything was happening simultaneously inside her body, so that tiny opening was my way in.

Later in the week we were invited back to Princess Margaret to hear the biopsy results. I held Sue's hand in the slow hospital elevator to alleviate her slight claustrophobia. She didn't appear nervous. I was. The elevator doors opened onto the corridor at the far end of the oncology wing. It was quiet that day among the greyness. Every door we passed was closed in cellblock uniformity. If hospitals were people, this one would be a high-school principal with an intoxicated liver: certainly esteemed, but you wouldn't want a private meeting with him, and you could be sure that whatever was going on inside couldn't be good.

"The results of the biopsy were not quite as expected," the kindly doctor said after we'd barely sat down.

"What does that mean?" Sue asked. I knew what it meant.

"It's cancer. And…"

"Well, it's not a death sentence," Sue said, straight-backed on her chair.

"No, it's not. You're absolutely right. These days most cancers are eminently treatable."

"So what do we do?"

There was a short pause as Dr. Callaghan considered her response. "If you weren't pregnant…"

"But I am pregnant."

"Yes, but if you weren't…"

"But I am."

"I know." The doctor paused again to evaluate whom she was up against. "You should know that you have the option to…"

"I'm not having an abortion."

Sometimes, albeit rarely, Sue could be talked out of her decisions. I was used to looking for the clues that there might be a chance she could change her mind: she'd speak softly, looking off into the distance and playing with her upper lip between her thumb and pointer finger. But there was none of that telltale uncertainty here. I tried to concentrate on the dialogue between Sue and the doctor, but I had already imagined the worst. Sue may have too, but within an instant she decided she didn't want to know about the tumour, what stage of cancer it was, or what influence it might have on her pregnancy. She didn't even try to catch my eye before she asserted her decision to keep the baby. I hadn't said a word, but even if I had, it wouldn't have made a difference. As usual she had the final word and I knew it. From that moment, I realized it was my job to back her up and, at least until the cancer was gone, little else.

That was usually my job. We had developed this pattern of behaviour early on in our relationship. I'm not suggesting she took more than she gave, but I definitely gave more than I took. She was the conscience in our relationship. Holding my tongue became a way of showing my devotion to her. Quietly, passively, I tried to be the perfect partner by not rocking any of the several boats she had on the water. She couldn't bear to be contradicted. If she was, she'd remind me why she was right, why I was wrong, how our marriage hinged on being aware of the difference between right and wrong, and that the entire world order under our roof depended on my never contradicting her ever again. So really, it wasn't worth it. But it was my decision to stand by her and I did it willingly. I never felt harassed or abused, and my love for her — always authentic, never compromised — still grew.

I didn't want the abortion either. This was our first child, and because of Sue's age — she was almost thirty-nine — it would probably be our last. Even the most downbeat thoughts concerning her prognosis were fleeting. But hindsight is only beneficial if one is unhappy with how things ended up. Had there been a clear indication that Sue would be dead in ten months, would I have held firm on behalf of termination? I challenge anyone who puts their child to bed each night to answer that question honestly.

"All right," Dr. Callaghan said. "I respect your decision. The option is there for you, just so you know."

"Nope," Sue said. Matter closed.

"With this type of malignancy, we would normally start some aggressive treatment quite soon … if you weren't pregnant."

"Find out what kind of treatment you *can* do then," Sue said.

"We're going to refer you to the high-risk pregnancy unit at Mount Sinai Hospital. Between us, we'll be able to determine what our plan of attack should be."

Dr. Callaghan handed us the referral form and ushered us back into the corridor for the long walk through the grey to the elevator.

Despite Sue's composure in the office, she was uncharacteristically quiet the entire drive home. As soon as she walked through our front door she went straight for the phone and called her parents. That's when she cried. Her belief that cancer was not a death sentence was brought down a notch when she had to tell her family. Not because she didn't believe she would beat it, but because she hated to cause them any undue anxiety. She knew she could count on me for comfort, but to her parents she was practically apologizing.

I sat quietly across from her as she made call after call to the rest of her family and mine, and to all her closest friends. Each conversation brought out a few more tears of regret while, at the same time, she absorbed their support. I watched with curious interest as those phone calls fortified her. It was, in many ways, a businesslike transaction. As she delivered the news, she reached out for the voices of solace, and in return received what she'd been after: the confirmation that those who loved her supported her unconditionally. Her tears were merely the residue of the exercise, like sweat. In the end she was more determined, more positive, and more certain of her decision to keep the baby.

"How was that?" she asked me.

"You were great," I said. They were the first words I'd spoken since she picked up the phone two hours earlier.

"I wanted everyone to know that I was okay with it, that I was confident."

"I think that was obvious."

"Yeah?"

"Yeah."

"I didn't mean to cry so much," she said. She may as well have made excuses for breathing. But crying wasn't part of her agenda. It was just the fine print she forgot to read.

"Nobody could blame you for a few tears," I said.

"Because even though it's bad news," she said, "it's not the end of the world. And we're going to have this baby, right?"

"That's right," I said. *This baby. This baby doesn't exist to me; it's like a fifth limb. This baby is complicating everything.* We were standing. Sue came up to me and put her hands on my chest. Her eyes, level with my chin, looked up at me softly.

"Are you confident?" she said.

"Of course I am."

Confidence. I had wrestled with it over the years. My convictions, such as they were, were rarely firm enough to convince even myself that I knew what I was thinking. As a young boy I was nearly always a follower, never quite sure enough to make even the simplest of suggestions. In my teens, when I was wooed by the stage, performing was more about compulsion than confidence. I relied on my talents — or what people told me were talents — because I didn't know what else to do. As a young adult, I was often loath to offer my opinions for fear of being proven ridiculous. I grew up with a practical outlook on my life; I saw the truth in situations and wasn't blinded by idealism. My pragmatism often stifled any ambition that may have been lurking within. When I met Sue, I fooled her into believing I was teeming with confidence. But she saw more in me than I saw in myself. Her own confidence assured me of what was right and true, even if I only saw it through her eyes. I was part of a unified team. Now, amid crisis, how could I not be confident? Sue made me believe, genuinely, that anything was possible. After listening to her curative phone calls, only an incorrigible cynic would not have been brought around.

* * *

My cousin Amy is sensitive and empathetic to a fault. Her tears were genuine and so was her kindness. I knew Sue's death affected other people too, but their losses meant little to me. Their sadness didn't cloud the sun. Their lives didn't change. They didn't feel the rope that pulled them toward some unreachable horizon.

So after three restless days in the comfort of my family, I was ready to welcome the familiarity of the restless road. My need to keep moving forward through unknown territory was stronger than the solace I found in loved ones.

Less than 800 kilometres due west of Oklahoma City is Santa Fe, New Mexico, where Uncle Jack lived. It would have been a day's drive if I wanted to motor onto Interstate 40, which cut across the top of Texas. But I didn't want to see another interstate, and frankly I didn't want to see Texas either. Something about the Lone Star State scared me. *People have guns there.* I was well aware this was a silly rationalization for avoiding Texas or any other American state, but I'd made up my mind. Besides, if I went the long way around, I could keep to the more picturesque back roads and also add a few more states to the list of those I'd seen.

Actually I did spend an hour in Texas on my way up to Kansas, nipping through the top-right corner. It was like taking a bite out of a gingerbread man's ear: it wasn't my favourite, and I'd had enough of a taste to appreciate what the whole cookie had to offer.

When we'd left Amy's house on the morning of August 10, it was already around twenty-five degrees Celsius, not atypical for a Midwestern summer's day. I kept the windows closed and the air conditioning on. By the time we stopped in Liberal, Kansas, to get gas and eat lunch, it was well over thirty degrees. Still, Myles and I shared a ham sandwich and grapes outside on the thirsty grass across from the gas station.

I noticed a one-storey white brick school and a low-rise office building, a strip mall with no cars in front, and some houses that might appear next to the dictionary entry for *bungalow*. More than one American flag flew proudly on staffs tall enough to endanger low-flying aircraft. Adjacent to the parking lot we'd stopped in was the "Land of Oz."

L. Frank Baum, the author of the original *Wizard of Oz*, never specified precisely where in Kansas Dorothy was from. The people in Liberal claimed, but couldn't prove, that she was from their town, so they built the "Land of Oz" in the hope they might attract tourists to a place known primarily for its beef ranches and annual Pancake Day race. To call it a museum is, perhaps, flattering. It's a converted shed with a corrugated roof and tin walls, around which a yellow brick road (sidewalk painted warning-sign yellow) winds its way through the classic story, complete with life-size figures of the characters Dorothy encounters. She was there too, in her familiar blue gingham dress, apron, and braids, giving tours to the masses who flocked there. I didn't go inside the enchanted tin shed, but I did see Dorothy take a very excited-looking family of four inside. I could only imagine the magical experience of the Emerald City that lay within.

With lunch finished and having had enough of the heat, I packed Myles back into his car seat — by now showing permanent imprints of his bum and head — and left the booming metropolis of Liberal with all its legendary Oz-ness. I followed my own yellow brick road, in this instance Route 83 north toward Garden City, about one hundred kilometres away. The stark landscape was as hypnotic as the blinking white lines I followed. In every direction, as far as my eyes could see, oceans of golden wheat grew and seemed to spread like a virus. The occasional farmhouse emerged from the fields with unassuming opacity. No such thing as close neighbours here.

I'd chosen Garden City as our destination because it met all the necessary criteria: a Super 8 Motel. Back in Indiana I had stayed in one of the chain's 1,100 locations and found it suitably clean and cheap. So I picked up one of their catalogues showing every Super 8 in North America. I was prepared, from that point on, to find my home-away-from-home wherever Myles and I happened to end up. I couldn't wait to reach Garden City, check in, have a rest, go for a walk, and find a place for dinner before retiring for the night. The quiet evenings in the Super 8, Myles asleep in his cot, were every bit as special as the daily drives. And I didn't even have to click my heels together three times.

"Oh, fuck! Myles, what have I done?" I said after a quick glance at the dashboard.

The red light of the gas gauge was on steady, the needle well below the big letter E that had reminded me to stop for gas back in Liberal. I thought about turning around and going back to the town where I'd obviously been too enthralled in the majesty of "Oz" to remember to fill up the tank. But I'd already driven around fifteen kilometres, so I looked on the map to see if there was another town before Garden City.

"Okay, Myles … It's okay. We're going to be okay," I said between anxious deep breaths.

According to the map, Route 83 met Route 56 about thirty kilometres ahead at the town of Sublette. *Thirty kilometres — can we make it that far?* It seemed like a gamble, and I was already sweating despite the air conditioning being on full. I'd never run the tank down this low before, so I didn't know how long I had. I decided this was an emergency and moments later, not seeing any other buildings, turned into the first driveway I came to.

"Farmers always have extra cans of gas, don't they, Myles? They drive tractors, they have generators."

I turned off the engine and looked back at Myles. As usual the short car ride had lulled him into a post-lunch sleep. I looked in my wallet to make sure I had some cash to offer what I hoped would be a generous and sympathetic farmer. I got out of the car and looked around the front of the farmhouse. The two-storey red brick home with white gables stared at me through its two upstairs windows. Fresh petunias and marigolds hung in pots from iron hooks. A football and a child's bicycle sat in the gravel driveway, only partially shaded by two enormous oak trees to the left of the house. I didn't see or hear any signs of movement. It was all-American, colourful and sun-bleached, tranquil but spooky.

The sun was at its peak. I wiped my forehead as I stepped up to the front door and broke through the quiet stillness by ringing the bell. I didn't hear any noise from inside, so I knocked on the door with the knocker, shaped like a cow's hoof. No footsteps, no answer. I wondered if Farmer Pete was out in the back forty doing whatever it is farmers do. Where was the good-natured farmer's wife if not baking pies in the enormous country kitchen? I stepped back from the door and followed the flagstones that led around to the left side of the house. The empty driveway abutted the side of the building and ended at a rickety iron gate at the back, beyond which lay a field of unidentifiable grain.

What did I expect to find? A tractor humming busily amid the acreage? A family of migrant workers huddled together over their lunch boxes? A barrel of gasoline with a sign above it saying "Help Yourself"?

It remained quiet except for the sound of the light breeze through the oak leaves and my feet on the gravel as I walked back to the car. In another life I could live here, I thought. If I'd never met Sue, maybe I'd have spent the rest of my twenties searching for some other place to belong. I might have journeyed through this part of America and met a beautiful country girl whose parents' farm grew produce for the whole town, the whole county. We'd all live communally in this fine farmhouse. I'd have learned how to drive a combine harvester, and known which fertilizer is best, and had a different pair of overalls for each day of the week. We'd have two healthy children — a boy and a girl, naturally — who'd grow up dreaming about the big city, but whose hearts were always here in Kansas. I might have learned to play the banjo. We'd grow old here, my country girl and I, happy that this homestead was our entire world. I could have lived a slower, more streamlined, healthier life where the twin beasts of Urban Stress and Illness were as fictional as flying monkeys.

It was a fleeting vision. One destined to blow away with the oak leaves. It must have been the heat of the sun.

I thought about stopping at the next farm, which was several kilometres away, but I was afraid of the same result. And how much more starting and stopping of the engine could my depleted gas tank take? I decided to cross my fingers and look to Sublette, having complete faith there'd be a gas station there. I shut off the air conditioning and opened the windows, my eyes as much on the dashboard — the needle couldn't go any lower — as on the road, which ran as straight as the Kansas border all the way to my fantasy filling station.

I imagined standing at the side of the road, Myles in one arm, trying to flag down a passing car with the other. But this stretch of road, like the farmhouse, seemed completely deserted. With the sun directly overhead, the trees offered little shade if we needed to take shelter from the relentless heat. It was the longest thirty kilometres I ever drove. Just as I was sure the engine was going to sputter and stall, the houses started getting closer together.

"I think we're going to make it," I said not too convincingly. "The town must be close."

Never had I seen a more beautiful sight in the entire continental United States than the bright red-and-white star of the Texaco station shining up ahead like Polaris burning in the night sky — a beacon to all widowed wanderers who were short of fuel. I swallowed my relief as I pulled up to the pump. I filled up the tank as if it were Myles who'd been starved, pouring in the gas until it nearly overflowed. I calmly paid the cashier, got back into the car, and drove away as if nothing out of the ordinary had happened.

But something had happened: I'd let my guard down. Before we set out, I'd been convinced that I could take care of myself and my son. It didn't matter if I was at home or a thousand kilometres away in the middle of nowhere. I was SuperDad. I could conquer parenting regardless of experience, gender, planning, or grief. This was Myles and Dad's All-for-One-and-One-for-All Cross-Continental Healing Tour. I was creating memories. But I could only imagine what Sue would have said.

"How could you be so stupid, Jonathan?" She'd always spit out my full name when she was pissed off at me. "How could you? You might be dumb enough to put yourself in danger, but don't ever put our son in danger. We're parents now; we are responsible for another life besides our own. I'm sick just thinking about what could have happened, Jonathan. Go away. I can't even look at you."

I would have apologized and told her she was right. Because she usually was right, and I was convinced that telling her she was right was the best way to ensure I'd remember the difference between right and wrong. And I'd have told her that it would never happen again, but it probably would because the pressure of my trying to be careful often led to carelessness. I wasn't always clever enough to learn from my mistakes the first time, so I relied on my apologies and made large gestures of atonement. Now there was only one person to apologize to.

"I'm so sorry, Myles," I said through tears of relief. "I never should have put you in that position. Your mother would've killed me. She never would have let that happen. I put us at risk ... I put *you* at risk. Listen to me, son. I love you so much. I will never, never, ever let anything like that happen again. I promise."

I looked at Myles's face in the mirror and then reached back to wipe the drool from his chin as he slept.

* * *

My second meeting in Dr. Grief's Grief Emporium was similar to the first. She stared at me blankly as I recapped what I'd discovered during our previous chat. I told her all about how happy I was to be with Myles while still figuring out what made me sad, what made me angry.

"Another thing," I said, "is that I was supposed to go first. Cancer runs in my family, not Sue's."

"Did you ever talk about that?" Every time the good doctor spoke it caught me off guard. I sometimes forgot that she had vocal chords.

"She actually thought the same thing. I still remember the conversation."

We had received Sue's diagnosis earlier in the day, a sunny June morning four months into her pregnancy and four days after the biopsy on the lump in her left breast.

"It should have been me," I said in a quiet moment.

"What are you talking about?"

"Cancer. I'm supposed to get it, not you."

"Why? Because your father had it?"

"Yes, my father and his sister, my aunt. It's in my bloodline. There was no cancer in your family. I always thought if either of us was going to get it, it would be me. It should have been me."

She was quiet as we held hands. Was she thinking I was right? Did she wish it were me instead? No. She just wished it hadn't been her.

"Just my rotten luck, I guess," she said.

"Sue reminded me that it was a lottery," I said, looking at Dr. Grief sitting statue-still on the other side of the room. "She used to say that we'd lost the cancer lottery, so we were due to win some other ones. Like karma or something. She used Myles as an example. Myles is so easygoing: he never cries, he's been sleeping through the night since he was three months old, and he always seems happy. He added no extra stress during her illness. Sue said, 'You're given what you can handle.' That's the karmic lottery she was talking about."

Dr. Grief looked at me with curiosity. "What kind of relationship did you have?" she said.

"We'd only been dating for one week when we had our first fight," I said. *Why is this the first thing I thought of? With all the things I miss about being with Sue — the laughter, the adventures, the companionship — why am I focusing on this?* "Years later, of course, neither of us could remember what the fight was about, but I know I was ashamed and apologetic about failing to do or say something she'd expected from me. But I wanted to be in a mature relationship, and she was definitely more mature than me. That seemed to start a pattern of behaviour that endured throughout."

"What kind of pattern?"

"Failed expectations," I said. "That became a common theme in our conflicts, which in the end eventually rolled together to form one giant, unresolved, overlooked flaw."

I welcomed the opportunity to tell the truth. The burden of sorrow was facilitated by these admissions. Just as grieving was a tool, so too was the acknowledgment of the reality I'd created with Sue. I discovered that it was okay to be sad and angry and confused all at the same time because that meant I was doing it right, if there was such a thing. Crying brought comfort. There was solace in the solitary. And yet...

"I just miss her so much." I paused as my eyes got wet. Dr. Grief let me stay like that for a while. She was paid to let me come to my own conclusions. She'd heard it all before. My friends, though I could confide in them, didn't have that standing. They couldn't just listen and ask the occasional helpful question. Friends had to be unconditionally supportive, caring, and sympathetic. But the dark cloud of my sadness must have been exhausting for my friends to stand under.

After an hour Dr. Grief told me my time was up and she'd see me next week. Where had the time gone? In no other environment could I talk for an hour straight. I left her grey quarters and wound my way back down through the maze of old folks cluttering up the Baycrest Centre and out into the sunlit parking lot. Sitting in the quiet sanctuary of my car, I reflected on what I'd said upstairs and breathed a deep sigh of consolation. If I could accept that Sue was gone; that the future I'd been promised was gone; that I was sitting on square number one of the great Snakes-and-Ladders game my life was about to become, then maybe I could believe that one day — one far-off day — things just might be okay again. But I didn't know if I could accept those things. Or if I even wanted to.

* * *

Garden City, Kansas, is an agricultural hub with a railway line that stretches all the way, some might say, to Kansas City. There is little else remarkable about this region. Though to be fair to all Garden Citizens, I wasn't exactly searching for anything remarkable. My fascination with the flat farmland of the rural Midwest had been quenched. Myles and I left after the complimentary Super 8 breakfast of dry toast and bitter orange juice and headed west again. After an hour of blanched wheat fields, we crossed the Colorado border where the landscape suddenly seemed greener, the vegetation more varied. It was as if the Governor of Colorado had legislated painting the countryside to distinguish the state from its washed-out neighbour to the east. Rambling stands of cottonwood trees sprouted from the moist woodlands that drank from streams fed by constant mountain runoff. The flood plains gave way to lush forests of willows and alders that dappled the coniferous stands. We were not in Kansas anymore.

Myles watched the Great Plains drift away in his rear-facing horizon while, about a hundred and sixty kilometres in front of me, I could see the approaching Sangre de Cristo mountain range fading into view as it arched its way down toward New Mexico. The reddish sandstone mountains were dotted with blue-green piñon pines and other small firs. After nearly a week of featureless views, I welcomed the sight of the mountains like a long absent parent. That's when I put Paul Simon's *Hearts and Bones* into the CD player. We listened to him sing about wandering Jews, one and a half of them to be precise — like Myles and me — moving through the Blood of Christ mountains. The song was written in 1982 about Simon and his then girlfriend, Carrie Fisher, and their efforts to heal their relationship. Travel and restoration are ancient bedfellows.

Driving had taken on a new characteristic by this time. It was no longer simply meditative and cathartic. It had become inevitable, each leg of the tour fulfilling an insatiable urge to be satisfied. Being in the car with my son was as necessary as breathing. To drive was to be. The vehicle itself became a part of our mobile family, an extension of Myles and me that sheltered and guided us and, in return, deserved our love and respect.

We were a threesome again. Like the trio Myles, Sue, and I never had the chance to explore. We could have been the exemplar of families. Sue and I might have raised Myles to be the perfect combination of his parents: from me he'd get patience, musicality, lightheartedness; from his mother shrewdness, dedication, and fire. Even before Sue was diagnosed — before the medical incentives — we only ever wanted one child. We thought we'd prefer to dedicate all of our parenting savvy to one child instead of dividing our time. As a threesome we would be complete.

With every visit to every doctor, this idea of *three* was paramount. We had to have this child. We trusted the insight of the various medical specialists; oncologist and high-risk obstetrician met like world leaders in top-secret underground summits, we imagined, discussing in hushed tones the pregnant cancer patient who refused to abort her baby. *Can we prescribe chemotherapy? If so, how much? And how close to her due date? What about radiation?* Yes. Not much. Until four weeks before. No way.

We believed they'd done their homework. The medical summit concluded that there were some dosages of chemicals deemed "safe" to administer during pregnancy. At the very least, they said, it would keep the cancer at bay until after the baby was born. Then they could ramp up the treatment to the necessary levels. In the meantime, the placenta should do its job by filtering out everything we didn't want the fetus to absorb. Most of their research came from a single, not-too-recent American study, we were told, carried out on a very small number of women. But it was all they had.

This information was enough for Sue — and therefore me. But it didn't take long for her to germinate an idea that would eventually blossom and thrive long after she'd gone.

"It doesn't sound like they have much to go on," she said. It was the end of June, nearing the onset of Toronto's humid summer months. Sue was four months pregnant. We sat in the waiting room outside Dr. Sermer's office, the obstetrician in the high-risk pregnancy unit at Mount Sinai Hospital. This setting, unlike oncology, was colourful and brightly lit. It was the jovial, heavily made-up secretary to Princess Margaret's headmaster.

"No. We're unique, sweetie."

"Yes but ... what did they say? One in every one-thousand pregnant women will get cancer. That's a lot of women."

"Overall it's a lot of women. But actually," I said, quickly doing the conversion, "that's only zero-point-one percent of pregnant women."

"But in North America that's still going to be thousands of women, don't you think?"

"Of course. But you know that research funding will go to the areas most in need. Zero-point-one percent is not very needy."

"There should be more information."

"I agree."

"So why isn't there?"

"We should ask Dr. Sermer about that."

"I will. Actually I've got a better idea," she said, getting that look in her eyes. It was the unmistakable stare of inspiration. I saw it when she worked out how we could afford to buy our first house; it was there when she suggested adopting a dog from the pound; it even showed up on our first canoe trip when she realized she could rough it with me. Something big was coming.

"We need to initiate our own study," she said. "There should be more research into the effects of chemotherapy on the unborn child. They can examine children, like ours, after they're born to see if they have any ... you know, deficiencies. And then people like us will have some information for making decisions."

"Yes, and..."

"And with my contacts in the media we can spread the word so that others can participate in the study. If I have to go through this then I'm going to make sure there's something positive to come out of it."

"Something other than the birth of our son, you mean."

"I'm gonna do this," she said. The look of inspiration turned more serious. Sue was looking off into the distance as if she could see her own legacy.

6

The Royal Gorge, about two hundred and forty kilometres inside the Colorado border, is home to the world's highest suspension bridge, which spans the kilometre-or-so gap over three hundred metres above the Arkansas River. I learned about it from the road signs pointing the direction just outside the town of Pueblo, where we'd stopped for lunch.

"Hey, Superman. Do you want to go see a big hole in the ground?" I had no idea just how big it was, but it sounded good. Besides, the Cañon City Super 8 with an outdoor swimming pool was only three kilometres from the gorge. "Maybe we can hike down into it. Take some nice pictures, eh?"

Whenever I'd seen a valley or canyon, I wanted to descend into it, just as I always wanted to climb a hill or mountain if faced with one. It must be something about wanting to see what it looks like from the other side. Here, so close to the Rocky Mountains, I looked forward to the generous offerings of peaks and valleys to explore. A gorge, I figured, was just a big valley. This particular gorge, it turned out, was too deep and too steep to walk into, with or without a baby on my back. It was a sheer drop down the sides of craggy red cliffs. That's why, I imagined, they built the bridge.

I parked the car, packed Myles into his pack — now as familiar to him as the car seat — and walked over to the edge of the canyon. The wind picked up as I stepped onto the bridge and started walking over the great span. I noticed immediately that the bridge floor was made of wooden decking, which is why it was meant only to be walked over. Like many planks of wood, they had spots where you could see through them, knots that had popped out, eroded grain. The view over the side was spectacular enough; I didn't need to look straight through the floor for any added perspective. We took our time crossing, enjoying the fresh air under the cloudless sky, the midday sun shining like a spotlight over this impressive, red-and-green chasm. I welcomed the vast expanse of colour and the reminder that I was just a speck on the earth, and that humanity, for all its brilliance and diversity, could be little more than a footnote in this universe. I stood over a hole in the ground that had taken three million years to get there, on a seventy-five-year-old bridge built in six months. Deep gorges and mile-high mountains are eternal and transcendent. *Those I love are dying and so shall I one day.* Yes, I felt small, and I carried everything I needed on my back.

At the far end of the bridge, the wind subsided as we approached the sheltering red rock. I saw flags and steel gates and heard the jingle-jangle of carousel music. I touched the solid ground, glanced nonplussed at the throngs of people on noisy rides and in the petting zoo, and then turned around and walked back across the bridge to where we'd started.

The last time I'd been to a gorge was with Sue in France. On our way down from Limoges toward Provence, we stopped at the Gorges du Tarn, in the Massif Central region. We hiked down narrow, precipitous paths into the valley and spent the day walking along the slow river. Above us, the white limestone cliffs feathered with tall pines protected us from the rest of the world. We barely talked. The birds sang and our feet scuffled over the white stones along the bank of the river. The only other people we saw were canoeists quietly paddling downstream. We sat on a mossy rock, where I unpacked our lunch from the rucksack: fresh baguette and cheese — whatever kind was recommended by the local *fromagerie* — grapes, and something sweet. All we had was a Swiss Army knife, a map, and each other. And there wasn't an amusement park anywhere to be seen.

Myles and I checked into the Cañon City Super 8 — *there's no place like home* — and immediately changed into our bathing suits. The cool water was a delight after the sticky Colorado drive. We had the pool to ourselves, so we could splash around without a care. I'd been taking him to swimming classes back home. It was one of the first things I did with him after Sue died. For a half-hour every Saturday morning, we pretended to be aquatic animals with a dozen other parents and their six month olds. He was never quite brave enough to let go of me, but I didn't mind. In the Colorado pool, Myles serenaded me with intoxicating giggles as we played, but he still wouldn't let go. I didn't want him to either. This was father-and-son time, face to face, skin to skin. In times like this I knew we had a burgeoning symbiosis, the likes of which, to my mind, fathers and sons had never before experienced. He needed me for his basic daily functions and I needed him for mine.

* * *

In mid-July, the weekend before chemotherapy began, Sue and I were in Stratford, Ontario, to see *All's Well That Ends Well*. We went to the festival every summer, enjoying the theatre and reminiscing on our respective careers as failed actors. To pass time before the show we walked through the town's red-bricked streets, passing cafés, antique stores, and countless souvenir shops. One shop window displayed colourful gemstones and crystals, spiritual books by New Age authors, and posters for yoga classes, acupuncturists, and a musician who played the zither. Sue and I went inside and were met with dozens of bins overflowing with glittering semi-precious stones sold like bulk candy. Over each bin was written an explanation of that stone's properties, qualities that were supposed to heal, energize, or encourage.

"I'm gonna get some of these," Sue said. "They're beautiful."

"What are you going to do with them?" I asked.

"I can use all the help I can get," she said.

She had already consulted a naturopath and a shiatsu therapist, and had switched to an all-organic diet. Some pretty rocks couldn't hurt either, I thought.

Sue spent half an hour sifting through all the stones, deciding based on their properties which ones best suited her needs. Once she'd made her selections, she had to find the right stone of each. It had to be the exact size, shape, and colour to suit her. I helped sort through them, but my selections were usually rejected. She settled on seven stones in all. The shopkeeper put them in a small green velveteen bag with a gold drawstring.

"Do you have a pen?" she asked me. I gave her one. She went back to the bins and, in tiny letters, wrote about each stone on the back of the shop's business card:

rose quartz — releasing impurities, peace, self-esteem

malachite — soothing, meditation, balances the body

jade — vitality, perspective, prolongs life

lapis lazuli — protect against spiritual darkness,
against depression

tiger's eye — energy, inner strength, balances yin and
yang

lepidolite — immune system, patience, self-
forgiveness

quartz — balance, purity, enhances all other crystals

Sue clung to that little green bag through three hours of
Shakespeare and all the way back to Toronto. The stones
immediately boosted her strength and faith. Even if it was
faith only in the need to have faith.

Her belief in a healthy future was contagious. So much
so that it disproved my entire ethos on cancer. To me,
cancer equalled death. My father, my aunt, close friends,
friends of friends, and mere acquaintances had all
succumbed. In my family, the C-word reigned as a
catchword for dying. But under Sue's tutelage all of that
was forgotten. I believed. I truly believed.

The Cancer Centre at Sunnybrook Hospital is the
beauty-pageant winner among Toronto hospitals. The
modern, low building doesn't threaten like other medical
facilities. Large windows in the concourse and all the
rooms welcome in natural light and offer views of the
wooded Sunnybrook Park and surrounding ravines.
Actual paintings, that seem to have been specially
commissioned, adorn the walls. Even the magazines are
up to date. This is an environment that knows how to
cater to its clientele.

Sue and I were met with a genuine smile by the
receptionist and had only a short wait in the comfortable

chairs facing the windows. At Sue's feet was her bag, packed with a water bottle, tissues, writing material, and her tiny green velvet sack of healing gemstones that she'd bought in Stratford the weekend before. It was July 25, one week before her thirty-ninth birthday and three months before our baby was due.

"Susan," a smiling woman called.

We both stood and walked over to shake her hand.

"I'm Clare. I'll be taking you through your chemo today," she said, flipping through the notes on her clipboard. "You're having the FDC, right?"

Sue and I looked at each other. "We're not sure what we're getting," I said. "What's FDC?"

"That's your chemo." She recited the names of the chemicals they'd be injecting into Sue's arm — long, serious names that bounced off my ears. "It's good stuff. Goes right to your cancer."

"Whatever works," said Sue.

"Amen," said Clare, pronouncing it *Ay*-men. Her unforced smile had an embracing effect on my nerves. She couldn't have been trained to smile like that. She had thick reddish-brown hair, no stranger to the blow-dryer, and a proud, arrowhead nose pointing out at us. She was small in stature, but underneath her regulation white coat, her little legs briskly guided us through the maze of corridors until we reached a small private therapy room. "Make yourselves comfortable. I'll be right back."

Sue sat in the treatment chair in the centre of the room surrounded by IV poles. I sat to her left and looked out the window. Through the trees, the sunlight shining in from behind her cast a halo around her head. She reached into her purse, pulled out the bag of gemstones, and placed them on top of her bulging belly just as Clare came back in.

"What are those?"

"Crystals," Sue said. "They'll help protect me and the baby."

"Ay-men to that," said Clare. "Okay. Do you want the ondansetron?"

"The what?"

"Anti-nausea medicine."

"Oh," said Sue, glancing over at me. "No, I don't. I've heard it could harm the baby."

"I hear you, sister," said Clare.

Surely, I thought, if the doctors considered this FDC to be safe, then wouldn't a little pill to hold down your cookies be all right? It was only offered for Sue's comfort, not that she'd need it anyway. She never got nauseated, not even morning sickness. Before she was pregnant, she could go on every stomach-churning ride at the Canadian National Exhibition and then down a hot dog and fries. I'd break out in a cold sweat just watching her.

"How far along are you?" Clare asked.

"About twenty-four weeks."

"Second trimester. The baby should be just fine. They wouldn't prescribe chemo in your first trimester. So nothing to worry about." Clare smiled.

"Okay," said Sue meekly, but she trusted that smile. "Clare?"

"Yes?"

"Will my hair fall out?"

"Yes," Clare said. "But it's not the end of the world. Hair grows back."

"I know," said Sue. "Just wondering."

She gave me a half-smile, half-grimace. She knew it was a probability she'd lose her hair, but she'd clung to the hope of keeping it. It didn't happen to all chemo patients, we'd heard. But it depends on the chemicals — the "cocktail" as they say in the cancer centre. During her tenure as a television reporter, Sue had spent enough time and money on her hair to qualify for some sort of lifetime salon membership. She meticulously chose just the right shades of blonde to highlight her natural chestnut colour. As trends came and went, she curled, flipped, teased, cropped, and coloured as required. But this summer she was working in radio and clearly realized she could afford to be less particular about her hair.

Clare found an appropriate vein on the back of Sue's hand and hooked her up to the saline IV drip. Sue turned her head, as she always did when a needle was going in. Then Clare picked up a small vial with a clear liquid inside.

"This is the F," she said. "Fluorouracil. A thousand milligrams. This'll get you going."

The vial of F was attached to the IV by an adjoining tube and Clare adjusted the drip rate. When she was satisfied, she left us alone to watch the dripping; to watch the magic of medicine going to work. Once per second a drop of the clear fluid popped out and mingled with the saline. It looked like water. I thought of the potent chemical swimming through Sue's veins, sniffing out the cancerous cells like a bloodhound. I imagined it taking bites out of the tumour in her breast and swallowing the cancer. It would do the job it had been trained for, I was certain. Occasionally I pictured it passing by Sue's womb, glancing over at the fetus and moving on. If the big F was going to do its job, it had to do it completely and properly, which meant ignoring the nascent, fast-growing cells of our son.

Ten minutes later the F was empty. Clare came back in and replaced the empty vial with a smaller one filled with bright red liquid.

"Doxorubicin," Clare said. "One hundred milligrams. This is the stuff that will make you nauseated."

"What's the stuff that makes my hair fall out?"

"All of it." Clare chuckled.

In went the D, filing through the tube in an orderly fashion just as its predecessor had. Only slower. This dog went about its job methodically, I decided. It sought out its target and ate slowly, savouring every bite and licking its lips afterward. It was forty-five minutes before Clare found it empty and exchanged it for the final ingredient of the cocktail.

"Cyclophosphamide. A thousand milligrams."

This one was clear like the first one and took its time like the second one. I wondered what was going through Sue's mind.

"Do you … feel anything?" I asked. It was a silly question, I know.

"Not really. It's a bit itchy on my hand where the needle's going in."

"You can't, like … feel anything flowing through you?"

"No," Sue giggled.

The whole process was, to borrow from the cancer phrasebook, quite benign. It was anticlimactic, unlike surgery. We could only wait and trust that the FDC would do its job.

At the end of the forty-five minute session with the C, Clare came back in, disconnected all the tubes, took Sue's vital statistics, and made a note of the itchy hand. Then she walked us out.

"I'll see you in three weeks."

"Will you be here?" Sue asked. "We like you."

Clare smiled. "I expect I'll be here."

"Good. As long as I have to be sitting in that chair, I may as well have people I like sitting there with me."

"Ay-men to that," said Clare.

In the intervening three weeks, Sue showed few signs of suffering side effects. No hair had fallen out yet, no nausea. She went to work every day at the CBC, and her radio voice sounded clear and confident as usual. She may have been a bit more fatigued, but that could just as easily have been due to being pregnant. So when we walked back into the cancer centre, it was with the confidence that Sue was strong, that her immune system was robust, and that the chemo would go to work without significantly distracting us from impending parenthood.

Clare, as promised, welcomed us back and took us into the same room as the first time. She took Sue's blood pressure, which was fine, then a blood sample. Clare left us for a few minutes while she tested Sue's blood. Sue seemed practically jovial sitting in her usual chair, bag of stones resting comfortably atop her pregnant paunch. She looked as though she had just sat down to a French pedicure.

Sue's white blood cell count — WBCs, which help boost the immune system — was "critically low," Clare told us. A low count is anything below 3,500. Sue's was 2,740. WBCs are formed by bone marrow, which has a tendency to be targeted by metastasizing cancer. However, chemotherapy itself can also be responsible.

"Just hang tight," Clare said with a smile, and she went off to consult the oncologist.

"I'm sure it's fine," I said after Clare left. "Your body is still adjusting to the chemo so the white blood cells are probably just reacting to it."

I had absolutely no idea what I was talking about.

Sue looked at me with a gentle smile. She may have actually believed me, but she only admitted I was right when it was something she needed to believe. I was playing the part of the supportive husband, showering her with positive thoughts and comments on how rosy the outlook was. If she said I was right, then I was.

"We're not going to worry about this," Clare said when she returned. "You can still have your chemo, and before you leave, I'll give you a prescription for some antibiotics, which should help with the low count."

"But you said it was critical," I said.

"Anything below normal is deemed critical. It's just the term we apply to the number. But it's not so low that we need to be overly concerned."

"I've still got enough?"

"You've still got enough." Clare smiled.

"Then let's get to work," Sue said.

"Ay-men."

Clare plugged the IV into Sue's hand and started the same routine as before. We sat quietly as the F bloodhound went to work — drip, drip, drip, chomp, chomp, chomp — and then the bright red D. When it was empty, we waited for Clare to return, but she didn't. I stuck my nose out the door to see if she was around and saw her dealing with another patient. I closed the door and stood over Sue who was being unusually tolerant. On the shelf to my right was Sue's file, which Clare had left behind. I casually opened the cover and tried to decipher the numbers and phrases on the chart. I had barely gotten past Sue's name and date of birth.

"Close that."

"Why?"

"We're not supposed to look at that."

"We're not?"

"No. Close it."

"But it's your file. It's about you. It just has the information on your chemo and notes and things."

"It's for the doctors. Not us."

"But…"

"Close it."

I closed it. And, though I wanted to, I never peeked again. I never saw what the doctors thought of Sue's prognosis. I didn't learn anything about how big the tumour was or what stage it was in. I only knew what Clare had told us about FDC and nothing more. It wasn't natural for me not to ask questions, to blindly sit by as my wife's life was being tossed around like a paper clip. I wanted to run out of there with the file under my arm until I found a quiet corner to read it at my leisure. I wanted to have the Latin words for the body roll off my tongue like a med student. I wanted to know. But if I knew, then Sue would want to know. And she didn't want to know. The conscience of our relationship loomed large.

Clare came bounding through the door, all apologies and ay-mens, and exchanged the empty D for the C. Sue sat perfectly still, eyes closed, clutching her belly. It always amazed me how a woman of such vigour could choose just the right time to meditate. She looked calm. I knew that she was channelling positive energy from somewhere to the medicine and to our baby.

Over the next few weeks, Sue began noticing hair on her pillow in the morning. Just a few strands at first, then gradually increasing day by day. She'd started taking baths instead of showers because it disheartened her to watch her hair go down the drain. Also she was afraid of slipping. But more importantly, the jets of water from the shower hurt the wound in her breast where the original biopsy had been performed, still open all these weeks later. Sue couldn't look at it. But I saw it every day, and I didn't like what I saw.

The three-centimetre incision had oozed with pus and blood for a couple of weeks following the biopsy. I changed the dressings three times a day, or more, and noticed that the cut wasn't closing as I'd expected. By late summer, what appeared to be red flesh was growing out of the incision. It looked like a small pair of moist lips was emerging from the top of Sue's breast. Our doctors had seen the flesh too but never commented on it, never confirming it was what I thought it was. Perhaps the doctors, all of them in their collective wisdom, decided the best thing to do was to let Sue concentrate on her pregnancy. Being pregnant brought her such obvious joy, why distract her with the grim details of her prognosis? Why add any more stress? So I never heard directly from any of the doctors — nor did I find the courage to ask — whether the red flesh sprouting from her breast was actually the swelling tumour.

In September we had two more visits to the fancy cancer centre before we were forced to take a hiatus. The baby was due in late October, and our medical team declared no chemotherapy four weeks either side of the birth. By day, Sue's energy was high, and her passionate faith drove me forward. But each night, after the lights were turned out and I waited for Sue to fall asleep, I came face to face with the unread file and the lingering shadow of that mysterious red flesh.

* * *

Until Sue was diagnosed, cancer always reminded me of my father, who was the first person I knew to have it. To those who remember him, Bruce Magidsohn — Dad, as I never called him — was a decent man, vociferously proud of his family. He was broad and heavy-footed, with a head of dense, almost-black hair, a beard to match, and a glowing, gap-toothed smile. He and his sister, Julie, grew up in the Detroit area with my dentist grandfather, Eliot, and former schoolteacher grandmother, Esther. Bruce went to football games and secretly smoked cigarettes and drove around in his dad's Chevrolet Bel Air and read books about architecture.

He met my mother, Kristine, in the summer of 1962 at a camp in Northern Ontario. A long-distance courtship ensued — Bruce in Detroit, Kris in Toronto — until their marriage in April 1964. Two kids later, Bruce finished his doctorate in architecture and picked up a professorship in Springfield, Illinois, at the local state university. He loved teaching and talking about art and architecture. He had a particular affection for the works of Frank Lloyd Wright and the British sculptor Henry Moore whose Hertfordshire, England, home and studio he visited with his students over two summers in the early 1970s.

He suffered his first seizure in the summer of 1972. Exploratory surgery in Springfield was unhelpful; whatever was inside his brain was too deep to be seen. This was before MRI and CT scans. He continued to work through 1973 and 1974 as the seizures persisted with occasional spells of aphasia. A new doctor in Detroit thought it could be a viral infection or a minor stroke. He couldn't be certain. By the end of 1974, Bruce's headaches became unbearable so more surgery was scheduled. In March 1975, the surgeon found a peach-sized tumour in the left lobe of Bruce's brain but couldn't remove all of it. In the ICU Bruce developed meningitis and for the next several weeks wavered in and out of consciousness. On the morning of Sunday, May 18, he died.

I was seven years old. He was thirty-four, forever in my memory as "Daddy."

The day my father died is one of my earliest memories. The spring sun blazed with the conviction of an eternal flame, casting heavy shadows under the gathering throng of mourners at my aunt and uncle's house. On a day when my cousins and I would normally be playing outside, we sat indoors in a collective muddle quivering with tears and whispers. I looked around at my family, faces wet with grief, and told myself I should be crying too.

For the next twenty-eight years the synergy between my father and cancer was as legendary as the story of the day he died. This was the legacy of cancer in my family. But to me, the hangover of losing my father to cancer inured me to all those I knew who suffered similar fates. While some around me bore the punishing blows of death, I felt numb. I grew up accepting that dying was simply an inevitable, sometimes tragic element of living. It was as if I looked at my life through a prism refracting the sunlight into its spectral colours. At one end, the fiery red and orange beams of childhood and youth merged into the mature yellows and greens showing growth and adventure. Then came the old-age blues. At the far end where the violet beam rounded out the band of colours, was death. It was just another part of the rainbow.

During my father's last months, my mother, sister, and I lived in Detroit with my Aunt Julie, Uncle Jack, and their kids, my cousins Marc and Amy. After he died, Julie was mother to all four children while Kris began her lifelong relationship with widowhood. (She was thirty-five years old, the same age I was when Sue died.) That short period in my aunt and uncle's home became the mantelpiece on which many of my childhood memories are perched. By the end of that summer, my mother had moved my sister and me to

Toronto. Uncle Jack became the prime male presence in my life, more than just avuncular, and for the next several years he always made time for me. One-on-one lunches came with every family visit. When I started university, he offered to pay my tuition. When I met Sue, he and Julie both vetted her and assured me they found her worthy of their nephew.

After my Aunt Julie died (also from breast cancer) in 1996, Jack spent a few years in South Florida before making the move to Santa Fe. I'd always considered Jack, a former oral surgeon, to be much cooler than he looked. A long-limbed scarecrow of a man, he retired to New Mexico, grew a beard, and spent his time hiking, skiing, and giving tours at a local museum. He and his new partner, Kathleen, whom I'd never met, lived on a low slope at the bottom of one of the mountains on the outskirts of the city with their two chows, Bear and Soleil. Jack's directions led me directly to their home, a sprawling adobe-style bungalow — painted white to stay cool in summer — on a gravel road surrounded by piñon pines and red earth. I parked the car in front and walked through a small wooden gate in a low adobe wall that encircled a splendid desert garden of silver sagebrush and creosote. Jack greeted us at the door barefoot and smiling.

"Myles and Jono." That's what he always called me. "Welcome to Santa Fe," he shouted. Jack had a way of imparting the enthusiasm of a spectacle into the most mundane comments. It was all in his manner and, for me at least, in the comical intonations of his Michigan accent. He knew we'd be weary from a long day on the road, so he shouted from his doorstep for the desert wind to carry his welcoming cry to the far reaches of America. We felt very welcome indeed.

Soon Myles and I were barefoot too, and Jack showed us around the house, pointing out in spectacular fashion every architectural detail and its relationship to the desert that surrounded us.

"We're enveloped by thousands of piñon pines," he told us. To this day, I hear Jack's voice telling me the name of the tree I'd never heard of before that day. "Pin-yan," he'd say.

I found Kathleen to be a pleasant, sober woman with a mane of thick Titian hair that matched the coats of her chows. Her love for her dogs was only equalled by her love of good food. She had just returned from a shopping extravaganza at Whole Foods Market when we arrived. I was looking forward to a good home-cooked meal after my latest succession of Super 8 breakfasts, variety store sandwich lunches, and dinners from any available restaurant. Later that afternoon, when I reached into the refrigerator to get Myles's milk, I saw a glorious rice and lamb salad tossed in a beautifully glazed terracotta bowl.

"This looks good," I said.

"What does?" said Jack.

"The salad. Is that our dinner?"

"That's the dogs' dinner."

My dinner was a steak as thick as my fist. Jack's barbecue on the back patio sent smoke signals up over the house that I was sure could be seen from the tops of the rusty, mystical New Mexican mountains in the distance.

August 12, 2003 — Santa Fe, New Mexico

Dear Myles,

A stunning drive today through Colorado into New Mexico. Often we drove through huge rocky valleys with red mountains on either side of us.

Spectacular views. Then we followed the Rio Grande — like in Joe's song, eh? — down from Taos to S.F.

It's nice here. Although, it's worth noting that there is a small degree of difficulty breaking out of our rhythm as we stay with others. Which is not to say we haven't been welcomed — we have. It's just that we have learned how to do this journeying, you and me, and now there are others involved. It will take some time.

I'm writing outside on the private deck off the guest room as you sleep inside. I just watched an awesome sunset. The back of the house looks over what appears to be desert, but is actually part of the Santa Fe National Forest. The seemingly endless rolling rocky outcrops are pocked with piñon pines. The crickets are deafening. Your mom would love it here.

Santa Fe is nestled into a lush pocket amid the high desert of the Sierras. The surrounding mountains ensure the city maintains its cool, arid conditions, insulating it from the inhospitable heat beyond. A cool, misty rain blanketed the area as we set out on a hike the next day: Jack, Kathleen, the dogs, and me with Myles on my back. The merciless southwestern sun I'd imagined was hidden behind low silver clouds. Footpaths wove through thick stands of quaking aspens, white firs, and junipers in countless shades of green, glowing in the mist like polished malachite. Fast-flowing mountain streams lined our path, occasionally rushing into boisterous waterfalls that settled into rocky pools from which the dogs drank.

"It's beautiful here," I said, pausing to rest in a small glade surrounded by young aspens.

"Yes, it is," Jack said. He and Kathleen were just coming into the clearing, their ski-pole-like walking sticks helping them up the slight rise. "We try to get up here every day. If we miss a day, I long for it."

"Do you see many wild animals up here?"

"Mountain lions, coyotes and wolves, jackrabbits, deer…"

"Any bears?"

"I've never seen a bear. But I know people who have."

"I've always wanted to see a bear," I said.

Jack sat next to me on a boulder and rested his hands on top of his stick. "Just up there," he said, pointing to a taller peak above us, "is where we usually go skiing. In the winter, of course."

"When did you learn to ski?"

"When I moved here," he said with a smile that read *Life is good.*

"I can see why you love it here." For a brief moment I felt like retiring and moving to Santa Fe. *Seriously, what's keeping me in Toronto? I could live here.* We listened to the sounds of rustling poplar leaves and the two dogs running through the tall grass.

"Jono. Kathleen and I would love to look after Myles tomorrow if you wanted to spend some time on your own up here."

He read my mind. I was itching for some time alone that wasn't constrained to a darkened hotel room. A solitary hike at my own pace might end up being the highlight of this adventure.

The next morning Jack gave a tour at the Museum of the American Indian, where he volunteered once a week. Myles and I listened as he told a small group about the local indigenous community and their lives in this area before it was known as New Mexico. After lunch, back at the house, I was given the all-clear and started out on my own. Just me, the coyotes, wolves, and jackrabbits. And bears.

For the first time in two weeks I didn't have Myles with me, which left me with a sense of release and at the same time incomplete. It was like going to a party and then realizing I was only wearing one shoe.

The morning had started out misty like the day before, the air cool and damp on my skin. But by the time I'd reached the trailhead the sun had come out and was directly over me. I took off my jacket and tied it around my waist. The mountain forest looked different under the sun: paler and coarser. The vibrant greens had dulled; the slick path was dustier. Birds that had sought shelter yesterday were singing excitedly today. I started on the same path Jack had led me down but soon climbed higher into unexplored territory, finding thicker stands of trees to meander through, taller grass.

There was an unbridled pace to my step. I nearly forgot why I was in New Mexico in the first place. Still my cleansing tears remained unguarded as my feet marched forward with the same momentum I'd been used to in the car. The silver-barked aspens glittered in the sunlight, and the pines pointed toward the borderless sky. My moist eyes followed their flight, lifting me skyward, weightless. I soared with the russet hawks that circled above the trees, looking down on myself from high in the air, freely resting upon the wind before landing softly among the tall grass and black prairie clover.

Ninety minutes in, I found myself walking down a large clearing on a wide incline. I stopped halfway and sat on the short grass; in winter this could have been a ski hill, I thought, but there was no lift. The warm sun was curative, not like the unyielding heat back in Kansas. I lay on my back, closed my eyes, and listened to the mountain: the birdsong, the crackle of leaves on the swaying trees. A bee buzzed around my face and I swatted it away, only for it to return. A distinct thud-thud-thud of distant footsteps vibrated the ground under my head. I sat up and looked around: dense trees fifteen metres to my right, another forest twenty-five metres to my left, nobody tramping over the hill behind me. I shrugged it off and lay back again, willing the arrival of an afternoon nap in the sun, the stillness continually interrupted by the indomitable bee. After a few moments my head trembled with the vibrations again; this time they seemed closer. I thought of the Native American hunter who put his ear to the ground to track his prey as I jumped to my feet afraid of what I might discover. I scoured all directions again, then crouched and put my palms face down on the ground to see if I could still feel the phantom footsteps. I remembered Jack's nonchalant reaction to my inquiry about bears. The feeling of being a solitary hiker on an unfamiliar mountain suddenly outweighed the curious desire to meet a bear in its natural habit. I set off running to the bottom of the hill, trying to convince myself it was the bee that compelled me to flee, but the mysterious footsteps had got the better of me. I looked back over my shoulder — *Can I outrun a bear?* — the momentum of running downhill carrying me faster than I would be able to propel myself on flat land.

My legs stung from the extra-long paces stretched out by gravity's exuberance. At the bottom I found another clearly marked path and took it automatically, running to my left into the thick woods. I thought of Myles at home with his great-uncle. What would happen if I were killed out here? Eaten by a bear or fallen down a mountain or abducted by some lonely woodsman straight out of *Deliverance*. How could I allow the possibility of Myles becoming an orphan at ten months? I ran — for my life and for Myles's — along the path until my legs lost the will, finally stopping to catch my breath and to listen for the sound of heavy footsteps. All was quiet except for my panting.

I walked out of the woods into another clearing. I knew I had come up westward from the main road so, judging the sun's trajectory, I headed east. The sun was inching over the far side of the mountain when I found the road, but I was much further up than when I started. I followed the winding road back down to my car, still a man in the wilderness.

"Did you get lost?" Jack said when I got back to the house. "We thought you'd be back two hours ago."

"So did I." I'd been gone over four hours. I told him about losing the trail and about my narrow escape from a rampaging grizzly. "Sorry to worry you. Myles okay?"

"Are you kidding? Myles is the man," Jack said in his cool, not-so-cool way. He didn't seem at all concerned about my brush with death. By implication, I may have been overreacting.

I walked into the kitchen where Myles was sitting on the floor watching Kathleen prepare the dogs' daily banquet. Or perhaps he was eating what had fallen on the floor. He heard me come in and crawled over to me for a sweet reunion. I picked him up and he gave me one of those perfect, restorative hugs that made me well up.

"It's so good to see you," I whispered into his ear. "I'm sorry I took so long. I won't leave you anymore." Myles smiled as if he knew exactly what I meant.

As I was getting into bed that night, I felt the gentle tug of the rope and knew I'd be leaving in the morning. Jack, of course, said we could stay as long as we wanted, but I craved the movement again. I was missing the momentum, the daily meditation over asphalt, even the Super 8.

There weren't likely to be any other opportunities on this trip to be on my own, but I didn't mind. Myles and I were a team. I lay on my back with my hands behind my head and looked out at the night sky through the French doors. In the quiet of the desert evening I heard the crickets marking the edge of the pine forest. Myles's soft breaths came from the dark corner by the door. I wondered if I'd really had a close encounter with a bear or if I was just feeling vulnerable — a solitary man far from home. There is innate danger in that anyway. Loneliness, my constant companion, had conspired to frighten the same way I'd frightened myself by nearly running out of gas. But this time, at least, I only put myself at risk. Sue couldn't have grumbled about that.

7

Contractions came fast and sudden on a Tuesday night in October at eleven o'clock when we were getting ready for bed. Sue froze on the spot, clutching her belly with both hands. She didn't look scared, but I called Crescence, our doula (a kind of birthing coach), immediately and told her what Sue was feeling: stomach cramps, tightness around her belly, nausea. Crescence — decidedly lunate in name and manner — rushed right over and, only a half hour later, cued us to go to the hospital. She helped Sue out to the car while I made room in the back seat for the two of them.

I didn't panic. At least I don't think I did, even though it was two weeks earlier than expected. If Sue remained calm — and she did — then so could I. *The baby is coming tonight. I'm going to be a dad tonight.* I didn't think about cancer or trauma or the remote chance of losing Sue. I was caught up in the excitement. That was all.

"I can't sit," Sue said.

"On your hands and knees then," Crescence replied without a beat, her long, thin arms wrapped around Sue's distended waist as she helped her flip over.

Sue took the hands-and-knees thing quite seriously, I thought, because moments after I backed out of the driveway, she started mooing. I wasn't sure how the staff at Mount Sinai Hospital would react to the cow imitations, but I didn't pass judgment as we drove on. A few minutes later Sue was silenced.

"What was that?" she asked.

"That was your water breaking," said Crescence.

I tried to look behind into the dark back seat but saw no signs of anything having broken. I thought maybe there'd be a noticeable sound like rainwater falling into a sewer — at the very least an audible trickle. But other than the mooing, there was silence.

"Sorry," Sue said. "It's made a mess."

"Don't worry," I said. Was she genuinely concerned about cheap Ford upholstery at a time like this? "It's not important, just keep doing what you're doing."

The initial examination at Mount Sinai showed that she was dilating quickly. Not long afterwards, we were marshalled into our private birthing room with medical personnel shuffling in and out like worker bees. The hermetically sealed room was surprisingly large and disconcertingly bright. I'd expected a more intimate, less chaotic setting for the arrival of my son. But I paid attention only to Sue and posted myself at her right side. On the daisy-yellow wall across from me was a clock; it was one in the morning. Sue was told that if she wanted the epidural, now was the time.

"What do you think?" she asked me.

What did I think? I thought her body had endured enough stress already, coping with the effects of chemotherapy during an already exhausting pregnancy. I thought if there were drugs available to dampen the discomfort of someone with a perilously low pain threshold, then she should just take them and not ask any questions. I also thought it was sweet of her to ask, but I didn't realize she might be asking because she was scared. Mostly I thought I wasn't the one who was about to pass a watermelon through a straw.

"It's your call, sweetie," I said.

"Would you think I'm wimping out?"

"No way." *Again? Really? At a time like this?*

"It's not just a question of strength," Crescence said, barely above a whisper. "It can help even the strongest women."

Spinal injection administered, it was time to push. Sue was never short on spiritual fortitude, but I'd never been very confident of her physical strength. Until this moment. Here was a woman in her fortieth year, weakened by aggressive, metastasizing cancer and by chemotherapy, who called up enough power to propel a small child through her birth canal. Nothing distracted Sue from her task; I could see the concentration all over her sweaty face. This was a display of pure, unmitigated determination. This was no made-for-TV birth. Although, the four or five times Sue paused to fix her wig could have been a scene from any sitcom.

"May I make a suggestion?" I'd asked Sue a few weeks earlier as we were putting an overnight bag together in preparation for a hasty, panicked (mooing) ride to the hospital. It included her favourite pillowcase and a new nightgown.

"About what?"

"About your wig."

"What about it?"

"I was thinking … you might consider not wearing it during the birth."

"Why wouldn't I wear it?" she said, looking at me with the same expression as when she'd ask, "Do I look fat in this?" She'd worn the wig stoically since late summer after the first six weeks of chemo. It had become a part of her that she actually learned to appreciate, and not just because it saved her thirty minutes during her morning routine.

"It's just … I mean … I think that it might prove difficult to keep it on straight. Maybe wear a bandana."

"I'm not wearing a bandana."

"Sweetie, it might…"

"I'm not wearing a bandana."

"All right," I said. I didn't normally make suggestions about her appearance, but with the best of intentions I thought Sue might feel silly if her wig was being pushed down over her eyes while she was busy projecting nearly seven pounds of baby out from between her legs.

"In fact," she said, "I want to go back to the wig place to get it styled next week so it looks good for the birth."

The wig place — I'm not sure it had another name — had been crucial in getting Sue to accept how she looked from the neck up. The fitting session was not entirely unpleasant; Sue was thrilled to have a complete follicular makeover, trying on every colour and length. When she was told her wig could be styled and coloured to look exactly like her real hair, the decision was made. But before Sue walked out of the wig place with her new hair, the wig maker suggested, sensitively but not sombrely, that she shave what was left of her real hair. It would, in her opinion, make the wig more comfortable and would mean Sue wouldn't have to look at her patchy scalp every morning. Sue agreed with surprising enthusiasm. The next day her colleagues at work didn't even notice, Sue told me.

So the coiffed prosthesis remained on her head for the entire birth with only the occasional adjustment. It did not derail her focus. My awe was only lessened by the anticipation of meeting my son, which occurred just after seven o'clock on Wednesday morning.

From first contraction to slimy, wailing neonate in eight hours.

"You did it," I said, kissing her. "I'm so proud of you."

Sue was my new hero. I'll never know from where she summoned the strength to deliver a baby. Some nights since her diagnosis, she'd sleep so soundly as to never even stir. She told me she often put her head down on her desk at work and closed her eyes for a midday nap. Despite her enthusiastic anticipation of motherhood, the cancer exhausted her. Now I'd stayed up all night with her and witnessed this act of superhuman fortitude. And the result was a beautiful boy.

At first look, all of the risks associated with cancer treatment during pregnancy appeared to have been overcome: ten fingers, ten toes, all requisite facial features, one shrivelled willy, and a sticky mop of brown peach fuzz pasted to his cone-shaped head. Physically, everything was in order. But it would be some months before we were assured the placenta had done its job of keeping out the chemicals.

After I cut the umbilical cord — a task, it must be noted, that requires significantly more physical effort than I'd imagined. I'd always assumed it would be as easy as snipping a piece of string. It turns out the cord tissue is firm, like gristle on a cheap chuck steak. Ideal, I realized, for safe transport of all essential nutrients to the fetus — our son was swaddled and placed under a warm lamp. I bent over him and whispered his name into his ear so that he'd be the first to learn what it was.

"My boy. You are Myles Day Magidsohn. And we love you very much."

As I was speaking to him, medical staff rushed around doing whatever they do postpartum. The grandparents gathered around with kisses and hugs and tears. Crescence fussed over Sue, as was her job. Then she told Sue and me she had an idea that required everyone else to leave the room for ten minutes. They obliged. She brought Myles over to Sue on the bed.

"Let's see if we can get him to nurse," she said, tucking thin blond strands behind her ear. Sue and I exchanged looks.

"We were told she shouldn't breastfeed," I said.

"I know. But there's no harm in trying for a few minutes on your good breast. Even the tiniest amount of colostrum will do him good."

"I'm willing to try," Sue said, uncovering her right breast. It was obvious the left one, bubbling with the aggressive, puckering tumour-lips, was off limits. But nobody said anything about the healthy one.

"Hold his mouth right up to the nipple," Crescence said. "That's it. Come on, Myles. Have a drink."

The nipple looked dry, but I was hoping Myles would have a good tug at it. He wasn't interested; he looked exhausted. The plan was abandoned. It was a disappointing result, but not unexpected, at least to me. Myles, it seemed, had decided what was best. Besides, we knew that plenty of children had grown into healthy adults without the benefit of breast milk. Sue and I were two of them, present setback aside.

We stayed in the hospital for about twenty-four hours, half of which Myles, thin and scrawny like his dad, spent in an incubator until he appeared to be the "right colour." I thought he looked beautiful the colour he came out. There was no danger in this procedure, we were assured, but given the circumstances by which he came into this world, I suppressed any thoughts of what this special attention might imply. I pressed my nose against the warm glass of the incubator, like a child at the aquarium. I took every breath with him as he acclimatized to this cold, waterless realm, his face literally changing by the hour. (For about forty-five minutes that evening he looked exactly like the actor-comedian Kevin Pollack.) But no matter whom he looked like, I was smitten. I knew from the instant I saw the top of his soft little skull poking out that he'd brought to me a purpose; a calling, the devotion to which had never in my life been revealed until that moment. I imagined him growing up, past infancy and early youth, into young adulthood; my visions were not specific, but through my eyes he became the paragon of children everywhere. My future was going to be overflowing with love, both given and received. I was already fulfilled — *kvelling*, as the Yiddish so aptly say. Swelling with pride.

I drank my fill of love that day, thanking my good fortune for this woman and this boy. It flowed in unapologetic stereotypes with such immediacy, such zeal, gushing out of me like broken water. Love flows like water, and water flows like love. Without one flood, there could not be the other.

The next morning we packed Myles into his baby seat — as carefully as bubble-wrapping Aunt Rose's antique cake plates — and took him home. I slept for the first time in more than two days, after which I quietly went outside with some cleaning supplies. I opened the back door of the car expecting to see the dark patch of upholstery that smelled like newborn baby. But I didn't. I felt around the seat and the floor below where Sue had been kneeling. Everything was dry. Not even a vague discolouration or watermark. I wondered if amniotic fluid evaporated faster and cleaner than regular water. How could I not trace where it once puddled? Could I have imagined the whole water-breaking-in-the-back-of-the-van episode?

If Myles's birth had been normal — assuming there is such a thing — then perhaps there would be less of a mystical quality to my memory. The evolution of Sue's pregnancy, from conception to delivery, might have seemed as ordinary to us as bringing a puppy home from the pound: a delightful day that ends with welcoming home a small, loveable creature. But if his birth had been normal, the mythical, biblical complications consigned to the thank-God-that-didn't-happen-to-us file, then Myles wouldn't be Myles, and I wouldn't be me. And Sue, well, who knows?

* * *

August 17, 2003 — Cortez, Colorado

Dear Myles,

Uncle Jack suggested we come back through southern Colorado before heading to the Grand Canyon. I'm glad he did — the drive here was stunning. New Mexico north of Santa Fe took my breath away. I literally gasped, driven, as it were, to tears at the majestic mountains, the colour of the earth and rocks, and the villages tucked into every nook. Not to mention the history and legends of the natives who still live around here despite being so callously displaced several decades ago.

Eighteen hundred metres up in the Rocky Mountains, the old city of Durango, Colorado, feels like a meeting between the Wild West and a modern college town. Strolling up and down the main street, I pushed you in your buggy as you chatted happily. We saw Colonial-style hotels, saddle makers, and saloons with those knee-high swinging doors. (I swear I could hear spurs jangling.) But there were also hip galleries and modern outdoor outfitters. We had dinner outside on a patio — the first time this trip — in an actual restaurant that wasn't a chain. It overlooked the old railway station complete with a Wells Fargo office, which I know is just a bank, but its name sounds like it's been around since the prospectors first staked their claims in this region. I would love to come here again with you when you are older.

We drove up Mesa Verde, which means "green table." But the green had all gone missing on top of the flat mesa. There had been a fire a couple of weeks ago, and all that was left was a forest of blackened tree stumps sticking up like used matchsticks. I imagined the road was usually hemmed in by a thick forest of junipers and piñon pines. But it looked rather like a charcoal graveyard sprawling over the scorched earth.

Harmony Moment: From the base of these burned trees grew some flowers; rising from the ashes, as they say. They had round yellow blooms like daisies but the centres were dark. I think they were black-eyed Susans.

We took a guided tour of Mesa Verde to see the cliff-side dwellings built thousands of years ago. For a few moments I forgot why we were there. Among the group of sightseers, I was just another tourist. Until I was asked to climb up a narrow wooden ladder, and I realized I was the only person doing it with a baby on his back. Perhaps like the original inhabitants — the women — of this community might have done. I wondered if anyone was looking strangely in my direction, or wondering where your mother was. But it never happened. Not since the border crossing in Detroit has anyone bothered to ask.

On the road between Mesa Verde and the Super 8 there were more black-eyed Susans lining the road. It's like your mom is following us — Sue, with her dark eyes and intense stare. Or better still, she's leading us in the right direction.

That night I put Myles to bed, dimmed the lights, wrote in my journal, did some sit-ups, and turned on David Letterman. It had been a lovely day.

Then I sat back and cried. The tears came from a different place that evening. They weren't simply tears of self-pity or loneliness because we'd been around other people that day. We'd mingled. But the loneliness of being alone is no match for the loneliness you still feel when you're among hundreds of people. Nothing accentuates isolation like being ignored. This was the day I went from being lonely to being invisible. I was as ethereal as the wind, a transparent, intangible visitor from another planet sent here to learn how to be a parent. And nobody could help me.

Part II

The Traveller Sees What He Sees

"I read somewhere it is psychologically beneficial to stand near things greater and more powerful than you yourself, so as to dwarf yourself (and your piddlyass bothers) by comparison."

— *Richard Ford,* The Sportswriter

8

I woke up on the morning after Sue died. Because that's what you do. Before you feel the warm mattress pressing up against your body; before the song that supplied the soundtrack to your dream downloads into your consciousness; before eyes are opened or salient memories reveal themselves — you wake up. And in that brief instant between darkness and light, between the old and the new, is that bewildering sense of nothingness, equal parts liberty and paralysis. You are sated from yesterday and empty for today. And you are powerless to fight the elemental force of nature that commands you to waken. So that's what you do. That ephemeral moment of waking is a fulcrum on which teeters a lifetime, a point stationed between past and future. We lie in the middle with a fleeting but hopeful sense of equilibrium.

But everything can change overnight.

When I'd gone to bed, I wondered if sleeping would ever again be restful or, if I did manage to sleep, whether or not I'd want to wake up again. The thought that I might find peaceful release was as far-fetched as thinking I wouldn't wake up alone. Then again, I wasn't afraid of nightmares.

I was awakened by the sun this new April Monday at Sue's parents' house. My eyes stung and I closed them against the glare. Then I realized it wasn't the sun's fault. My mind buzzed as the day woke up with me. I lay frozen, alone in a hurricane's eye with a hopeful but fleeting sense of equilibrium. I watched images of Sue, waking up and smiling, projected onto the insides of my eyelids. I could watch that smile forever. Finally I sat up, perched my weary body on the edge of the bed — the left side, *my* side — and forced my eyes to stay open. My shoulders hunched; my feet touched the floor. The carpet was soft on my soles but firm enough to stop me from floating. The sense of being grounded filtered its way up through the rest of my displaced body. Everything was awash in sepia; the sun cast a tattered, threadbare light.

An "Angel of Courage" — for that's what it said on the box she came in — stood on the bedside table. The little ceramic figurine, which I'd brought here the night before, had spent the past week at Sue's bedside offering its courage. But to me it was mute. I was still balancing precariously on that delicate pivot point, yesterday and tomorrow weighing me down from both sides.

I took in the rest of this room that Sue and I shared when we stayed with her parents in Burlington, less than an hour's drive from our home in Toronto. Frilly linens and cushions. Bedskirt. Throw pillows used for decoration only. The familiar smell of the sheets. Dresser scarf — I had never even heard of such a thing before I met Sue. Towels folded in thirds and then in half the other way placed neatly on the shelf. Curtains over blinds. Matching bedside tables topped with matching bedside-table lamps with matching TRIWATT bulbs. An area rug resting redundantly atop plush wall-to-wall carpeting. Except for that last item, it could have been our house. Only the colours differed.

On that first morning without Sue, however, there were no colours. I could only see her lying in the hospital bed, struggling to breathe. My ears echoed with the humid crackling of her last moments. I could still feel the cold touch of her skin after I'd kissed her that last time. I wished these lingering sensations could shelter me, tiny and hidden, like a cloak.

I looked at my tabletop angel. A cellphone with a dead battery lay next to her. If I'd held it to my ear I might have heard, like the sea raging inside a shell, its last conversation from a few hours earlier.

"Hello."

"Mom."

"Jonathan?" The tone of her voice was recognizable even in those few syllables. If my mom receives a phone call at two o'clock in the morning she immediately knows why. It's happened to her too many times.

"She's gone, Mom."

"Oh no. I'm so sorry."

I told her we were all heading back to Sue's parents' house, and I'd call her in the morning. Then in the earpiece, a crackling followed by another silence.

The angel and dead phone sat as a quiet still life on the table; they'd done their jobs. I didn't feel much like calling my mother back. I didn't feel like talking to anybody. It was quiet in my in-laws' house. Sue's parents, George and Joyce, might have been waking up with their usual morning coffee. Her sister, Nancy, definitely hadn't emerged from her basement quarters. Myles, barely six months old, was with my mother an hour away. *Oh God, Myles. I could use one of his hugs.* He'd just lost the mother he'd never know. My only consolation: his age precluded me from having to break the news to him.

Finally wrenching myself off the bed, I got dressed (I must have), wordlessly moved to the door and out of the house. There was only one place to go.

The sun poured in through the glass ceiling onto the white marble-ish floors, chrome banisters, and towering faux palm trees of Mapleview Mall, deep in the suburban jungle. Footsteps echoed amid the chatter between women and their pram-pampered youngsters. I floated along the hospital-white corridor to the Bell Mobility shop on the top floor. *What the hell am I doing here? Is there even any money in my wallet?* I knew I needed control: the new phone battery. I wanted something to hold, buy, stroke, heal — something that would react sympathetically to my desperate touch. And it was right there across from the food court. After months of freefalling I found myself grasping for the rip cord so that, perhaps, my landing might be softened. But it was still a long way down to the ground. Sue had been dead for about ten hours.

Surely my ripening grief was evident on my face. Among the throngs of preening teenagers and yummy mummies, I must have been the blackest of sheep. Mourners don't shop in suburban malls. They wear black suits and sit in wingback chairs in the corner; they stare at the ground while loved ones hold their hands and talk at them; at best they parade down Bourbon Street to the strains of "When the Saints Go Marching In." I just wanted to walk invisibly into the shop and take what I needed. I didn't want to be asked, "May I help you?" by some clueless, pimple-faced employee. Even if he could help me.

I bought what I'd gone for and left the mall. Driving back to my in-laws' house, I looked toward the horizon and I saw nothing. The world around me — trees, sky, cars, shops, people — was a collection of vague shapes in muted hues. They neither attracted nor repelled me. My vision obtuse, everything was peripheral. My only reality was that my wife was dead, and I was solely responsible for our child. I shouldn't have been allowed behind the wheel.

"I'm going to go home tonight," I told Sue's family when I got back. "I just … I need to … I think I'm going to go home."

"Oh, sure," Joyce said.

"Okay, Jon," said George. "That's…"

"Will you come back tomorrow?"

"Yes."

"Good," said George. "Then we can plan the … uh…"

"Yes. We will. I'll see you tomorrow."

How did I get home? I have no memory of saying goodbye, getting into the car, or travelling the sixty kilometres home to Toronto. No memory of pulling into the drive behind the house on Humberside Avenue or going inside. Did I eat? Did I make any phone calls? Did the house seem empty, larger, wrong without Sue?

The memory fast-forwards like a hissing blank tape until faint images start to emerge like faded photos in one of the well-loved albums Sue had industriously compiled. The photo albums that still rested on the bookcase where Sue had put them. Every January she started a new album, and by the time she installed that year's Christmas photos, she had bought the album for the next year. All had stickers on their spines indicating the year documented inside the covers. We'd been together for ten years, but there were more than ten albums, owing to the special editions: Wedding, Honeymoon, France 2000, Childhood Photos.

I picked up the album from our honeymoon — two and a half weeks in the Greek islands — carried it upstairs and spread it open on our bed. The two cats, Sydney and Seattle, followed me up as usual, and Mika the dog stayed downstairs. Turning the album pages slowly, I relived our dream vacation. We'd travelled to five different islands and finished with four days in Athens where we scaled the Acropolis and shopped at the Agora. On Crete we hung out on a nude beach and visited the palace of Knossos. On Paros we took a self-guided history tour. On Naxos we slept. One night on the island of Mykonos, after a seaside meal of lamb and rice, flaming cheese, baklava, and ouzo, we talked about Sue's metaphysical beliefs and faith in reincarnation. Reading horoscopes always gave her a tingly delight, and she was soothed by the conviction that she might someday return to this world as someone else. She was certain that we were destined to be together not only in this life but every subsequent one. I never shared her belief, but her resolve was so undeniable that I often thought I did. She decided on this night in Mykonos that whichever one of us died first should find a way to prove to the other that they were okay — a signal from the afterlife that would allow the surviving spouse to gain some peace. She suggested that the spirit should leave the honeymoon photo album open on our bed. I was unsure how this could be achieved, but we kissed on it and stared out at the boisterous Aegean waves crashing into the seawall at our feet. I never thought about it again.

On Santorini we rented a moped. Taking turns driving, we scooted around the tiny island like Peck and Hepburn in *Roman Holiday*. In one photo, I'm sitting on the moped halfway up Santorini's highest peak during a rest stop. I'm smiling at Sue as if the mountain we are scaling is love itself. Looking at that picture in the album on our bed, almost eight years after it was taken, I started to laugh, a big, beefy laugh that shook the bed and my overloaded emotions. Inserted into the slot that held the photo was a small piece of red fibreglass, a shard from the moped's broken front fender. Moments after that photo was taken, I had lost control and driven into a parked car. Sue had collected a piece of the shattered fender and put it into the scrapbook as a souvenir. She thought it was hysterical and teased me about it for the rest of her life. I laughed out loud at the memory of my bruised pride and at Sue's cheekiness for keeping the souvenir. Then through the hilarity came the piercing memory of the agreement we made by the sea in Mykonos. Her message had been received.

I threw my head back until it hit the pillow. With my eyes closed, convulsing, I could hear Sue laughing with me. She held my hand and stroked my cheek while giggling more enthusiastically than I was. Like an inconsolable cartoon character, my nourishing giggles promptly morphed into wrenching tears. The unrelenting vigour with which I cried caught me off guard. I thought the dam had already been opened, but until now it had only been a trickle. Not since I could remember had I cried with such abandon, freely and unedited. These new tears were born of a deeply plaintive well, of necessity, of truth. They came from a place so mysterious, like the source of the Amazon, that its reservoir might forever remain hidden. They were thick but generous. They were in fact, though I couldn't admit it at the time, welcome.

The sound of my own crying was foreign to me, like some tribal gulping and clucking and indiscriminate mewling. In all my years as an actor and singer, I had never made these sounds with my voice. I was lost in a bombastic symphony whose overture and finale washed together in an endless unresolved cadence. The true song of sadness.

I opened my blurry eyes and looked up at the impenetrable white cloud of the ceiling. From somewhere below the cloud, among pillows and photographs and broken fenders, I heard a voice. At first it mumbled something from far away like chatter on a distant radio. But it quickly grew louder and clearer until the radio was blaring, its gut-twisting bass stirring my bowels and the treble ringing inside my head. "Sue," it shrieked. The voice rang out in abrasive, pulsating tremors, slashing through the cloud and echoing back down to the bed. My mouth was dry and my face was wet. "Sue," the voice cried out again, "I … miss you … so much."

Like driftwood on an open sea, the merciless waves cradled and rocked me in endless undulations until, at last, the turbulence stilled and I glided out to float in the middle of a vast nothingness. There was only that moment and then the next, each growing quieter and calmer, begging for equilibrium. I caught my breath. I craved and feared the sleep that was approaching. My eyes stung. The first day of my life without Sue ended as it had begun.

* * *

The Four Corners region of America's southwest is so named because it's the only example of four states — Utah, Colorado, Arizona, and New Mexico, four of the squarest states in the union, geographically speaking — meeting at one juncture. And it's not just declared on the map, it's on the ground too. From the Colorado side I followed the road signs pointing toward the Four Corners until I found a parking lot for the visitors centre beside a huge paved concrete slab surrounded by flags. The borders of the four states were embossed on the ground in compass formation. The spectacle made over this site was greater than I thought was deserved. It was a quick stop on the tourist trail that required little more than a photograph of Myles sitting in four states at once. He even removed his sun hat to show his reverence for the momentous occasion. From the small podium positioned for just such photo-taking, I looked around in every direction and wondered why this spot in the middle of the featureless desert should be chosen to delineate state borders. Why did the USA, so nationalistic, still regard state borders with such eminence? I imagined dozens of bearded, bespectacled men in black coats and stovepipe hats sitting around a map of the nineteenth-century territories, one of them chosen to close his eyes and point to a place on the map. "Let this place now and forever be known as the Four Corners." I might not be too far off.

The truth is, like mostly everything else I saw, I didn't care why it existed. It mattered simply that I was there. The amusing and mystifying randomness of this location mirrored other random moments that I'd been reflecting on, those inexplicable events during a lifetime that can't necessarily be traced back to choices being made: falling in love with someone you met by chance; the joining of a sperm and an egg; contracting a deadly disease. Randomness was all around me.

Nobody else came to visit the Four Corners while we were there, making it lonely and wanting. I picked Myles up from that celebrated spot and quietly carried him back to the car. There was an eerie calm in the desert despite a light wind blowing in no distinct direction. There were no voices. No sounds of animals or cars. I wondered if it was possible to get lost out there. The sun was poised directly over our heads, suspended in a cloudless sky. The desert had been bleached by the sun, whitening the redness, the consistent light suggesting it was never any other way.

I had the sense that, although I was still heading west, I was about as far from home as I could be. I'd been deposited into this austere otherworld because someone or something wanted me to take note of the emptiness, the colourlessness, and the vastness, deeming it to be far more critical than any other setting I'd previously been shown. But what was I supposed to learn? What could I discover here that might elude me in the real world? I was there but I wasn't. I was alone but I wasn't. I was free but I wasn't. With this mystery fresh in my mind, I drove deeper into the desert.

We headed north into Utah, a state I knew only for references to the Mormons and an inaptly named NBA team. The desert took me out of my comfort zone and out of my head. Those reds and greens didn't exist in steel-grey Toronto. Neither did the panorama or the dry air. To me, this vista was in a place of fantasy, a land of artistic interpretation. The desert was Georgia O'Keeffe paintings and old Hollywood westerns. It was Frank Lloyd Wright and Sam Shepard. It was part wasteland, part kaleidoscope. By the time I'd arrived, I found it was the ideal landscape for lamentation.

Having barrelled through the Valley of the Gods — a vast, uninhabited, prehistoric landscape — I charged down Route 191 with the windows down and the volume up. I screamed into the rushing wind along with Sting and the Police that all I wanted was to be "next to you." Myles settled into his morning nap, disturbed by neither the wind nor my boisterous singing. I was certain the music was getting through to him despite his effortless napping, certain that the louder I screamed the greater chance of his subliminal absorption. I kept looking over my shoulder to check if he might be tapping his toe or "grooving," as we used to say.

Back in the heady days of Still Life, my old band, when making music was as close to a job as I'd ever known, singing was a joy. Gig after gig, the opportunity to open my mouth and let loose with poetry delivered over incisive melodies was the only therapy I needed. Singing brought definition and regeneration to my life regardless of what may have been happening elsewhere. Every note I sang was born in a private place deep within me, a place of peace, of stillness. From that place I could project — in various degrees of intensity — hope, yearning, wonder, joy, love, sadness, or just a story. After Sue died, I no longer felt the peace that compelled me to sing for people; the thought of publicly celebrating my joy was not just unappealing, it was completely alien. But I still sang for myself and for Myles. A familiar melody was as much comfort as a hug from an old friend. Melodies could heal. So I never suppressed the songs swimming through my head. Each song was a step toward finding that peace again; of reaching the stillness without the dark, unsettled subtext of grief. I'd often sing Myles to sleep and lay him in his crib as my tears dripped onto his face. He didn't mind; tears were a part of the music. Singing in the car, whether shouting at the desert wind or quietly serenading the rolling green hills, defined the momentum. It was a response to the tugging rope.

The mysterious state of Utah welcomed us with some small examples of the sandstone formations I was looking forward to seeing in Monument Valley. Proud, craggy shapes that stood like enormous, crude root vegetables: multi-limbed carrots, harlequin potatoes, and ginger sprouting from the orange-red clay earth, their tuber-arms raised to the sky for having triumphed over millennia of erosion. The backdrop of pale blue sky accentuated their dark rusty bodies, opposites on a colour wheel.

The sun was nearing its zenith, and the sandstone now glowed, inflamed by the sun's relentlessness. Up ahead, ten o'clock on the compass, something distracted me from the perpetual soundtrack and the red vista. Through the fluttering terrestrial refraction, it appeared to be alive — *are there black bears in Utah?* Moving closer it looked less threatening. A camper's tent maybe. Soon it became clear. I pulled over onto the shoulder as I reached a burned-out pizza delivery car, left to languish at the foot of one of the magnificent sandstone figures. The hood was raised to ninety degrees, its charred engine lying prostrate like carrion under the sun. The windows were blown out and there were no tires on what might formerly have been a Honda, but the magnetic sign on the driver's door was still intact and legible. I stared at the incongruous, once-green pile of steel superimposed against the rich red sand.

Someone might have died here. Lives may have been altered. A loved one could be driving around the desert seeking solace and momentum, looking for signs of life.

I looked up the road and then back from where we'd come. We were alone, my sleeping son and me, and the inscrutable Honda. We were kilometres away from any town; I hadn't seen a house in hours. Who could have ordered a pizza around here?

Utah has some of the most interesting geography in the US. In Bryce Canyon there are terrific examples of hoodoos, towering rock-capped spires of sandstone. Salt Lake City sits by a large inland sea. Further south is the Arches National Park, where massive sandstone archways rise over the desert. I would have liked to see it all, but we drove only as far as the Natural Bridges National Monument, nearly one hundred kilometres inside Utah's southern border. Myles and I trekked down into the valley sculpted millions of years ago by winding rivers that carved through the siltstone leaving, as the name suggests, bridges of stone to span the valley. Here the earth was less red, more sand-coloured, and the erosion had left it with a wrinkled, elephantine texture. Small pines dotted the rocks and valley floor. My sandals kicked up clouds of warm brown dust from the path with every step. I had to stop frequently so Myles and I could rehydrate in the dry, searing heat. On the way down Myles giggled at a small snake we found hidden in a crevice; I identified it later as a milksnake. I didn't know anything about snakes — I still don't — but I figured if it had been poisonous, it wouldn't have stayed so tranquil in the wake of Myles's giggles.

We met one couple climbing up the valley path as we were heading down — a slight smile and a cursory "Hi" — and an older, single man who was kind enough to snap a picture of Myles and me in front of the most impressive formation, called the Owachomo Bridge. Otherwise the valley belonged to us and to the snakes, and again nobody asked questions as to why I was out there in the desert alone with a baby on my back.

The next day was the one I'd been looking forward to since we left Toronto. I'd always wanted to see Monument Valley and the Grand Canyon. Since I was a kid, pictures of these immense, distinctive places fascinated me. These formations were evidence of the mysterious nature of nature … in epic proportions.

Route 160 took me directly through Monument Valley — though I soon discovered it wasn't the part of Monument Valley I'd seen in all the movies, the part with formations that look like massive mittens. But I didn't care. They were still the large stone buttes, flushed red with iron oxide, sticking up from the desert floor with monumental immodesty, as I'd hoped. Besides, I was already familiar with the place thanks to the esteemed film repertoire featuring the Road Runner and Wile E. Coyote. The compulsion to move forward reigned, if only for the secure knowledge that there was a Super 8 at the end of the road. I located our home-from-home in Williams, Arizona, about sixty-five kilometres south of Grand Canyon Village. I figured we'd have a solid three hours to enjoy the view.

When you think of holes in the ground that had been incised by a river — something I witnessed on a much smaller scale at the local ravine down the road from where I grew up — you wouldn't expect anything like this. But the Grand Canyon is suitably named. It is four hundred and fifty-five kilometres long, at times thirty kilometres wide, and in many places two and a half kilometres deep, tearing through the layered landscape in a jagged swath of dusty red earth. By now, the desert colours had blanketed my vision as if I'd been wearing rust-coloured glasses. I carried Myles in his pack along the rim of the canyon, sitting occasionally in an attempt to recognize the heft of this moment; to pay heed to this giant earth, us tiny humans merely rambling over its canyons, gorges, mountains, and oceans. Among the swarms of tourists, I was once again reduced to near invisibility. Young people scuttled over rocks perched precariously at the edge of the void, proving their youth and fearlessness. Retired couples strode hand in hand thrilled, I imagined, to finally be having that adventurous holiday for which they'd saved their whole lives. Everyone took photographs to share in sentimental delight for years to come.

I took pictures too because I didn't have the words. I saw the canyon only because it was there. I was lost in thought under the big sky, hundreds of metres above the canyon floor, but could find only wordless images to bubble in syncopation with one another. Thinking of Sue made me sad, and my sadness made me think of Sue; I would be talking in circles. Most days I only had to say "hello" and "thank you." Otherwise there was no need to say anything at all.

Despite feeling invisible, I thought the sight of a man crying at the top of a two and a half kilometre drop, baby in tow, might not be part of the traditional Grand Canyon experience people had come to expect. It hadn't lived up to my unreachable expectations either. It turned out to be just another hole in the ground. We left after an hour.

On the way back to the car I paused in the gift shop and bought a Grand Canyon t-shirt with "The journey is the destination" written on it. I'd heard people say that phrase before, but I'd never read it. Most people say it stressing the word *is*, as if emphasizing one as the definition of the other. When I read it, I stressed the word *journey*, as if it alone was sufficient to underscore where I was going.

Scattered around the desert states were other holes in the ground I'd heard about: colossal craters formed by meteor collisions thousands of years ago. I'd also heard it alleged that these craters may actually have resulted from an alien spaceship crash. I knew Area 51, the US Air Force base suspected of housing proof of these aliens, was nearby, but I didn't know exactly where and I didn't feel like searching for it. If it hadn't been for the television series *The X-Files*, I wouldn't have known any of these things. If there is life on another planet — and who am I to say there isn't? — I'll need more proof than a hole in the New Mexico desert. I'm not convinced there is such a thing as paranormal phenomena. I've never bought into life after death, and I'm convinced ESP is trickery. I definitely don't believe in fate or destiny. Or even prayer.

Sue believed in all of these things. She had an inherent gift for finding explanations for the unexplained and always insisted she'd obtain proof that everything happens for a reason. "Be careful what you wish for," she was fond of saying. She was prepared to move through her life completely trusting that it would turn out just the way it had been predetermined. Despite a healthy agnosticism, she drew comfort from the belief that we were somehow meant to follow a certain path. She told well-rehearsed stories about how she and I met to prove that our meeting hadn't been accidental. In her mind it was all part of something much larger than both of us. So when we talked about death — before her diagnosis — from this life or any other, she took it very seriously.

"Which one of us do you hope dies first?" We were lying in bed shortly after we'd gotten engaged and she casually asked this question as if she wanted to know what kind of puppy I wanted.

"What?" *Please no, not this question.*

"Do you want to die first or do you hope it's me?" *I like Dalmatians!*

"I couldn't answer that," I said. Oh boy. I needed time to prepare for this question. I couldn't just improvise.

"It's a simple question."

Simple? "What about you?" I said.

"I asked you first."

She could take my stalling no longer. Here I was, stark naked with my arm around the woman to whom I'd committed my future, knowing that we were about to tread on some very sensitive ground. Whatever I said, no matter how sincere or well-intentioned, Sue was bound to be ready with some spiky comment to prove I hadn't given the issue much consideration. She'd probably been thinking about this one for months.

I stared at the pale clouds through the skylight over the bed, trying not to look like I was thinking too hard.

To Sue, so many things were simply common sense, and as far as she was concerned everyone thought the same way she did. But what was common sense to her was not necessarily common to me. She'd get frustrated by our differences. "How were you brought up?" she'd say, or if I vigilantly chose my words and spoke slowly: "Who talks that way?" Sometimes, the harder I tried to be clear, the more she'd question. This was the quagmire through which I walked.

The obvious response would be to say, "Me. I hope I die first because I couldn't bear to live without you." And that would have been true. I should have just said that right then and there. Just spat it out so she could be sad for a little while and wonder if perhaps I really did want to die in order to free myself from her "captive spell." But then I thought about how sad she would be if I died. I wouldn't want that. *She loves me. She just told me she loves me.* After a reasonably judicious amount of time passed, I tried, martyr-like, to make it sound as if I would suffer her death so that she could be spared suffering mine.

"I hope it's you," I said. "Because I'd hate for you to have to live without me."

In my head that sounded selfless and sincere: I had put her happiness before my own. Out loud it sounded selfish and heartless. Sue got very quiet and then started to cry.

"I can't believe you said you wanted me to die."

We never spoke about it again.

I'm sure she remembered the conversation; she remembered every conversation. I wouldn't have been surprised if she had thought of it years later while she was lying unconscious in her hospital bed. Because I, while watching her in that bed, waiting for her life to end, couldn't shake the memory of it from my own mind. There was a large index finger jabbing me squarely in the sternum saying, "You ... wished ... this."

Of all the wishes I'd made throughout my entire life, voiced aloud or otherwise, the only one to actually materialize was the one I wanted least of all. But it wasn't a wish. It didn't mean anything. I couldn't possibly have prophesied my wife's death simply by preferring it to my own. Could I? It was just a game — one of those games that's supposed to help couples know each other better. A game I knew I would lose.

I vowed I would avoid those games if I were ever in a relationship again.

There was no danger of my losing any games when Myles and I got to Las Vegas the next day. I wasn't there to gamble, nor did I have the means or the inclination. But after the Grand Canyon and a brief look at the Hoover Dam, Vegas was the next logical place to go. We pulled into the Super 8 — complete with a twenty-four-hour casino though it's well off the main drag — early enough to wander up and down Las Vegas Boulevard: the Strip. That's where I discovered that Las Vegas is an amusement park with suburbs.

Driving into Vegas was not unlike entering any other American city. Sporadic rural homes started to get closer together until they melded into tightly knit peripheral communities. The freeway led to the centre of town, where the commercial and social core of the city flaunted wealth and poverty within the same city block. In the daylight, the panoply of colours fronting the Las Vegas shops and casinos seemed an attempt to make up for the neutral-coloured desert that surrounded them. By night — though Myles and I were in bed early — the neon and fluorescent lights on every surface, each building trying to outdo its neighbours, made you forget that there was even such a thing as daylight. I saw marquees that reminded me of performers plugging their gigs on Johnny Carson: Siegfried and Roy at the Mirage, Don Rickles at the Stardust, and Celine Dion at Caesars Palace. For our supper, Myles and I shared a twelve-ounce sirloin steak at the Outback Steakhouse. Ever since Jack's barbecue that night back in Santa Fe, I'd been hankering for another slab of red meat.

I didn't see any other dads — or moms, for that matter — pushing children in Las Vegas. I wondered if carrying a young child through the Bellagio casino was reason to be stopped and questioned. Apparently it wasn't. I was curious to see what the inside of one of these places really looked and felt like. Myles looked around at the infinite flashing lights and was stunned into silence, his consistent smile momentarily neutralized by input overload. I thought maybe I should protect his sensitive ears from the incessant blips, beeps, bells, pings, and whirs. But I'd seen enough; I literally walked in one side and out the other. Outside we watched the Bellagio's famous fountain "performance": an aquatic ballet of sorts, incandescent colours above and below the water glistening in the early evening half-light. Beside us, a young couple canoodled against the Romanesque balustrade. He stood behind her, his arms wrapped tightly around her torso just underneath her perfect, healthy breasts. Their eyes were on the fountain; they were blissfully unaware of the single dad and baby next to them.

The next day Myles and I would cross the state border into California, our week in the desert nearly over. By this time, the desert had come to exist as one idiosyncratic moment; a single piece of red clay rolled into a giant ball. Between Santa Fe and Southern California, it was a week of sameness. The Southwest had become:

mesaverdefourcornerspainteddesertmonumentvalleygrandcanyonlasvegas

The infinite redness, at some point, turned colourless, as if the sun had become threadbare. Where was the colour, the green of forest-lined back roads, the arable vegetable-producing farmland that fed America? Where were the seasons? Where was the variety, the choice of where to look so that the eye could, in a single moment, receive nature's full spectrum? In the desert, the rainbow had been dulled to a monochromatic pencil sketch. In the produce department at any roadside supermarket, I might find every missing colour I craved. But out on the road, driving for the sake of driving, amid the sandstone and dust, I felt galaxies away from the bright green hues of broccoli or lettuce, the glowing yellow lemons, or the vibrant, non-rusty red of a crispy pepper. Was this the lesson I was supposed to have learned?

The desert was beautiful, but it lacked freshness. It felt dead.

9

Death Valley didn't seem like a good place to go. After the Kansas fiasco, I was wary of being too far from a gas station, and it didn't sound like it was exactly heaving with places to top up. Also I wanted to see Joshua Tree National Park, which meant veering south toward Los Angeles, the city I thought I might head toward next. But mostly I didn't go there because it's called *Death* Valley. So I drove into California, put on some music, and waited to see some green.

I'd selected my CDs three weeks earlier with no other predictive reasoning than what I might enjoy listening to. I didn't have specific music in mind that would relate to any particular moment, but occasionally it worked out that way.

"This is *The Joshua Tree* by U2," I said, as the California sun settled into a hazy afternoon nap. "All of these songs were written about this part of the world."

I told Myles how the songs we heard upheld the band's mid-eighties obsession with America: songs about desert communities, about patriotism, about searching for an identity.

"There's that familiar guitar again."

The instruments resonated out of the speakers as if they were echoing across the very desert Bono sang about. I was certain many fans of the group had spent countless hours searching the Joshua Tree National Park — covering more than 3,100 square kilometres of the Mojave Desert in Southern California — for the very tree photographed on the album cover. A tall order indeed. From the road, I thought every tree I saw could have been the one. It seemed only appropriate that I should play this CD loud and often as I drove under the blue sky along streets with no names.

I wished I could have closed my eyes and driven at the same time. My forward momentum married the music, the rushing wind, and my restlessness, but occasionally the visual noise deflected the melodies and the mood. There was too much to look at considering I couldn't see anything.

At the western edge of the park, nearing San Bernardino, I saw a sign telling me it was only 160 kilometres to Los Angeles. If I continued straight ahead, I could be in LA before dinner. I'd never been there before, but from where I'd been that afternoon, it seemed like a dead end. I'd had enough of the desert, certainly, but I didn't want to substitute it with one of the largest urban areas in the world. I turned right and drove 160 kilometres north to the town of Ridgecrest instead. I pulled into the Super 8, unpacked the car, and then took it across the road for an oil change while Myles and I ate dinner at a nearby roadhouse. After dinner, as usual, we rolled a ball around the hotel room floor until Myles got tired enough for one last bottle of milk, which he drank from the comfort of my lap. I laid him in his bed and he drifted off quickly, as expected. I turned on the television, did some sit-ups, had a shower, and wrote in my journal. As I wrote, the sun set outside our ground-floor window, and I acknowledged the peacefulness of my world inside this room. Everything I needed was here, familiar like a habit. *Who needs stupid old LA?* I got ready for bed, prepared to tackle the Sierra Nevada mountains and Yosemite National Park.

My nights alone were as beneficial as my days with Myles in the car. They were two sides of the same coin — all a part of the same job. Hearing him sleep while I wrote or watched television was the perfect soundtrack to my evenings; his soft inhalations and exhalations like distant ocean waves that would pacify me and, when needed, lull me into a vital sleep.

* * *

It's impossible to describe Yosemite without reverting to descriptions of Ansel Adams photographs. Because what is most remarkable about the park is not simply the magnificent granite mountains, half domes, and wooded valleys thick with black oaks and dogwood trees. Nor is it the satisfying drive along the winding, sometimes dizzying roads running through the park with breathtaking views in every direction. No, most extraordinary is the indescribable light cast on all of these things, at once robust and fragile, subdued and rhapsodic. A shadow on a cliffside can stop you in your tracks. Beams of sunlight filtering through delicate cloud cover could introduce God to even the most ardent non-believer. These light pictures told stories that Adams suspended in time and, in the process, set the bar too high for any other Yosemite storyteller to reach, let alone surpass.

I discovered that the park was too big to appreciate in the amount of time I was prepared to dedicate. I hadn't planned on camping; I didn't rent a lodge. It was merely another marker on this non-stop forward-moving extravaganza. A brief hike with Myles on my back was about all I could take. I'd found a clearly marked path that set out from a parking lot near Yosemite's centre. After one bend in the trail, the cars were no longer visible behind us. The ubiquitous granite boulders closed in on us like the walls of a shrinking room and the thick grasses grew taller, tapering the path. The trees in this part of the park were thinly dispersed, so I could still see the sky. I felt no danger, even after the path seemed to end, so I kept walking through the tall flora, stopping now and then to show Myles some happy bees pollinating the wildflowers. When I'd gone a few hundred metres further, I stopped. If I'd been there by myself, I might have explored more and considered setting up camp. I'd spent enough time in the Ontario wilderness to feel at home without street signs, porcelain facilities, or a thick mattress. I would have gladly gotten lost in there. But I recalled the virtual bear encounter in New Mexico and the ghostly conversation with Sue back in Kansas. My priorities were to keep Myles safe and to keep myself moving forward. In my mind, if I couldn't see all of Yosemite, then I wouldn't try to see any more than this. I found the way back to the car and drove out the western gate. We'd spent only about three hours in one of the most beautiful places I'd ever seen.

In the tiny hippy town of Mariposa, sixty-five kilometres west of Yosemite in the Sierra Nevada foothills, we settled in for the night. I phoned my friend Rob, whom I'd promised we'd visit in San Francisco, to tell him we'd be arriving the next day. After I put Myles to bed, I sat back with my feet up and picked up my journal, but I was at a loss for what to write, still reeling from what I'd seen that day in the park. Maybe it was a trick of the light, but part of me was still there. Instead I reflected on my willingness to feel pleasure in the wake of so much sadness.

Sometimes it's difficult to allow myself to have

a good time ... without guilt.

But we were having a good time, Myles and me. Most of the pleasure was simply spending every hour with my son, driving, finding places to eat, checking into hotels: the minutiae of our new normal. Myles's steady smile and consistently mellow disposition suggested he was enjoying himself too. But I also had to acknowledge that I'd done the right thing by leaving the confining four walls of home, where I was nearly always sad. That was my job: to work through the grief. Out here I was allowed to appreciate the joys often overlooked when distracted by the mundaneness of daily life. Sometimes those happy moments were dulled by the sadness superimposed onto them. But other times the day's pleasures seemed greater, given the sadness with which I had awakened. Either way, I had given myself permission to find happiness. It didn't mean I was over Sue, far from it. It meant I didn't have to be estranged from the rest of my life; I could experience my grief as a part of it. Somehow I recognized that I would eventually get through this; someday I would be happy again, full stop.

* * *

The 260-kilometre drive from Mariposa to San Francisco took us through the lush Sacramento Valley — part of the great Central Valley of California, which is sandwiched between the Sierra Nevada to the east and the Coast Ranges to the west — into Oakland's dense industry, across San Francisco Bay to the Golden Gate Bridge. I was no longer landlocked. Reaching the Pacific Ocean felt like how I imagine a sailor would feel upon seeing land after weeks at sea. Only in reverse.

Rob lived just north of the city with his fiancée Hilary, whom I'd never met. I really didn't know Rob that well either — at least not as an adult — but his stepfather and my father had been professorial colleagues at the same university in Illinois and became close friends. When we were kids, our families got together for most holidays. Rob and my sister, Lainie, were similar in age, which helped bond the families. The last time I'd seen Rob was at my wedding, where he briefly stood between me and Sue and read a poem about the power of relationships, how they would endure despite the obstacles of time and space. I believed him then and I still did, which is why I felt comfortable dropping in after not seeing him in eight years.

We drove into San Francisco from the Oakland side, crossing the Bay Bridge as the late-morning fog lifted. By the time we'd driven through the city, crossed the Golden Gate, and arrived at Rob's house in San Rafael, the midday sun was at its peak. When I got out of the car, I thought my feet would sink into the melting asphalt. I carried Myles up to the door past Rob's Toyota Prius, parked in the driveway. He was the first person I knew with a "green" car. It echoed his lifestyle despite living in a car-centric country and working in IT. He answered the door in a pair of shorts and nothing else, his sweaty chest glistening.

"Jon. Myles. Come in," he said, as if we were neighbours popping by for a cup of coffee. There was little eye contact as we entered. "Hilary," he called out, "Jon and Myles are here." He closed the door and then gave me a sticky, shirtless hug, his scratchy beard and hairy chest sticking to me like Velcro. I discreetly wiped my chin.

So far his welcome did not live up to the standards set by Uncle Jack, but I was not deterred. I remembered Rob as being warm and kind, exemplified by the times as kids when he used to let me ride his bicycle with the drop handles, which was far cooler than my own bike with the banana seat and pedal brakes. There was no doubt in my mind that he would once again prove his generosity.

Rob and Hilary paid great attention to Myles that first day, which I welcomed, but the subject of Sue never surfaced. I didn't mind not talking about her — she was always on my mind, so the occasional distraction was appreciated — but I didn't appreciate feeling like they were avoiding the topic altogether. It was part of my job to talk about her, the gasoline in my engine of bereavement. Rob's uneasiness, if that's what it was, was not surprising. I'd experienced it many times after Sue died; more intimate friends than Rob said they wanted to come see me, but that they expected I needed time alone. It wasn't my discomfort they were concerned about.

I gave Rob the benefit of the doubt and waited for the opportunity to speak openly with him.

The next day, Rob and Myles and I went to a baseball game with Rob's daughter, Jessica. I wanted to see what was then called Pacific Bell Park, where Barry Bonds was currently in the habit of hitting balls into McCovey Cove by the truckload. Being a Giants fan, Rob acquired tickets before I'd finished suggesting it. As we drove down to the ballpark, I tried to lure Rob into my emotional jurisdiction.

"I owe you an apology," I said.

"What for?"

"Because I didn't get in touch with you after your mom died," I said. Lillian had been like a special aunt to me. She had four boys of her own — Rob was the youngest — but always gave me the kind of love destined for her fifth. She'd died three years earlier. Sue and I lived in Windsor at the time, and we were deep into our own lives, far away from death and sadness.

"Oh, Jon. Never mind about that."

"No, really. I never even sent you an email."

"It's not important. Really. In fact I wouldn't have remembered unless you told me."

I think that was meant to let me off the hook. But I wanted to talk about Sue.

"Anyway, I'm sorry," I said. "I wanted so much to tell you how important your mother was to me but I couldn't find the words. The longer I put it off the more difficult it became."

"It's fine. I understand."

We went back over the Golden Gate. The famous deep-orange towers glowed in the midday sun like large, stone buttes flushed red with iron oxide.

"Besides," he said, "I'm not so sure you heard from me when Sue died."

"Yes, I did. You were one of the first I heard from."

"Oh. Well…" He paused. "It's not a competition."

"Of course it isn't," I said. "But the point is I've learned something from all this, which you might find interesting. When my father died, I was seven years old. Learning about death that early in life gave me an understanding that death was an obvious, unavoidable fact of life."

Rob listened as he guided me through Pacific Heights and Russian Hill toward the stadium.

"I thought nothing could be worse than me losing my father at a young age," I said. "So every time I was faced with dealing with death — whether it was my grandparents, my Aunt Julie, your mom, or anybody else — I just felt … impassive. Almost apathetic. I was sad, but I wasn't changed by the experience. My father's death had numbed me against being moved to any great extent. So that was it. I figured that was his legacy to me: to inure me against grief."

Rob said "Uh-huh" a few times as we inched along the Embarcadero. He knew my father and certainly had his own memories of him.

"Until Sue died," I said. "That was when I discovered true sadness, and that was when I realized the effect my father's death had on me. That numbing sense had left me unprepared for the depth of grief ... of the genuine grief I have right now. So I think it hit me even harder, if that's possible."

"I think we all deal with death differently," Rob said. "There's no right way to do it. But for what it's worth, it seems to me you're doing really well."

"I've got Myles to help me."

"That's obvious. He's an amazing kid ... Hilary and I just love him."

"Thanks." I wasn't sure if he was trying to change the subject or not. "Anyway, I don't know if that justifies my behaviour, but I hope that from now on I'll be more sensitive to other people's losses."

"I suspect you will be. But you don't need to justify anything. Our families have a bond, Jon. It's something I appreciate."

I think I needed that reminder. Sometimes recognizing a historical bond is enough to draw the present into perspective. I hoped the history I was striving to make with Myles would somehow be linked to the history of the rest of my life, despite the jagged cleft cut down the middle of it. Sue's death had left a scar in my history, marked like the rings of a tree that has lived through great hardship, yet there was only one way forward. Forward.

"I'd love to hear more about Sue," Rob said.

"I'd love to tell you," I said.

That afternoon we watched the Florida Marlins beat the San Francisco Giants 7–4. Myles paid little attention to the action on the field — to be fair, even the most exciting baseball games don't have a lot of what might be called "action," especially for a ten month old — but he seemed to enjoy being among tens of thousands of rowdy sports fans. For the rest of our time in San Francisco, Rob and I spoke with greater ease about why I was there.

Back at Rob and Hilary's house, Myles crawled around the ground floor while I helped prepare that evening's meal. I was setting the table when I looked around to see what Myles was up to. I spotted him nearing the landing at the top of the first flight of stairs.

"Hey … you've never done that before," I said.

"What's that?" Rob asked from the kitchen.

"He just climbed his first stairs," I said proudly.

Things were moving forward.

10

The Pacific wind picks up speed as it careens across the water eastward toward the California shore, where it vaults over the cliffside and assaults whatever happens to be driving along the Pacific Coast Highway — Route 1. On this twisty, often vertiginous road, my car, which had sheltered me through the desert like an armoured tank, seemed vulnerable. The gusts challenged the little silver Toyota's traction — and my skills as a driver — as it tried to force me out of my lane. This was the stretch of highway on which road-trip dreams are made: aerial shots of the handsome leading man, right arm around the dishy blonde, driving a cherry-red Alfa Romeo convertible, majestic views on both sides of the two-lane highway. But I couldn't appreciate the scenery for fear of driving over the edge. No hot blonde either, just the adorable bald kid in the back. Still, it was better than the interstate.

We'd been on this road since we left the Bay area. Like the desert and Grand Canyon before it, the ocean made me feel small. As I drove north, the gentle arc of the sea's horizon seemed to hang like an enormous, ghostly umbrella over my little world. It quieted me. My thoughts drifted. I was sure the mighty ocean would swallow me up on its way to quenching the dusty terrain of Southern California and the Sierras' burning rash. I was torn between following the invisible rope that pulled me toward my unknown destination and the desire to stop and absorb the panorama to the west, to experience stillness beside the great rumbling waves.

Somewhere approaching Mendocino, the road followed the curve of one of the coves that dug into the cliff as if a great undersea giant had taken a bite out of America. At the far end of the cove, as the road swung back toward the sea, I saw a small sign with a picture of a picnic table, then a turnoff on the left that led to a small, empty parking area surrounded by grass and picnic tables. Making a quick decision, I pulled in and parked. I lifted Myles from his car seat, carried him over to the cliff edge, and sat down on the rough grass looking toward the boisterous sea. The wind tore into the cliff from the seaside and gushed over the edge, making sure we stayed seated. To our left, the jagged brown rocks of the cliff wall that formed the cove we'd just driven around; to our right, the largest body of water in the world. Down below, the whitecapped waves crashed through dozens of rocky obstacles sticking up above the waterline like spiky dorsal growths from that same giant, America-eating, underwater beast.

"Look, Myles," I said, pointing to something lying on top of one of the rocks. "A sea lion... Or a seal. Down there, do you see it?" I don't think Myles could distinguish the languishing animal from the grey-brown rocks in the cove. The sun seemed to be following us since we'd left Rob's house and the Bay area even though we were driving north. I continued to point at the creature, fifty metres or so below us, in the hope that it would move. But it didn't. I'd never seen a sea lion in its natural habitat before. I wanted Myles to be as excited as I was.

"Maybe it's a statue? Or a walrus, a young one? What do you think, Myles?" It could have been a mermaid for all I knew.

If Myles was excited about seeing the wild sea animal, he stifled it. Still, he smiled for the camera as I photographed him sitting at the top of the precipice, the sea-lion thing just visible over his left shoulder. He may have been slightly too close to the edge, but he wasn't one to roll around inexplicably. He trusted me so I trusted him.

We sat up there for a while. I don't know how long, because in those few moments overlooking the endless waves, the white noise of rushing water, I thought about Sue and lost track of the time. *She would have loved this view, this moment with her family.* And then I thought about the memory of Sue, as if it existed independently of the Sue who'd lived. Perhaps, I thought, the quintessence of Sue would still exist — would *always* exist — whether I was here to remember her or not. Like the old conundrum about a tree falling in the forest. We might all be distilled into a larger memory of humankind, forever immortal as an idea of what we once were. People live on in memory, this I knew. But maybe people continued to live in the DNA of humanity, beyond the memory of those who knew them. If there was life after death, I thought, surely that's how it must exist.

In that moment, clinging to Myles as we stared out to sea, my mind wandered in the wordless labyrinth of meandering images and concepts and sensations and visual themes. It was one of those moments when my thoughts were so vast that I couldn't see where they began or ended. Only after returning from the wander might I finally put words to where my thoughts went. Some of these memories are put to music — a soundtrack for the cinematic meanderings. Memories of Sue, and of the life we were supposed to live together, rose and fell like the ocean waves and seemed just as unforgiving.

In one of these memories, we'd been walking along Bloor Street, around the corner from our house in west Toronto, on a sunny but crisp October afternoon. Sue was eager to get outside and stretch her legs and, more importantly, show off her new son. We bundled young Myles into his cotton one-piece inside a knitted sweater and his fleece snuggly-thing, lay him in his buggy, and covered him with the blanket his Aunt Nancy had made for him. All we could see were his eyes. Sue was dressed for the biting autumn wind in her favourite black coat, fuchsia boa scarf with matching gloves, and black hat secured tightly over her wig. We walked slowly away from the bright sun, into the wind that whipped down the tunnel-like street, window-shopping and people-watching.

In front of the library a little old lady, as if delivered from central casting, stopped to peer at the swaddled contents in our buggy. The lady's grandmotherly gravitas and floral babushka tied under her chin gave her licence to poke her nose in. As she leaned over, she held her jute carrying bag with both hands so it wouldn't swing into the buggy and disturb Myles.

"What's his name then?" she cooed.

"Myles," Sue sang.

"Myles. What a precious little thing."

"Thanks." Sue smiled. *This* was why she wanted to go out that day.

"And so tiny too," the Babushka said. "How old is he?"

"He's five days old."

"Five days? Oh my. And look at you walking around. How are you feeling?" she asked like she was Sue's grade-three teacher.

"I feel great."

"Good for you. You look great. Keep that little bundle warm now."

"Thanks. Bye." In that brief moment of pleasant small talk, Sue got to show off her new son and prove that newborns don't have to hide indoors, and to her delight, she was permitted to proclaim to the world — or at least to the babushka — that she was feeling great. There was no mention of cancer.

We'd reached the end of the strip, so we crossed the road at the traffic lights and headed back on the other side. The wind was at our backs now but the sun was in our eyes. I pushed the buggy while Sue rested her right hand on top of mine. It was the perfect little family outing.

Sue stopped at the health food store. "I want to see if they have my vitamins," she said. "I'll be right back."

I moved Myles in his buggy beside a tree so that we wouldn't block the sidewalk and rocked him gently as he slept. People passed by quickly, a few glances toward Myles but no more peering grandmothers. Sue came out sooner than I'd expected. Her face was pale, her bright eyes had dimmed, and the corners of her mouth pointed down. She came over to me, grabbed my arm, and put her forehead to my shoulder.

"What's the matter?"

"There was a song playing in the store," she sniffled. "This woman just kept repeating 'Will you remember me?' I had to get out of there."

"I know that song. Jann Arden," I said, unsuitably proud of naming that tune and the Canadian songstress responsible for it. Sue muffled her tears and stayed quiet while I thought of something more appropriate to say. My powers of compassion were being tested. For the past five days, Myles had been my priority. I'd almost forgotten Sue still needed my help, especially after her superhuman performance in the delivery room. Did she think she was going to die? Did she truly believe she could ever be forgotten? How do you reassure someone that her reactions are unwarranted?

I put my arm around her, holding her tightly as the faceless people walked by. Our long shadows pointed toward our home. "It's just a song," I said.

The song lingered in my head as I picked Myles up from the windy clifftop and carried him to the car. This moment had been ours and ours alone. Back on Route 1, heading north again with the hypnotic sea to my left, I glanced every so often at the rocky coves in the hopes of spotting one more resting mermaid. The song of memory hummed along as I looked at Myles in my rear-view mirror.

* * *

Sue loved to dance. With me mostly, but sometimes she danced alone, completely surrendering to the music, if there happened to be some. She let her body move without pretense or preconception. With me as her partner, she preferred if I led, which I did when I wasn't stepping on her toes or elbowing her in the temple. Often I led simply by following her lead.

I complied with this love of hers despite my fierce sense of inadequacy on the dance floor, and in time I learned to actually enjoy it. Whether slow or fast, we danced staring into each other's eyes, touching as the rhythm or music dictated. It was conversation; it was foreplay. We cha-cha-ed, we discoed, we waltzed, we slam-danced, we gavotted, we two-stepped, we even line-danced once. I let her talk me into taking adult-beginner ballet lessons together one winter. For Sue, dancing was a reminder that there was more to life than daily obligations and following the rules.

We danced at work functions, Christmas parties, and weddings. We went to clubs despite the fact we'd surpassed the unofficial age limit. Wherever it was, Sue wanted to be the first one on the dance floor. After securing drinks, she'd grab my hand — *Dance with me* — and away we went, eye to eye, cheek to cheek. At home she would play music loudly as she took care of chores. That way she could dance in her own way to the cranked-up wailings of Alanis Morissette or Peter Gabriel as she carried the sorted laundry into the bedroom, smiling and singing along at the top of her lungs. The more she needed to get out of her busy head, the louder the music, which was particularly controversial when we lived in our third-floor apartment in the Beaches. But she didn't care about the neighbours.

Occasionally, if she were in a particularly silly mood, Sue would take to the floor in the style of what can only be described as the *Caddyshack* gopher. Channelling the movie rodent's enthusiastic hustle celebrating its continued victories over groundskeeper Bill Murray, Sue inexplicably took on the same puppet-like choreography. It started with a hiccup-rhythm stutter-step shuffling directionless across the floor, which automatically generated a cute little bum wiggle. Her arms joined in next, bent at the elbows, hands fisted and chugging at her side like a steam engine. Finally her face would scrunch up gopher-like, buckteeth and all, looking completely out of character but cheekily proud of herself. She no longer played the serious journalist preparing to take the Canadian press by storm. I loved watching it and usually joined in.

The last time Sue and I danced together was toward the end of her last winter during a weekend retreat at a resort on Lake Couchiching, an hour and a half north of Toronto. We left Myles with my mother and drove out of the city up

Highway 400 anticipating a welcome respite from the obligations of being guardians to cancer and our young son. Like most of Southern Ontario that time of year, the overwhelming colour was grey: sky, water, half-melted snow, and the lifeless grass it revealed. Sue's pain was relentless, and she'd hoped a relaxing weekend in the woods with a lakeview Jacuzzi would be just the antidote. The hot bubbling water felt great on her aching body, but stepping in and out of the deep tub was like climbing a rock wall. Even with my help, the struggle and the pain made her angry, and the anger made her sad.

"Dammit! Why does it still hurt so much?" she asked, taking more Extra Strength Tylenol with codeine.

"It will pass, sweetie."

After helping her out of the hot tub one last time, I wrapped a towel around her and held her closely but not too tight. She was angry but didn't struggle. We both looked out the window to the grey waves gently lapping against the frozen shore as the vague sun passed behind the clouds. She started to calm down, enfolded in my arms. I rocked her and sang softly in her ear, assuring her that long after the Rocky Mountains had eroded to become flat, stony plains and all evidence of us being together had been archived as ancient history, "Our Love Is Here to Stay." I sang to prove that no matter what happened for the rest of this life or any subsequent one, we would never be apart. We danced a quiet, private, stationary dance in the fading light. She put her head on my chest and let me lead until her tears stopped. Gershwin worked every time.

* * *

August 26, 2003 — Fort Bragg, California

Dear Myles,

Today your mom and I should have celebrated our eighth wedding anniversary. Instead, all I could do was miss her. I cried a few times today (I don't only cry in the morning anymore) as we drove up the coast. It's no coincidence we are taking this trip during the month of August. I thought a lot about our wedding today. Up until the day you were born, it was the greatest day of my life.

The most important thing is to have people around you to love and who love you in return. Outside of family it's all about finding a mate. We were supposed to be together forever, your mom and me. Love is real, Myles. You'll know it when you've found it. And don't be afraid just because I lost my love. When you have found your love, you must do everything in your power to keep it. You never know when you're going to have another chance to tell someone you love them.

We found what was probably the fanciest restaurant in this tiny seaside town known for its fishing and lumber industries. I even cleaned Myles's face before we went in and sat down at our corner table by the window. Every table had a window and a view of the rocky seashore. I ordered a glass of white wine so that I could silently toast Sue on this non-anniversary. I was sure Sue's parents back in Burlington were raising a glass themselves. My mother would solemnly wonder where I was, what I was doing to mark the day. No doubt others would pause in front of their calendars to remember that day they had shared with us eight years earlier.

To say that our wedding was memorable would be to suggest that it was memorable only to us, as most weddings are to the couple being wed. It's one thing for a wedding guest to greet the couple with, "That was a beautiful wedding," no matter how sincere. It's quite another to be told years after the fact that it was the most beautiful wedding they'd ever been to. And we had been told many times.

Sue decided, with the welcome support of her parents, to host the wedding at her family's cottage, in an exclusive community only a half hour north of their home in Burlington. Set at the edge of Bronte Creek, which runs all the way to Lake Ontario, the old wooden cabin had been owned by Sue's family since she was a little girl, and she and her sister, Nancy, had spent their summers and weekends growing up there. It was an ideal setting: the rocky, rippling stream lined with tiger lilies; the grounds surrounded by tall cedars and maples and accessed by a meandering dirt track.

Sue's parents, George and Joyce, had spent that summer lovingly landscaping their property in preparation for the event. The lawn was pristine; the foliage trimmed back just enough to straddle the line between rustic and decorous. Tiny white lights were threaded through the trees and around the two massive white tents that had been rented for the evening. The ceremony began that clear August night just as the sun began to set over the Niagara Escarpment.

Our guests gathered in a circle on the lawn as we joined together in the middle. We spurned the customary vows and recited Shakespearean sonnets instead ("Let not my love be called idolatry..." Sue said. "Betwixt mine eye and heart a league is took..." I responded). There was an interactive element to the proceedings: we'd had our families and closest friends each create a design on a small piece of cloth, all of which were then quilted together to create a *chuppah*, the traditional covering underneath which a Jewish wedding service takes place. It was, however, a secular ceremony; a neighbour of Sue's family, who happened to be a family court judge, married us, adding his personal touches. Afterwards we dined from a splendid buffet — part Thai, part summer barbecue — and enjoyed the endless supply of Inniskillin Pinot Grigio and Upper Canada Lager. Until finally dancing into the night to the six-hour homemade mixed tape I put together — everything from Sinatra to Seal — so that we didn't have to suffer the relentless patter of a DJ or cheesy wedding singer.

But that's not what made it special. It was, I think, distinctly ours. We proved that we had put significant thought into every element of the evening to make it meaningful to us — and when I say "we," I mean, of course, Sue. That meant the inclusion of everyone who was there. Because what would be the point, we thought, of showing the people important to us how much love we had for each other and for them — as you do at weddings — if they were not allowed to share their love in return? In our minds it turned out perfectly, and we were thrilled that so many other people found it just as unforgettable.

In retrospect, a wedding is a wedding. It's not too dissimilar from a funeral, with the possible exception of more dancing. Of greatest importance is the opportunity to publicly acknowledge the commitment you're making to each other. Whatever the setting is, and however the occasion is remembered by the guests, we mark the date each year to remind ourselves why we are still together. Ultimately the wedding fades, but hopefully the reasons for being together do not.

As Myles and I enjoyed our Pacific salmon in California — always preferable to its east-coast cousin — the piped-in music, to my amazement, provided the ideal soundtrack to this non-anniversary dinner. First came Enya, whose songs Sue had chosen to be part of our wedding ceremony, and then Nat King Cole came on singing "Our Love Is Here to Stay," the same version I used to imitate when I sang to Sue. After our meal, we went out to the parking lot to find a rusty red Volkswagen Fox parked next to the RAV4. It was identical to the car Sue owned when we first met, the same car on which she taught me how to drive a standard transmission.

On any other day these would have been notable Harmony Moments. But this evening's Anniversary Edition Harmony Moments sang in the full voices of a four-part choir.

Myles and I settled into our Super 8 while the sun was still setting. From the open window I heard a cacophonous honking. It was a curious chorus of off-pitch, off-time wailing in various dissonant ranges, like an orchestra of trombones being played by tone-deaf six year olds. I picked Myles up and we followed the noise down toward the sea, where we eventually came upon hundreds of sea lions nattering under the setting sun like a harem of gossiping mermaids. Their voices and voluptuous bodies filled the cove as they sang their appreciation for the warmth, the water, and the rocks. Myles pointed at the throng of beasts and giggled like Bart Simpson on helium. The sea lions heard him laughing over the din and turned their heads toward us.

I wondered why I was so fascinated with the animals. Afterward it dawned on me that I was seeing them through Myles's eyes. He had broadened the scope of all that was intriguing in the world. Through his eyes I found joy in moments that might otherwise have left me cold. Sea lions became objects of captivating charm; a ball rolling across the hotel-room floor offered hours of giggling amusement; climbing the stairs was an adventure.

But what could Myles have been thinking? Not just about this gaggle of sea-beasts, but about the entire excursion. Where did he think we were going? Were his needs limited to those I fulfilled for him? What did home mean to him? Who was I to him? Did he miss Sue? More questions than answers.

I called Sue's parents that night. Then I called my mother. Nobody mentioned our anniversary, but they didn't need to. They knew why I'd called. Sometimes you need to mark an occasion by not marking it.

* * *

The next day we reached the top of California. The lofty Pacific Coast Highway was sufficiently entertaining, but added to the mix was the consistently remarkable view and the opportunity to pass by towns with names only California could pull off: Eureka, Honeydew, Peanut. Before checking into the Crescent City Super 8, we went for a hike around a forest of giant redwoods, trees so mammoth they could barely be recognized as trees. They were like giant earthen dwellings in which a family of four might have comfortably lived. Some of the trees had vast black scars of scorched bark from where they'd been struck by lightning, their crowns towering over the rest of the forest. In my journal that night I simply wrote: *Big trees. Really big trees.*

The next day we crossed the state line into Oregon, where the fog began to thicken over the coast road. After a few hours of not being able to see anything — a condition for which the road is known — I turned inland and joined up with Interstate 5, which took us to the city of Eugene. Somewhere along the interstate, a CD got stuck inside the player. I panicked. What was I expected to listen to without it? The radio? Not only that, but the disc that was jammed held the song of the day, which I'd been playing on a loop: "Salvation" by Elton John. Elton had been telling me all day about this long, long road, and I was beginning to see his point. Firstly, because we were getting into that mid-trip funk — that part of the trip where you feel like you've been away from home for an immeasurable amount of time and you're unsure of what toll the rest of the trip will take. I wasn't ready to go home, but I was relieved that I couldn't go any farther west. Secondly, Elton kept suggesting that it would take salvation and a helping hand if we were going to find the end of this road. Myles was my salvation, that much had become perfectly clear. And with every chorus Elton and I sang together, I became more and more convinced that Myles would help me, in no uncertain terms, along this road that we would navigate together for the rest of our lives.

I'd known that song since I'd been small — the album on which it appears was released in 1972; my parents listened to it — but the word *salvation* never had any meaning for me. At most it held a lofty, religious connotation suggesting faith in a god I didn't believe in; all you had to do was trust in a greater-than-earthly power, and your worries for eternity would be resolved. To me that meant you didn't have to take responsibility for your own actions because someone or something else would take care of that for you. Salvation. The word just dripped with condescension. But suddenly I'd discovered a new context in which to define it. My salvation was helping me navigate, keeping me on the road, and saving me from this life, all the while strapped into his car seat and napping across North America.

I hoped the Toyota dealership in Eugene would repair my CD player and rescue Elton. They took care of the oil change with expected efficiency, but the CD player would have to be removed and sent to their manufacturer's head office, which could take two weeks. I told the nice mechanic I had no intention of being in Eugene any later than the following morning and took my freshly lubed vehicle back to the Super 8 where I spent the night wallowing in the mid-trip funk, now without a soundtrack.

I was eager to get to Vancouver: to see some friends, to be back in Canada, to know that afterwards I'd surely be heading east — back home.

So I hastily motored through the rest of Oregon and most of Washington. In Seattle — *Oh, Seattle. I wonder how the cats are doing* — I stayed an extra day to explore the city that gave birth to Hendrix and Pearl Jam, scaled the famous Space Needle, and took Myles to Safeco Field to watch the hometown Mariners hammer the visiting Baltimore Orioles 13–1. I also bought four jars of flavoured honey from the stall in Pike Place Market on the waterfront. We'd had it before; Sue always preferred the lime-flavoured one, so I got two of those.

I contacted Sue's sister, Nancy, to let her know that we were getting closer to her. After Vancouver, we would go directly to the Okanagan Valley to visit her. She assured me she was ready for us but cautioned me about the forest fires that had been burning wildly all summer in British Columbia's interior. I remembered the matchstick graveyard at Mesa Verde and told her I'd keep my eyes and ears open for any danger warnings.

Danger, such as it was, seemed to be a regular subtext to this adventure. But despite the rare oversight or my lofty imagination, I never thought we were in any actual peril. I drove on.

11

Vancouver had been an important place for Sue. It was the city where, in the summer of 1997, she chose to do her journalism internship. She worked for six weeks at the CTV affiliate in Vancouver, and afterwards she'd hoped to land a full-time reporting job there. Her sister had lived in Vancouver for a short time, as did some close friends. We loved that we knew people there.

From the twelfth-floor balcony of our hotel room, Myles and I could see all the signs of what I regarded as special about Vancouver: to my left Stanley Park, occupying half of the peninsular west-end; ahead of me the great waterway of Burrard Inlet welcoming ships to Vancouver's port from the Pacific. Beyond the inlet, North Vancouver nestles into the base of Grouse Mountain, which, at nearly 1,200 metres, is a mere hill compared to its neighbours in the Coast Mountains. Among other things, the city is renowned for its rain and outdoorsy people, not always a compatible combination. As soon as the clouds disappear, the hardy citizens emerge like worms after the rain to partake in their swimming, surfing, skiing (both snow and water), jogging, cycling, or hiking. Sue and I once pictured ourselves living there.

Myles and I spent our first afternoon in Vancouver with my high-school friend Gil and his infant son, Joshua, at Jericho Beach on the shore of English Bay. Gil, a small, serious fellow and a talented musician, had genuine affection for his friends, often so sincere as to be intimidating. Whenever I was with him I always wished I could be as good a friend as he was. But we hadn't seen each other in a few years and, as with every other person I spent time with on this trip, I didn't know what to expect from him. We'd worked together in some musical projects in Toronto, but in Vancouver he was practicing law. Gil had always proved his worth as a friend, making our time together easy and welcoming.

After dislodging the beach sand from Myles's every orifice, we went back to Gil's house in Kitsilano for dinner with his wife, also named Sue. While sitting around their dining room table, I remembered the last time I was there. It was two summers earlier, and both Sues had just told each other that they were pregnant. The joy of that moment was tempered by the coincidental miscarriages both of our wives had weeks later before each became pregnant a second time, with happier results. This visit was less joyous; I was thrilled our children got to meet each other, but there was one Sue missing.

We had a busy schedule in Vancouver, with other friends to see and the essential tasks of hiking around Stanley Park and buying a woodcarving. Every time Sue and I visited this city we bought a wooden animal carving from one of the galleries in Gastown. We had four of them from previous visits. My otter, carved by the well-known west-coast native Canadian artist Glen Harper, was number five.

The next day we had lunch with Sue's former colleague Dennis, a jolly man who'd adored and respected her. During their time together in Ottawa, when Sue worked for a cabinet minister and Dennis in the Prime Minister's Office, he was Sue's constant protector, ensuring she was always safe and never taken advantage of by a hovering paramour. The first time I met him was at his wedding to Rachelle in rural New Brunswick. I'd had a gig the night before, but we reached the church just in time after driving through the night from Toronto. Dennis was grateful and amazed at our commitment to attend, but it was indicative of the lengths Sue went to maintain relationships with those she loved.

"I'm really glad you're here," Dennis said before biting into his sandwich. We'd met him in front of his Vancouver office building, where he worked for the Insurance Bureau of Canada, and wandered to the nearest café.

"I was in the neighbourhood," I said.

"I think it's great you're taking this trip. I can only imagine, but I'd guess it's just what you need."

"Seems to be working out that way," I said, giving Myles a taste of banana. "I needed to get out of Toronto and find some unfamiliar territory to clear my head."

Dennis nodded and swallowed. "When you called me that night," he said, "to tell me Sue had died, I was blown away. That you took the time to do that so soon afterwards meant a lot to me." His soft smile and gentle manner belied his flat-footed stature, but I always knew he was sincere.

"It meant a lot to me too," I said. "It was two-thirty in the morning and I wanted to hear a friendly voice so I thought, 'Who do I know on the west coast?'"

"It was the most decent act, Jon."

"I thought the people who meant the most to Sue should be the first to know."

Dennis had a way of showing love that was contagious. He was built like a linebacker — as a football fan, he probably always wished he were one — but had a heart that reminded me of my grandmother's old friend Melba back in Detroit. When you were with them, you knew that they had time for you — they weren't just pretending. He couldn't be refused.

Dennis needed to get back to work, so we bid each other goodbye in front of his building again, and Myles and I went off to do our Vancouver errands.

That evening we had dinner at Jeremy and Karina's tiny west-end apartment. Jeremy and Sue had grown up together in Dundas, Ontario, sharing walks to and from school since they were nine or ten years old. He was, according to Sue, her best friend until I came along. A professional jazz guitarist, Jeremy put on an impromptu performance with his band at his own wedding. Always soft spoken, Jeremy liked to use language straight out of Miles Davis's era, calling people "cat," describing things as "hip." To him, my musical tastes made me a "pop cat," a moniker I wore with pride.

At the end of the evening, Jeremy walked us to the elevator. He hugged me and quietly said, "I still consider Sue my best friend." There was a slight wavering in his voice and moisture in his eyes.

"That's nice to hear, Jeremy," I said.

He shook my hand as the elevator door was closing and said nothing more.

How could Sue still have been his best friend? *She was my best friend. Wasn't Karina Jeremy's best friend now?* I'm aware that it's possible to maintain strong friendships with people you grew up with, but isn't it likely you might find a new, grown-up best friend by the time you get married? Or was I just thinking that because this best friend happened to be of the opposite sex? What did this say about his relationship to Karina? What did it say about me and Sue? Could Jeremy have thought those were words of solace? Once again, more questions than answers.

Maybe Sue really was my best friend or maybe I just gave her that title because I spent more time with her than anyone else. I fell in love with her for different reasons than those I'd sought in a friendship. I'd never fallen in love with a friend before, so it's possible I fell in love with Sue and subsequently became her best friend as well as her lover. Because although I had several good, reliable friends, both male and female, there wasn't one whom I could categorically describe as the best. Perhaps Sue was my best friend by default.

Or did it even matter? Jeremy and Dennis had long, significant histories with Sue and, by association, with me. Now that Sue was gone, what difference did it make what they thought about her? It wasn't going to bring her back, and it wasn't going to make her loss any less. They proved their friendships by continuing to let me and Myles be a part of their lives, confirming that Sue was an excellent judge of character.

Myles and I went back to Kitsilano on the morning we left Vancouver to say goodbye to Gil and Sue. Gil and I chatted in the kitchen over a cup of tea while Sue slept in. Myles and Joshua sat on the floor together looking at each other as if they'd just met. It looked like Joshua had inherited his father's swarthy skin and conspicuous curiosity. I heard Sue call to Gil that she was awake, so he took Joshua in for Sue to breastfeed while I gathered up our stuff in preparation to leave.

"I'll just wait until you're done and then say goodbye," I said.

"Don't be silly," Gil said.

"Come in, Jon. It's okay," Sue said. "It's nothing you haven't seen before."

Well, I hadn't seen *hers* before, but I knew what she meant. A woman feeding her son was perfectly natural. Why would anyone be offended? What possible damage could it do to either party?

I entered the room, Myles tucked in the crook of my arm. Gil was in the corner folding clothes. Sue was sitting up in bed, topless, with Joshua suckling on her left breast.

Breasts! Breasts! I could see nothing but breasts. Big breasts, small breasts, bouncy breasts, pert breasts, sexy breasts, and great, swollen maternal feed-bag breasts. I saw smooth, young supple breasts and old wrinkled breasts. Round, firm breasts. Long, pendulous breasts. I saw every breast I'd ever desired to cup with my sweaty, teenage palms. I saw beautiful, healthy breasts and sick, cancerous breasts. Then I saw Sue's missing breast; vast, empty patches of skin where a breast had been hacked off in an attempt to save her life.

I thought about my dedication to Sue during her illness and my old mantra: "Stand by your woman. Show her you love her and don't hold back. Be strong but let her be the boss. Find happiness in her happiness." I lived by it even more after her diagnosis. I thought of her needs before I paid attention to my own. However, my stoic, sentry-like devotion and everlasting optimism was put to the test the first time I looked at her mastectomy scar.

I had been anticipating the moment with a sanguine resignation. Having seen photos of women who had undergone the same procedure, I thought I knew what to expect. The photos usually showed proud, defiant-looking women proving to the world that missing a part of their anatomy — of their femininity, no less — was merely a blemish, a symbol of their successful slaying of the Beast. In some cases it even seemed they wore their scars as medals of honour. At least that was my misguided male interpretation. It didn't take long for me to accept that I would spend the rest of my life with a one-breasted woman.

Our relationship went far deeper than our physical connection. Our bond in marriage was reinforced by the experiences we'd shared and by our singular togetherness. We were united, I felt, as if of one discrete, idealistic mind. So even if she were missing a breast, I thought, at least I'd still be allowed to share my life with her. The important thing, I kept reminding myself, was that the essence of Sue was still there, which she had already proven in her attitude toward her illness and her body.

She was in good spirits when she came home from the hospital a few weeks before Christmas. Myles, six weeks old at the time, brought her an endless supply of cheer. Within hours of coming home she had formulated mock ideas about a memoir and a movie of the week. "I'll call it *My Left Breast*," she said with a smile. "If it's good enough for Daniel Day-Lewis it's good enough for me."

Her mother was the first to see Sue's scar post-operation. We were given some moisturizer for the skin around her incision so that it wouldn't dry out around the stitches and rupture. Sue didn't feel up to looking at the result of her surgery, let alone touching it, so Joyce quickly volunteered to help and followed Sue up to our bedroom. When they came back down, nothing was said. I was strangely envious of Joyce for being allowed to help Sue. It had always been my job.

My turn came the following day. It was a chilly December morning and Sue awoke from another typically restless sleep complaining that her scar was itching. She asked me to apply the cream for her, so I got out of bed, walked around to her side, and turned on the bedside light. I recalled the defiant picture of Sue I had in my mind, and I prepared myself for that first glance. Perhaps it would be slightly red, I thought. I expected to see a nice, clean line of supple, healing tissue on her chest where her breast used to be. She handed me the moisturizer and took off her nightie.

I looked. No shock, no gasping. Maybe all those years of acting lessons paid off. *All right. Big deal. She's still the woman I love. She's just missing a body part. It could be a finger. Or a foot.* I saw a large area of bright red skin with a line running through it. That much I expected. Then I looked closer and I clenched my teeth, squelching any compulsion to react in a manner that Sue might perceive as either frightening or in any way suspicious. The red was like the worst skin rash I'd ever seen. In places it was patchy with brownish spots about the size and shape of an almond. The entire area was larger than the diameter of what had once been her breast. More than the colour, though, it was the texture that surprised me. It wasn't smooth like I had expected. It was raised and rough and pitted with lumps and craters like a bright red topographic map. Some of the hollows were so distinct I could see shadows filling them.

"How does it look?" she asked.

"It looks fine."

"Fine? That doesn't tell me anything. How does it look?"

I tried not to appear as though I was studying her chest for signs of cancer. I tried not to take too long answering her, to have her sense my dread. I tried not to look like I wished none of this had ever happened to us.

"It's kind of red and swollen," I said. "But I'm sure that's normal since you've just had surgery. It's going to be red as it heals."

"Does it disgust you?" Subtext: *Do I disgust you? Have I become so grotesque in my deformity that you will never want to touch me again? Will you love me like this until the day I die? Do you just want to run away?*

"Of course not, sweetie," and I dipped my fingers into the cream.

I started applying the moisturizer and within an instant of touching her I thought something was wrong. Her skin felt firm. Really firm like a dried-out orange peel. The irregularities in her skin didn't yield to my fingers; rather my fingers followed the rigid contour of each bump and crevice. The suture line was stiff and rough with dying flesh. As I gently rubbed in the cream I found that wherever it was red, it was mercilessly hard. It felt, to my untrained hand, that the mass was not just on the surface but ran deep inside of her. The flesh-embossed Braille of her chest read, "There's cancer in here." My fingers caressed her skin and I wished that my loving touch would soften it. But the scar stabbed at my fingertips with its unforgiving artillery.

I thought of my own small, inconsequential scars sustained during any number of freak childhood accidents. The wonky bone in my left wrist from a break when I was five. The one tiny stitch I received on my left cheek when a neighbour's cocker spaniel bit me. The strange one on my right thumb from getting gashed by a schoolmate's braces. All of these faded away as soon as I saw Sue's scar. Hers, unlike mine, would last forever not only on her skin but in her mind and in her spirit. It would leave an indelible "sell-by date" imprint on her body and on her identity. For me, it would signal a "before" and "after" moment, forever corrupting my memory of who she was and what she had suffered. It would endure in my index of remembrances as a signpost on the road to losing her. Worst of all it became a violent perforation slashing through our marriage and our ability to talk about what the cancer meant to us and our future. It cut us off from everything we used to be.

Maybe I did think something was wrong, but I justified what I saw in her appearance with naive hope and by censuring the facts. It's just healing, I kept telling myself. Was I being the perfect husband by telling her what she wanted to hear, or was I setting us up to be mortally disappointed? Was I standing by my woman, or was I running away from her? Through my denial, a part of me surely believed what I was ultimately forced to acknowledge as the truth: removing Sue's breast did not remove the cancer.

Some sensations, for better or worse, are just impossible to forget: the smell of your grandmother's perfume; feeling your newborn child grab your finger; the elation of watching your favourite team win the championship; or the nervous anticipation of starting a new job. I wish I could forget what Sue's skin felt like, but I can't. Because it wasn't just what it felt like on my fingertips that stayed with me — it's what that feeling meant. It meant the months of considering the cancer a temporary episode were proven right, but not for the reason I had once believed. It meant I could no longer comfort Sue just by offering her all the love I had. It meant the end.

I'll never shake that.

I tried to maintain eye contact with Vancouver Sue as I carefully leaned in, kissed her on the cheek, left the house, and left Vancouver.

12

Smoke hovered over the mountains, obscuring the sun like an urban haze. The morning light, trying to push back the grey, painted a pinkish hue on the canvas of smoke. The Trans-Canada Highway eastbound out of Vancouver should have been pointing directly into the still-rising sun. Instead it rumbled tentatively toward a menacing wall of ashen clouds that hovered over the Okanagan Valley over 160 kilometres away. I wondered if I was getting into another dangerous situation. Where we were headed, the forest fires, I'd been told, were under control but that didn't necessarily mean they would remain that way. When you can't see beyond the next ridge, the mountains can be unpredictable.

The capricious nature of this excursion appealed to me. Not in a dangerous sense; I certainly had no desire to drive through acres of burning mountain forests. But if the eastward road was impassable, then I'd happily go in a different direction. I knew I'd end up in the right place eventually. Wherever that was. Among the familiarity of friends in Vancouver, I almost forgot that I was meant to be on the move. But eventually, the sight of healthy people with healthy lives and healthy breasts can take its toll.

The tragicomic images of Vancouver Sue's breasts continued to flood my mind's eye as I drove through the mountains. Her hungry baby was happily nourished, but they were the first naked breasts I'd seen since Sue died. In my mind, though, there was only one set that mattered, and the last time I saw them, half of them were missing.

Breasts, despite their function, their beauty, their politics, and all their innuendo, are funny things. Men will do anything to see them, women will do anything to hide them, fashion designers spend their life's work obsessed with them, and entire books have been written about them.

I was lying on my back looking up at Sue, who sat over me on her bed when she first revealed hers to me. To Sue, nudity was not something she grew up appreciating. Her modesty, though genuine, was perhaps coloured by her conservative upbringing in suburban Ontario in the seventies. Even her teenage rebellion, the way she explained it to me, was fairly mild by most standards, consisting of little more than applying bright red streaks in her new-wave haircut and tying a bandana around her thigh. She never wore anything that came close to showing cleavage, and her bras, always chosen for support over style, were firmly fastened to avoid any embarrassing bounces.

So when she showed me her buoyant, symmetrical C-cups for the first time during a quietly passionate romp one afternoon in her apartment on Madison Avenue, I not only appreciated their design and presentation but also the fact that I was one of very few people to ever witness them close-up in person.

"You're beautiful," I said.

She smiled and blushed as she rubbed my bare chest. "Really?"

"Uh … yeah." As in *Duhh*.

"Even my saggy boobs?" she asked, expecting another compliment.

I looked at them — how could I not? — and thought they were the biological equivalent of Paradise. They were ice cream for every dessert, the right music for every occasion, and a peaceful sleep every night. I could have gone blind right then and I'd have been happy, the image of them embossed into my darkened canvas.

"They're perfect," I said.

She smiled again as if I'd just told her the secret of the universe. "Thanks."

Her perfect breasts stayed perfect over the next ten years. Until cancer found the left one and made a home for itself there. I wondered if the tiny, evil cancer cells were inclined to search for perfection while they sought sanctuary. Do brain tumours seek the smartest brains to inhabit? Does testicular cancer prefer beautiful balls?

Sue's comparison of cancer to a lottery was appropriate. She appreciated more than anyone the randomness of cancer choosing her. If cancer could land in her breasts then nobody was safe, I thought. And if that was the case, then how could I ever look at another pair of breasts the same way ever again?

The mountain smoke stayed ahead of us as we reached Okanagan Falls. We arrived in the early afternoon when the sun had heated up the pavement and continued to scorch the vegetation. The grass had been burned brown, the deciduous trees looked withered and thirsty. Nancy's building of white concrete, reflecting the sun's persistent flame, blinded me as we parked next to it.

Inside, Nancy kept the curtains drawn in an effort to save the apartment from turning into a sauna. It was a small two-bedroom with a tiny kitchen and living area, all decorated in a kaleidoscopic colour scheme: red and orange walls, South American fabrics of striated purple-green-blue, paintings from Nancy's own hand in bold primaries, homemade dream catchers, hanging mobiles, pendants, and all manner of tchotchke. Most notable, however, were the items Nancy had acquired that were once in our house. Sue had kept a small collection of celestial decorations: suns and moons and stars expressed in all manner of tchotchke. Nancy took those. She also took some of Sue's clothes. Around Nancy's neck hung two of Sue's necklaces. Most of Sue's jewellery had come from me. I knew each piece's history and what it meant to Sue. I knew where all her clothes came from and the origin of every knick-knack. To Nancy, they had once belonged to her sister. To me, they were parts of Sue.

The night after the Celebration of Life, I'd arranged for several of Sue's girlfriends, her sister, and mine to sort through Sue's clothes closet. That was one task I had no interest in participating in. I couldn't have done it for fear of having to stop and recall every occasion she'd worn each item of clothing. There were about ten women who came over to help sort through the clothes and have a private celebration of their own. Some of the clothes were adopted by her friends, some set aside for donation to a women's shelter, and the rest bagged for Goodwill. Nancy took quite a lot. By all participants' accounts it was a beautiful evening. While it was happening, I went out for chicken wings and beer with two of the partners of the women in Sue's closet and Dennis from Vancouver, who was still in town. There was enough laughter that night to make up for the lack of joy during the week since Sue died. The laughter was a release and a relief. When I returned home, Sue's closet was empty. The laughter had ended and the tears returned.

Nancy was only fifteen months younger than Sue, an age difference that practically demanded closeness despite great dissimilarities. Sue took after their mother; Nancy their dad. Sue sought recognition; Nancy looked inward. Sue was a city dweller; Nancy fled the urban jungle. She'd moved to Okanagan Falls from Vancouver, where she'd relocated years earlier to escape Ontario's conservative lifestyle and her familial obligations. The mountains, forests, and rivers brought her the peace she had been looking for. In OK Falls, as it's known, she managed a recreation centre where she was particularly keen on helping wayward youth.

"I didn't think you'd have wayward youth here, Nance," I said.

"They're everywhere," she said, chuckling. "At the moment, though, I'm supervising the supply warehouse for the firefighters. That's really cool."

"You said the fires were gone."

"They're gone from OK Falls. It was pretty nerve-racking a few weeks ago. We almost had to evacuate, but they extinguished them before it got to that point. They're still burning around Kelowna."

"How far is that?"

"About eighty kilometres away," she said, carrying Myles outside onto her rooftop balcony.

I followed. "I can smell the smoke," I said.

"They set up the base camp for the firefighters down there on the common," she said, pointing toward a patch of grass nestled among the evergreens. Beyond it was Skaha Lake, a vital source of irrigation for the arid Okanagan, part of the Great Basin Desert. "The fires are still close enough to keep the base here. And it keeps me employed for the next month or so."

"What do you do at the warehouse?"

"I keep the inventory and make sure all the equipment is signed out and returned. The firefighters are really cool, I hang out with them. They bring me wine." She chuckled and I imagined her with a wine glass in her hand, gesticulating coyly, surrounded by several sweaty firemen with flirtatious smiles on their faces.

It was comforting to know Nancy's life continued as she'd hoped it would, with independence and adventure. She was a free spirit, something Sue always claimed to be but in fact fell well short of. Sue's spirit, defined by her love of dancing and her desire to travel, was often grounded by her innate adherence to the practical. When she spread her wings — quitting her cushy job in Ottawa to pursue acting in Toronto, for example — she'd only soar freely for a predetermined length of time before landing as planned, her nest egg precariously close to slipping over the edge. She was both wild and reserved, romantic and pragmatic, somehow managing to keep both sides of herself balanced.

From Nancy's balcony I saw an enormous rock. It appeared to rise from the earth as a perfect dome pocked with craggy crevices. Patches of grass and a few determined young ponderosa pines sprouted from it at random like a teenage boy's beard. The rock was one of several that roll up from the shores of the skinny Skaha. The grey-brown earth that smothers them disappears on the far side as these low hills rumble through the Okanagan on their way to the proud granite slopes of the Rockies. I wanted to climb that rock.

It wasn't very high, maybe sixty metres, but it beckoned for me to scale it as if the top held some sacred shrine to recently widowed fathers. I always get the same sensation whenever I'm in the mountains: Must. Climb. Standing at the bottom, it's not enough just to imagine the view from the top.

I asked Nancy if the rock was climbable. "I've done it," she said. "You can get up and down in about an hour."

"I'll have Myles on my back though. Is it safe?"

"Yeah, it's safe. There's an obvious trail going right up to the top. If you walk up the road from my building and go through the gate at the end you'll see the bottom of the trail. I'd go in the morning before it gets too hot."

Nancy cooked us a plate of vegetable pasta for dinner that we washed down with some beers. Myles had apple juice. It was a quiet evening, and the heat of the day meant we were ready to turn in early.

The next morning, after breakfast, Nancy went off to OK Fire Headquarters, and I prepared for our hike. I changed Myles's diaper, slid him into the backpack, and slung him over my shoulders. Just before we went out the door, I grabbed a bottle of water and an orange. We'd only be an hour.

It was a steep but easy ascent, even with Myles on my back. The path had clearly been trod many times before, so the footfalls were relatively smooth compared to the rougher terrain on either side. I was anxious to get to the top — it couldn't have taken much more than fifteen minutes to reach it. There was nothing much up there besides one lonely pine tree and sparse bunchgrass softening the austere rocky surface. But I could look out over the town and the lake beyond. Behind me the sun continued to rise over mountains that I might have considered trying to climb if I hadn't been carrying a ten month old.

I took off the backpack with Myles still in it, and I opened the aluminum legs so it would stand up. I fixed his sun hat and sat beside him in the small shady spot below the tree. All I could hear was the wind as I looked down at the lake and peeled the orange. The sweet tang of citrus cut through the dust and the smokiness from the distant fires.

"Nice here, isn't it?" I said, handing Myles an orange section. He savoured it like it was the finest chocolate truffle. "It's so quiet." This was our daily moment, the time I looked forward to each day when we weren't driving or finding a place to stay or setting up his bed or changing diapers. This was the time, tranquil and plaintive, when I could look at him and think of Sue. *Look how beautiful he is. I can't believe you're missing this.*

The sun rose higher and our shady spot shrunk. "Shall we head down now?" We each had a sip of water. I stood up and put the backpack on. "How about we find a different way down? Just for fun."

I returned to the trail going back the way we'd come, down to the right, but I turned left. The hilltop path was rugged, as if paved with uprooted cobblestones. After fifty metres or so, the path ended, but I kept walking anyway, certain we would find our way down on the other side. The dry grass was longer and its scratchy blades were leaving marks on my bare legs and sandalled feet. Some rocks up ahead stuck out of the dirt forming natural stairs going down so I followed them. The stairs ended, the rocks loosened and became smaller. I continued on, but more carefully. Looking for a smooth descent I kept to the flattest areas, but the loose rocks made all progress tricky. I had gone down from the top about fifteen or twenty metres when I stopped to look back. I couldn't tell where I'd walked. The rocks and dirt and grass were all the same amber colour.

"The town is still in front of us, Myles. We may as well keep going in that direction." Myles was falling asleep.

It was getting harder to gain purchase. I slid a few times and needed to use my hands to balance myself. Every time

I slipped, I stopped to look at the terrain around me and up at the sun, whose rays, it seemed, were heating up by the second. A few more steps and a few more skids. My foot pushed some stones ahead of me and they tumbled like a mini-avalanche toward a sharp drop-off. I heard them land with a crunch on the ragged earth below. I froze. This rock was not a dome at all.

"Shit." Once again my high-flying freedom had distracted me from all notions of safety and sensibility. And my son was at the mercy of my recklessness. I'd broken the promise I made to him three weeks earlier when we nearly ran out of gas driving through rural Kansas. I had put him in a dangerous situation that day. *I will never let that happen again. I promise,* I'd written in my journal. Running out of gas was a joke compared to nearly falling off the edge of a cliff.

"Your mom wouldn't be too happy about this, Myles."

This wasn't the kind of predicament I would have shared with Sue. I heard her chastising voice again, just as I did back in Kansas. "What were you thinking, Jonathan?" She'd stare at me incredulously with her arms crossed, her head tilted to one side. Her perfectly plucked eyebrows would drop and meet in the middle to make an evil V. "It was obviously dangerous. You might be stupid enough to put yourself in danger, but don't ever put your son in danger."

"I know. You're right."

"I can't believe how fucking stupid that was."

"I know. It was stupid. But we're okay."

"Doesn't matter, Jonathan." She would have held on to Myles as if I were a murderous intruder. "What's done is done."

"I'm sorry, sweetie. I figured I could get down the other side."

"Well you couldn't, could you?"

"But how could I know until I tried?"

"You should have figured it out when the path ended. Duh!"

"There's no need for that."

"Then think before you speak."

"Please don't talk to me like I'm a child."

"Then stop acting like one."

I wouldn't know what to say at this point because I'd realize I didn't have a leg to stand on. Not only could I not defend myself against something Sue considered indefensible, but I'd simply run out of things to say. Sue never did.

"Get away from me. I can't look at you."

She'd storm away from me, and I'd be left sad and scared on the edge of a precipitous rock, waiting for the ground to crumble under my feet.

"I'm sorry," I said. "I'm sorry, Myles."

I took a sip of water from the nearly empty bottle, cautiously turned around, and started walking back into the sun toward the top of the rock. The few slips on loose rocks didn't seem so bad going uphill. At the top I found the trail again and walked back down the way we'd come.

I breathed easier but kept thinking about Sue's condemnation of my carelessness. It didn't matter to me that she would never actually know about it; what mattered was that I recognized how much more sensible she would have been about the risk in the first place.

Back on level ground I carried Myles down to the park by the lake where I bought a frozen lemonade and some Fig Newtons. We sat on the cool grass in the shade. The soft wind coming off the lake felt like summer. Myles woke up, none the wiser to our brief moment of peril on top of that rock. I lifted him out of the pack so he could crawl around, and I took off my sandals. With my naked toes in the grass I looked up at the amber rock, which from there seemed to loom larger above the town. *Stupid, that was so stupid.* I looked back at Myles and suddenly saw him with different eyes. I was no longer simply viewing our son with fatherly love and my longing for Sue to see what I was seeing. She was now watching him through me. She was also watching me watching him. Myles's well-being was being scrutinized by his mother from the beyond. I was putting him in too many risky scenarios, I was an irresponsible father, unqualified for the only job I was interested in doing. Baby Myles sat like a rocky mountain dividing his parents' tranquil plain into two frayed patches of desert.

Maybe every parent feels inadequate on occasion. I'd be shocked if I were the first father to feel he wasn't doing enough for his child. No doubt other men have scoffed at parenting advice and empathic insight. But my moments of inadequacy — fleeting though they might have been — were not the only symptoms of woe bubbling around in my head after this incident.

Sue and I never got the chance to learn how Myles would have fit into our family. The natural volatility of our marriage could have been exacerbated by having a baby around, despite our best intentions. We may just as easily have disagreed on how to raise Myles as we would have agreed on how much we loved him. One of us, at some point, might have been pushed to the limit of our tolerance. I could imagine Sue getting tired of arguing about the smallest things, of giving up on waiting for me to prove myself to her. As loyal as I'd always been, I might have given up on trying to find firm footing on her foundation of common sense; I might have insisted on doing things my own way. Conversations like the one I'd imagined up on the rock might have become more frequent. Certainly adding a child to the mix would have altered our dynamic. But her death meant we were not afforded the opportunity to unite as parents. We were unproven. Could we have relearned how to communicate? Would we have wanted to?

I tried to be the husband Sue wanted me to be, not necessarily the husband I knew I could be. It wasn't anything she forced me to do. It was my choice because I loved her. Maybe it had something to do with meeting Sue during a time when I was lonely, compelling me to behave in ways that ensured I didn't lose her. But eventually my choices painted me into a corner where she'd chosen the colours.

We knew we weren't the perfect couple — agreeing on every issue, treating our differences with respect and graceful acceptance — but we still loved each other. I admitted to loving her despite sacrificing more of myself than felt comfortable. But sometimes I wondered why she still loved me.

I still missed Sue, of course. I still ached for the lost future I had been promised. The grief had not lessened. But in that one precarious moment sixty metres above OK Falls, I recognized the problems embedded in our relationship as those that parenting — and the wisdom of middle age — may have exploited. Perhaps love, as faithfully as I'd always clung to it, would not have been enough.

13

Unlike the previous stops where we'd stayed with people, visiting with Nancy made me anxious. There wasn't the same sense of respite from the road; I was less relaxed. Her tangible connection to Sue was less comforting and more frustrating. In OK Falls, my memories of Sue were seen through the prism of Nancy's life. It's possible she felt, as I sometimes did, that Sue had often been the object of our competing affections. Perhaps Nancy, too, was unsettled by my visiting. She no longer felt like my sister-in-law, the woman who, for ten years, had been there for birthdays, graduations, Thanksgivings, and Christmases, and whose almost-daily phone calls with Sue I'd overheard. I wondered who had changed more. Or, indeed, if either of us had changed at all.

Nancy had been a long-time smoker, a habit Sue had always discouraged in her sister. She didn't smoke heavily but certainly daily for the better part of twenty years. To me, this contradicted her character as someone who preferred to live outside of large, polluted cities, among the forests and mountains and lakes. In her work she promoted physical fitness and outdoor education. She was a vegetarian. She read and talked about books on self-improvement and spiritual awakening. But the sessions of espousing what she'd learned about healthy minds and a healthy lifestyle were often interrupted by smoke breaks.

She didn't get cancer.

I was ready to go home. It wasn't Nancy or the mid-trip funk that got me down, it was the need for something else. I may have already gained everything I could have hoped to gain from this exercise. There was nothing left to look forward to — no more friends or family to stay with. No more expectations. I craved the comfortable, familiar surroundings of the home I had left five weeks earlier. Amid the hours of meditative driving, bonding with Myles, underappreciated sightseeing, Harmony Moments, and nightly Super 8s, I felt the need for firmer footing, the kind travelling had all but eliminated.

To begin my journey home, the first step was to cross over the border back into the US. I'd never seen the northern states before.

September 6, 2003 — Sandpoint, Idaho

Dear Myles,

Idaho is one of those states I never thought I'd be forced to visit. I don't know any more about this place than I did before. In other words: potatoes. Fortunately, Idaho is very narrow.

Today was basically a travel day. We crossed the border — again without incident — into Washington State and stayed on the winding, green back roads until stopping at the Super 8 here in Idaho. We went into the local Walmart to buy a portable CD player for the car, thanks to the emailed suggestions of a few friends. It plugs into the lighter. I can't believe I didn't think of it

sooner. The music is back. When we get home, it
will go into your room so you can have music to
fall asleep to.

I stayed on Interstate 90 through Montana, Idaho's
neighbour to the east. It's the third largest state in the union
— not including Alaska — surely home to some dazzling
geography and wildlife. But I simply grabbed hold of the
rope that pulled me headlong across half the state. The only
noteworthy moment occurred near the town of Missoula,
when I got wind of the now-familiar smell of smoke from
the forest fires that continued their tour of the Rockies.

The next day, I detoured south into Wyoming to take in
Yellowstone National Park, famous for its natural hot
springs and geysers, including Old Faithful. It's normally a
heavily forested park but, in keeping with the summer's
theme, several acres of lodgepole pine, Douglas fir, and
aspen had fallen victim to fires. It was a rare overcast day
— rare for me on this sunlit adventure but not, apparently,
for this part of the world — and the effect on the park was
strangely brightening. The scorched grass appeared golden
against the grey sky; the ragged silver rocks glowed with
occasional flashes of orange-oxide ribbons running through
them. It was the opposite effect of the sun in the southwest,
which, though it had been less than three weeks since I was
there, seemed like months ago.

Most exciting for me were the hundreds of bison that
wandered the park. The massive cattle-like beasts roamed
the area freely — or seemingly freely — even along the
roads, showing a complete disregard for the parade of cars
filled with wide-eyed onlookers, their cameras pointing
through rolled-down windows. As I stopped the car and

reached for my camera, I couldn't help thinking of the moose — equally magnificent and imposing as the bison — I commonly encountered on my visits to Algonquin Park in Northern Ontario. My bandmate and friend Norm first took me there for a six-day canoe trip in the early nineties. From then on, it wasn't summer unless I had a visit to the park where I'd fallen in love with the oil-painting landscapes, clean lakes, quiet, moonlit nights, and moose. The animals epitomized the region for me: larger than life, handsome if a bit unwieldy, peaceful and calming, even when they wandered onto the highway just as these bison did.

It always amazed me that, in a land as massive as Canada, you only needed to drive about two and half hours north of Toronto, its largest city, to reach moose country. I had taken that drive many times before I met Sue, but she'd never had the good fortune to be in the regal presence of a moose before. It took three years before I could convince her to "rough it" with me in Algonquin, one of my favourite places. I'd planned a relatively easy four-day trip for her inaugural visit to the park, one that included a good blend of lakes, rivers, and some manageable portages.

Our campsite on the first night was on Pen Lake, one of the 2,400 lakes navigable almost solely by canoe. It had its own rocky beach and plenty of cover thanks to the maples, white pines, and fragrant cedars — so many shades of green. After setting up our tent on a soft bed of pine needles at the top of a rocky rise about twenty metres from the water's edge, Sue and I gathered firewood and settled into our evening.

Cooking over an open fire in the woods is one of life's great pleasures: the speed at which a pot of water boils; the sparks flickering off the dry logs and rising up into the tree canopy; everything tasting smoked. That night, while eating our pasta with freeze-dried vegetables, we watched the sun finish its slow orange-pink-silver cascade over the opposite shore. (At home we'd probably have been watching a *Friends* rerun.) Afterwards, we took our charred enamel pots and bowls down to the lake, the soft water already cool for an August night, and began washing up by flashlight. The stillness of the night had descended onto us. That spot was our whole world shrouded by the pure night.

"What was that?" Sue asked, turning to the willow bushes that framed the edge of our beach.

"I didn't hear anything." We stood still in the hushed darkness. All I heard was the fire gently snapping its fingers back up the rise. Then suddenly a crackling from among the willows.

"There ... did you hear that?"

"Yeah."

"What do you think it was?" she asked.

I shined the flashlight toward the bushes, which even in the daytime cloaked whatever lurked within them. There was definitely something in there, but in the vast silence of the woods even the slightest murmur is amplified. When the night is deprived of all the activity, clamour, light, and human influence, it's amazing what a racket a snapping twig makes.

"Probably a squirrel."

"It's a moose," she said, shuffling behind me and grabbing me around the waist.

"No way," I said with a chuckle. I was a seasoned moose-spotter and in all my experience, I'd never seen one just walk up beside me on a beach. They'd typically spot you coming around a river bend and then, with a few hulking steps, disappear into the scrub like the baseball players in the *Field of Dreams* cornfield. But Sue's senses were finer than mine that night.

In my flashlight beam, two agate eyes reflected back at me through the leaves. Then the sound of rustling branches as the eyes floated toward us. In a few quick seconds, a magnificent bull moose was standing in front of us staring into my light and methodically chewing what was left of his evening snack. Though his eyes were level with mine, his adolescent antlers gave him a distinct height advantage. His spindly legs and knobby knees seemed insufficient to support a head, neck, and torso built like a Buick. He chewed peacefully, each crunch echoing over the glassy surface of the lake. His fur shimmered in the dim light like rich caramel.

Sue and I stared back at him, me with a big smile on my face and she with a tentative giggle, her fingernails still digging into my ribs. My skin tingled in delight and my heart raced.

"Stand still," I whispered.

"I can't. My knees are knocking."

"Oh." I laughed. "Don't be scared."

"I'm not. Just a bit freaked out. Do you think it might charge at us?"

"I don't think so. We aren't threatening him and anyway moose are herbivores."

"What about the light in its eyes?"

I couldn't bring myself to turn the light off. I was closer than I'd ever been to my favourite animal, less than five metres away. I'd always known moose, despite their size and gangly appearance, to be extremely mellow creatures. In keeping with the tradition of North America's indigenous people and their totem animals, I'd adopted the moose as mine. So if one was going to trample me into that beach for shining a light into his eyes then, I resolved, that was how I was going to go.

But he'd decided it was time for him to leave. I kept the light on him as Sue and I watched him turn to his left and silently glide up the rise toward our tent. As he passed behind our campfire, the flickering amber glow projected a wraithlike halo around him and cast a grand shadow on the trees beyond. He disappeared as stealthily as he had arrived through the brush, but for the twigs snapping under his heavy footsteps, leaving us once again alone in the calm of our night.

Of the dozens of moose encounters I'd had in Algonquin, that one was the best and not just because of the great beast's proximity. It's because it was Sue's first moose.

But more notable was that taking Sue through Algonquin was one of the few times in our marriage when I was in control. At home, Sue held the compass and I followed. She earned more money than I did, paid the bills, booked the vacations, chose what to watch on television, scheduled our nights out with friends, decided when to have a child and how to manage the cancer and the pregnancy. But the park was my territory, and Sue had no choice but to defer to my expertise as the experienced tripper. I appreciated the control for a change but somehow it didn't seem right. The balance usually tipped her way but I was strong enough — or so I thought — to keep it from overturning completely. With me in command I felt as though the balance could capsize at any moment. Despite the autonomy, I couldn't wait for normal service to resume.

The bison didn't quite have the same effect on me as the moose did, but I appreciated them for who they were. I let them be, scattered as they were around Yellowstone, their thick black-brown coats matted now in the rain, and left the park as unceremoniously as when I'd left Yosemite a few weeks earlier. From there we drove through Shoshone National Forest where the rippling, creviced reddish rocks sprouted out of the earth like ancient, wrinkled hands reaching from a grave. Cascading lodgepole pines lined the road as I descended from the mountains toward flatter terrain. I passed a sign telling me I'd just crossed the continental divide.

That night Myles and I had dinner at the pizzeria across the road from the Super 8. The beer was ice cold and the pizza was hot and greasy. The perfect end to a long day of driving. Myles was particularly keen on the slices of pepperoni I plucked off the cheesy crust for him. From our table by the window, I glanced over at the only other diners in the restaurant. A man and a woman sat across from each other, mugs of beer in front of them. To the woman's right sat a boy no older than twelve, talking animatedly, about what I couldn't tell. The boy was thin and pale. He was also bald.

Baldness meant cancer. It meant enduring months of chemotherapy treatment, sleepless nights, pain, and doubt. If it had been so arduous for me and Sue, who used adult reasoning to rationalize everything, how must it be for a twelve year old and his family? How did they justify their agony? Sue and I had been assured by our team of doctors that our son's exposure to the anti-cancer chemicals was minimal. My instincts for Myles were to love and protect him, to get him through each day without incident or illness. He'd proven to me that he was strong, healthy, and happy. But what if, years from now, he was found to have cancer? How could I have prevented that? How would I deal with it, having already lost his mother? That could be me eating pizza with my bald son.

I wanted Myles to understand what I was thinking and feeling. I wished he could grasp how devoted Sue and I were to him, how Sue thought of his well-being before thinking of her own. Yet I didn't want him to catch on to the things I knew I couldn't control. Because although I had no fears about the type of person he'd grow up to be — he'd already shown that he was decent, kind, funny, smart — I couldn't shake the fear that he might never have the chance to grow up at all.

This angst was superimposed against the approaching anniversary of the September 11 attacks. Every night there had been television programs marking the day. Many of the interviews with New Yorkers talked about getting back to "normal" and the guilt they suffered by resuming their routines and careers. But they all seemed to agree that trying to live as they did before the attacks would help them heal. I related to their sorrow but I couldn't help recognizing the differences between their scenarios and mine. New Yorkers grieved with the collective might of a city more than eight million strong. I didn't have that many people watching my back. Even if I did, how could they alleviate my entrenched anxieties about my son's welfare that started before he was even born?

Myles ate his pizza in complete oblivion to our surroundings, or so it seemed. How lucky, I thought, that he should be allowed to enjoy his meal without the white-noise subtext of our surroundings. Baldness didn't mean anything to him, whether he'd noticed the boy or not. For my son it was just another day out on the road, another meal with Dad, more songs and smiles. I wished I could live my life in the same void as Myles.

I nearly broke down, not the best thing to do at a Pizza Hut in rural Wyoming. I watched Myles chewing on a pizza crust and wiped some tomato sauce off his face, every so often looking over to see if the bald kid with the wan complexion was showing any other signs of illness. Perhaps he'd be wheeling around one of those portable oxygen tanks, or he'd spontaneously spit up some blood onto his meat-lover's slice. Part of me — the secret, hard to justify, "schadenfreudian" part — hoped this random family, clueless to pain and sorrow, would have to learn the same lessons I did. I almost wanted to wink at them to let them know that I could anticipate how they were going to feel. But the genuine part of me hoped they would never know the sadness, loneliness, and confusion I knew.

They paid their bill and got up to leave. Only when they walked past our table did I notice that the boy's head had been shaved. As if by choice. He wasn't sick at all, unless you count bad judgment in hairstyle as a sickness. The truth was a relief, but I was discomfited by my assumption. I was still suffering the aftershocks of cancer, while these people took their full stomachs and bald son happily out of the Pizza Hut into the tranquil Wyoming night. *You got off easy. Have a nice day.*

14

In the six months between my son's birth and my wife's death, Sue never held Myles for more than five minutes at a time. Even at his birth weight, a paltry six pounds, ten ounces, she couldn't bear the extra burden of Myles lying on her lap. He was too heavy.

"Jon, can you take him from me now please?" and she would smile at Myles as I lifted him off her tired legs. Despite her physical pain and the unavoidable attention she paid to her metastasizing cancer, Sue never stopped smiling at us, her two men. It seemed to give her as much pleasure watching us bond, father and son, as it gave me being a part of that equation.

Overnight I became a one-armed dad, effortlessly preparing baby bottles with my right as Myles rested comfortably in my cradled left. Entire meals had been cooked and served the same way. If Sue needed anything, I was confident I could fetch it for her without having to put Myles down. I'd worked out the best approach to every doorway in the house, allowing for the most geometrically sensible passage, so that Myles, resting on my hip, would not be concussed along the way.

Being the primary caregiver of my son and my wife was like breathing to me. No sooner had my life turned unrecognizable than I discovered the role I was meant to play in it. Becoming Dad was inevitable; it found me with the primeval muscle memory for parenting.

More importantly, Sue's death defined my role as a father more than I had originally been able to admit. It turned out to be the single most important influence on my parenting. My new job was to take care of my son's needs first and then take care of my own. As it turned out, taking care of him was virtually all I needed to do to take care of myself.

Being a dad, I discovered, was my calling, something I often wondered whether I'd ever find. Most people I knew had already found theirs. Until now I'd followed my interests and so-called passions in an effort to forge a "career" doing something I loved. I'd been an actor and a singer; I learned a trade and had my own solo business; I even dabbled in sales. But not until I became a dad, a *single* dad, did I truly learn why I was here. I'd found something I could take seriously, do well, and enjoy, and it didn't matter that I wasn't getting paid for it. I would not have made this discovery if I'd had to share parenting duties with Sue. When she died I was forced to accept being a single dad, but it also made me the father I wanted to be. It made me better at my job.

So this trip we were on, however loosely it had been planned, could only have occurred in this scenario. Despite the unforeseen encounters and adventures along the emotionally treacherous landscape, I had needed to get out of Toronto, and I was certainly not going to leave my son behind. It wasn't a question of "how"; it was "how could I not?" We were a team; I looked after him and he looked after me.

When I'd excitedly told Dr. Grief my plans before we left, it was almost as if I were asking for permission. I wanted her approval even though I'd have gone regardless. I might have been looking for reasons not to leave home, but as it turned out she only gave me more reasons to leave.

"I'm going on a road trip," I'd told her.

She stared at me from behind her dark-rimmed glasses and gave the best example I'd ever seen of her smile. I waited for a response that mirrored her face but she remained typically taciturn.

"Myles and I are going to drive around for a while. See where it takes us."

"Good," she said after another short silence. "I think that's a good idea."

"I think so too," I said.

After seeing Dr. Grief for six weeks, I'd grown accustomed to speaking without many responses. I'd learned to talk without looking at her, listening to myself in order to understand what I was feeling. I became immune to the cheerlessness of her office. But I think I expected a bit more than just affirmation of my decisions.

I told her about what I'd learned about myself while rebuilding the front and back decks of the house — about breaking myself down to my basic elements in order to rebuild myself. She seemed moved, but I couldn't be sure. I decided to take the fact that she didn't challenge me as a good sign.

"What else have you been doing with your days?" she asked, sounding almost interested.

"We've gotten into a routine, Myles and me," I said. "Most days he's awake by six, so I am too."

"He wakes you up?"

"Yes, but nicely. He doesn't cry and demand attention right away so I can wake up slowly, which I'm thankful for. He's ready for breakfast right away. I give him a bottle while I prepare his food."

Dr. Grief stared blankly. I was fairly certain she wasn't a parent herself, so I stopped short of telling her about what Myles liked to eat for breakfast or his pooping habits.

"Afterwards we play for a bit. What's really good is that I can leave him alone if I need to. I can go clean up the kitchen while he plays in the living room, and he's fine. He doesn't need me around a hundred per cent of the time. I guess he's used to being shuffled between grandparents and my sister, who all help out a few days a week. He seems perfectly happy on his own, like I was as a kid."

I waited for a reaction, thinking this might be an opportunity to talk about my childhood. *Can't everything be traced back to the incident with the garden hose when I was three?* Dr. Grief didn't bite.

"Sometimes we'll go see friends or to the playground. Or I might just go to the mall."

"The mall?"

"Yeah." I chuckled. "Some days I'll drive us over to Sherway Gardens. Not to shop — I almost never buy anything … I can hide there. I'm just another faceless buggy-pusher among the mall traffic. It's usually good for two or three hours until I start to get depressed … I hate malls."

The ambience of Chez Grief was particularly harsh that day. Outside, the charcoal sky grew murkier until day looked like night. I wished I could hear the sound of the rain bouncing off the tops of the air-conditioning units, but the double-paned windows of tempered glass took care of that.

"Do you like hiding?"

"I have enough time every day being present with myself. I like being home. Sue is there … I can be as sad as I want to be. But it's also like an office. That's where I do my work. My grieving work. Sometimes I need to leave work. So I hide at the mall."

"Does any work go on there?"

I'd never considered that. Whether I was at the home office or doing field research, wasn't it all part of the same work? Wasn't this the same objective I had by taking a road trip? Part of my commitment to healing myself was to find elements of normal in a self-governed environment of abnormality. Some days that meant wrapping myself in the dark cloak of my sanctuary/office/prison, other days it meant attempting a daring daylight escape. So if this were my job, as I'd considered it to be, then every choice I made would have to, in some small way, help me meet my job requirements.

"I suppose so," I said. "If nothing else, the anonymity is comforting."

Dr. Grief looked at the forbidden clock and said it was time for me to go. It had stopped raining outside, but the sky was still draped in greyness. Inside me, the sun was shining as the doctor wished me the best for my trip and asked me to contact her when I returned. I said I would, my head still dizzy from the hour of confession. It was the same every week: as if voicing my sadness made me lighter. Not empty, just less satiated from the daily doses of despondency. I glided from her office into the tomb-like corridors of the Baycrest Centre that smelled of old people and chimed with quiet echoes of imminent death. I was ready for whatever the next few months of fieldwork were going to bring me. I stepped out into the charcoal afternoon, not exactly anonymous but barely myself.

15

South Dakota. We woke up on the west side of the state, where the sunny faces of Mount Rushmore — surprisingly impressive — rise above the western plateau as a testament to American patriotism, ingenuity, and bizarre tributes. To my Canadian ears, people here spoke with the kind of drawl you might recognize from any cowboy movie. On the other side of South Dakota, a short day's drive about five hundred kilometres east across a time zone, people spoke in the flat, Midwestern tones I'd been used to hearing from my Michigan family. We spent the night in Sioux Falls — pronounced "Sue" Falls — before getting back on Interstate 90 again the next morning. For the next two days, Minnesota and Wisconsin flew past my open window with barely more than an acknowledgement.

The work I'd been doing on this adventure would surely have pleased Dr. Grief. But I didn't give the woman much thought. Instead I wondered how I was going to reconcile my discoveries when I got home to Toronto. Out here I was filling a need without distraction, unless you included the distraction of driving. When I got home, more of Sue would be there. I still had no palpable desire to loosen my grasp on her, but I feared her presence might force me to take a few steps back from the progress I felt I'd made out on the road. I feared her presence.

The soundtrack for this leg of the drive featured Rush. The Canadian band's legendary guitars, bass, drums, and vocals — each distinctive in their own right and collectively peerless — propelled the car along the tree-lined but otherwise featureless highway. One song in particular caught my interest in this different context. "Dreamline" is a song about wandering the face of the earth, restlessly searching for those things that can make dreams come true. It could be love or heroism or adventure itself. The song reminds us, however, of our immortality (as if I needed a reminder) by suggesting our search is for a limited time only.

"Listen," I said to my budding musicologist in the back seat. "You'll never hear another bass played so precisely — you'll never hear a better rock drummer than Neil Peart. They've been together for thirty years. Two of the guys grew up in the same neighbourhood I did. Listen to this line."

I paused to let singer Geddy Lee tell Myles that the only time it felt like home was when you were on the run.

"We're on the run," I said. "Is this where we are supposed to feel at home?"

I listened to the words more closely. He wasn't advocating running, neither away from or toward anything. So what was it about the "running" I found so appealing? Perhaps it's the searching that's the key. Maybe the fulfillment of a dream is simply in being able to pursue it. Realizing the dream is, in some sense, irrelevant. Whatever I was searching for, now almost six weeks after leaving home, might not even reveal itself until years from now in the flickering light of memory. I might always be searching. We all might be.

Peart is not just an extraordinary drummer, but he's also the lyricist for the band. His love of literature is evoked in their songs and his compulsion to write is proven by the four memoirs he's written, one of which, *Ghost Rider*, was instrumental in getting Myles and me out on the road in the first place. Peart's wife and daughter both died less than a year apart, compelling him to spend what turned out to be two years riding around North and South America on his motorcycle. He documented his time on what he called the healing road. I'd already decided to take a trip before I read his book, but when I learned how his adventure helped him heal, it confirmed for me that I'd made the right decision.

Sometime during my drive through Wisconsin, the singer Johnny Cash died. By the time I'd checked into the Super 8 in North Chicago, all the news channels were airing video tributes to him every hour. I didn't know much about Johnny, other than that he always wore black, but I learned during the unavoidable televised obituaries that one of the songs he was most famous for was called "A Boy Named Sue." I never would have predicted Johnny Cash being responsible for a Harmony Moment.

The next morning I took Myles on a stroll through the city that Sue and I visited one long weekend a few years before.

"Your mom and I ate lunch at that restaurant, Myles," I said as we made our way up the Magnificent Mile of Michigan Avenue. I tried to remember all the famous Chicago buildings Sue and I saw during an architectural river cruise. "There's the *Tribune* building," I said, pointing at the magnificent neo-Gothic skyscraper. "And I think that's Trump Tower over there."

I also remembered seeing a terrific view of the iconic Sears Tower from the lakefront. I wanted to take a picture of Myles there. Not far from the famous Buckingham Fountain I found the spot I was thinking of and snapped the photo. A little farther south along the lakeshore is the famous aquarium. Outside this building was a sign advertising the Museum of Natural History and an exhibit showing some of the earliest dinosaur bones ever found, which they had named — harmoniously — "Sue."

Being in Chicago reminded me of how well Sue and I travelled together. We enjoyed seeing the same things, going at the same pace, sharing our experiences. This symbiosis was evidence of a connection that went beyond what we did together. But I couldn't help thinking, as I peered past the Chicago shoreline smoothly outlining this part of Lake Michigan, that this connection between us belied the inherent volatility in our marriage. How could we each have been so much in love with the one person who compelled us to act so irrationally?

Among all the spats, quarrels, and grudges that peppered our history, one specific fight stuck out. We were living in Windsor at the time, married about five years. Sue's broadcast career was in full bloom, my upholstery business self-sufficient. But we were in an unspoken rut, ready for the next challenge in our lives but too comfortable in the present to risk making any changes. There was a mysterious restlessness in our house as we blindly went from day to day as a temporarily unsatisfied couple. As was the norm, the initial kernel of this particular dispute had long been forgotten — in retrospect it's irrelevant — and we were at that point, as usual, arguing about the argument. We floated between the bedroom and the office, heavy footsteps dampened by the carpet.

"Where were you brought up?" Sue shouted. "Who talks that way?"

I tried to stay calm, certain I was being the voice of reason. "I'm just trying to choose my words carefully," I said, "so that there's no misunderstanding of what I'm trying to say."

"You're failing miserably."

She walked away from me. I followed. She began putting clothes away, fluffing up the pillows. Sometimes she would prepare a whole meal while we argued.

"Can I just try to make my point please?" I said.

"It's too late, Jonathan. You said what you said. You can't take it back."

"But what you think I said is not what I meant to say."

"I think you meant what you said."

She turned away from me again and went into the bathroom to brush her teeth, cleansing her mouth of the vitriol. I followed again.

"Can you please stop and listen to me? I'm trying…"

"I'm done listening. You can talk as much as you like but you're not saying anything to make this better."

"I can't even remember what it is I'm trying to make better," I said.

She reminded me as she stormed downstairs, recounting, like a court reporter, every word I said. Or what she thought I said. Her memory rarely let her down even if it often coloured things slightly in her favour.

"…and if you really think you're right about this," she went on, "I may just have to divorce you."

That wasn't a word we used.

"Divorce? Seriously?"

"Of course, seriously. You can take the dog and the car, I'm keeping the cats and the house."

She'd given this some thought. I couldn't believe how quickly she'd come up with the division of assets. And yet I did believe it. Every time we fought I wondered how long it would be before she decided this was the last straw. If I wondered if I could take it much longer, she certainly must have.

"Sweetie…" I said quietly.

"Don't call me that."

"Calm down, you're…"

"Don't tell me to calm down."

"Just listen…"

"Shut up. Shut. Up." She started to thrash me around the shoulders and across my chest, nearly hitting me in the face. "I hate you … right now." Even in the heat of battle she was always careful to add that last part, to distinguish her disgust in that moment from any long-term feelings about me.

"Stop hitting me," I said, grabbing her around the wrists.

"Let go of me." She tried to pull her hands away. "Don't you dare grab my hands. That's abuse."

I paused, waiting for her to stop struggling before I let go.

She scurried up the stairs. I grabbed my keys from the hall table, ran outside, and jumped into the car. I started it up and drove, I didn't know where. There aren't too many places in Windsor to drive to when you don't know where to go. But I found myself on Riverside Drive pulling into one of the dark parking lots that overlook the bright lights of the Detroit skyline across the river. I turned off the engine.

I suppose I could sleep here. She wouldn't care. She's got this all figured out anyway. She wants a divorce. This is it. This is really it.

I was tired of fighting with the woman I loved. Tired of feeling like I was the one making compromises and she was the one making decisions. I moved to Windsor so she could be a journalist. I was tired of being a second-rate citizen in my own marriage.

I remembered that first fight we'd had years earlier and how I still fell in love with her soon afterwards. I remembered how I threatened to breakup with her a few months later and she forbade it. By the time we were married, she ignored the common marital theory of not going to bed angry. She was happy to tromp off to the bed in the spare room if she was pissed off enough, determining at that moment, I assumed, that sleep was more important to her than resolution. But I always brought her back to bed. Ultimately I begged for her forgiveness and convinced her of my genuine belief that love could conquer all. It seemed to me that, as volatile as this was, we were going to last.

It was getting cold down by the river. *Don't go back there, not tonight. Tonight she can try to bring me back to bed. I'm sleeping here.* The Detroit skyline paled as the moon rose higher, the sky glowing under its light.

Less than an hour later I started up the car, drove back home, and walked into our house. All the lights were off, and I slowly walked up the stairs to our bedroom. Sue was on the bed but she was awake; she rolled over when I entered the room, putting her back to me. I sat down on my side of the bed.

"I'm sorry," I said.

"I know," Sue said. We both bathed in the unsettled silence, a tiny thread of light coming through the bedroom window from the street lamps. "I'm sorry too."

The need to offer explanations for my behaviour rumbled within me, my proficiency in contrition by this time perfected. I wanted to remind her that my love for her had made me fight every compulsion I had to contradict her. I wanted nothing more than to avoid all conflicts with her because quarrelling made me sad.

Arguments were rarely resolved, and every one of them seemed pointless to me. Moreover, as she knew, I was a terrible opponent for her because I could never state my case as boldly as she could. I walked on eggshells to ensure I didn't tread on any of her sensitive toes. But she knew all of this. She'd heard it from me many times.

"Sometimes I think I'll grow old all alone," she said. "Just me and the cats. I'm going to be an old cat woman with wild, grey hair and plastic bags on my feet."

"That's impossible," I said, putting my hand on her back. "I'm not going anywhere."

* * *

I had to go home. I knew that I had only just begun to piece together this new life of mine, but I sensed that I'd learned everything I was going to learn from running away. Taking myself out of my comfort zone, if there is such a thing during a period of grief, had provided much-needed perspective. But I had grown aimless. No wandering minstrel, I. From here on, I thought, I'll have to meet the ghosts at home head-on. It was time to face the music.

Myles woke up in the Chicago Super 8 like it was any other morning. But on this day he had no idea that by nightfall he'd be sleeping in his own bed. I packed up his travel cot — its blue fabric fading now, seams starting to fray — his bags of toys, clothes, and food, and I threw it all into the car to prepare for the last day of driving. My system of car-loading had long ago been perfected, yet the RAV4 bulged with the clutter of six weeks' worth of dirty clothes, food wrappers, CDs, souvenirs, blurry memories, and Harmony Moments. It would be a long day, ten or eleven hours on the road, but

Highway

I knew I could make it home from Chicago. And home is where I wanted to be.

I had tunnel vision and a heavy foot as I hit I-94, which cuts across the bottom of Michigan. Back in familiar Detroit, the road numbers got smaller: 9 Mile Road, 8 Mile Road, 7 Mile … Eventually we reached the river and another unchallenged border crossing. Rising out of the tunnel into downtown Windsor, I barely looked to my left or right. I just continued on until I reached the 401 and the sign that said *Toronto 360*. Three hundred and sixty kilometres. If I didn't stop, I'd be home in less than four hours. The sun was setting behind us; in front, the nighttime sanctuary of Toronto welcomed us into its darkened hearth.

Every last bit of adventure, meditation, and insularity had been drained out of me. The thought of being home lured me with the same delight as if Sue would be there to greet us so I could tell her all about Myles's and my life for the past six weeks. Including my epiphany from our hike in British Columbia on the state of our marriage.

That lingering feeling of ambiguity hovered in the car like the scent of old flowers. The past I'd been mourning and the future that I'd been denied had, until this point, been connected by one constant. Sue was meant to have been a part of the entire timeline. Now there was a division. It wasn't simply that she'd died; it was the understanding that, had she lived, I may not have been able to keep her. My unknown, unlived, unforeseen future — the future I should have had with Sue — now seemed burdened by an enduring tear. Living without her may have always been unavoidable.

September 17, 2003 — Toronto

Home: The Final Frontier

Dear Myles,

> *Here are the totals:*
>
> *14,807.5 kilometres door to door*
>
> *23 states, 2 provinces*
>
> *4 time zones and back again*
>
> *2 oil changes*
>
> *1 entire box of Cheerios consumed, one Cheerio at a time*

I have to baby-proof the house. When we left almost seven weeks ago, you were only just beginning to crawl. Now you can't keep still and you have become quite accustomed to exploring. In fact I should be doing that tonight, right now as you sleep, but for the moment I'd prefer to sit quietly and put some of my thoughts down for you.

It's been nearly five months since your mom died. I'm feeling her slipping away from me, and I don't want that. There is comfort in feeling sad because then I know she's still with me. Perhaps one day I might lose my sense of her completely, but for now I need her as much as I need you.

That's why we're home now. I still feel her here. Being home means starting the next step of healing, whatever that is.

I'm aware that hearing a lot about your mom may weigh down on you after a while. I know what that feels like. After my dad — your grandfather Bruce — died when I was seven years old, people who knew him kept telling me how I reminded them of him. I didn't begrudge my grandparents or my mother their memories, but because I had so few of my own, it became a burden for me to carry their memories around with me. If my memories of Sue become a burden on you, Myles, then I'm sorry. I'd completely understand if you asked me to keep some of my thoughts to myself. However, if you ever want to know anything about her I would be happy to tell you. And I'll try to be as objective as possible.

Coming home has confirmed that going away was definitely the right thing to do. A lot of healing took place (still a long way to go) even though the road has led me right back here. Now instead of long drives with obligations as basic as eating and sleeping, my healing must be conducted under a new, more domestic set of guidelines. I'm okay with that. Because I learned a lot while we were travelling: about you, about me, and about your mom. Now that we're home, I hope to be able to take what I learned and use that to guide me toward our future.

Tomorrow I'm going to get my second tattoo. I got my first one, the moose, two years ago in Windsor. My next one will be in memory of your mom. It's an infinity sign. It means eternity, forever, never-ending. Sue was going to get an infinity tattoo, but she never got around to it. So I'm doing it in her stead as well as for myself. One day I'll get a tattoo for you too.

I want to thank you, Myles, for everything you have done for me without even knowing it. Thank you for travelling with me. May it be the first of many excursions you and I take together, and may you be bitten by the travel bug. Find out what life is all about by seeing how the rest of the world lives. Thank you for helping me through the most difficult time of my life. If it weren't for you and your smiles, laughter, and joy I would see no light at the end of this dark tunnel. You are my reason for getting up in the morning. You are my inspiration for forging ahead into an uncertain future. Forever you will have my love and fatherly devotion. As you grow, I hope you will be able to rely on me as much as I've relied on you. I'll do whatever is in my power to ensure that. Whatever your future brings, you will always have people in your life who love you. With love you are empowered. With love you are never alone. I love you, son. Thank you for being you. Thank you for being.

With infinite love,
Dad

Part III

Having New Eyes

"During the middle of the day it was no longer the sun alone that persecuted from above — the entire sky was like a metal dome grown white with heat. The merciless light pushed down from all directions; the sun was the whole sky."

— *Paul Bowles,* The Sheltering Sky

16

One of the ironies of cancer is how pervasive it is but how seldom people talk about it. It's always there, sitting just over everyone's shoulder in various personae like those imaginary little angels and devils. But nobody is quite sure which one to listen to.

The word itself — *cancer* — looms large in the lexicon of our unconscious as one that we dare not speak. It is at once sacrosanct and taboo, as if saying the word might somehow curse the person who has it or pass it on to someone in the vicinity. When the word is actually spoken, it is done quietly, almost politely, so as not to aggravate the temperamental God of Terminal Illness. It is inherently self-editing, the harsh sound of the first C muted by the sibilance of the second one. *Come-here-go-away*, it says in a radio-static whisper.

When Sue was only months away from dying, I could see her cancer, whether I admitted it or not. It was literally in her. From the tumour in her breast it spread, in time, to her liver and bones. But it was also there in her eyes, masking the twinkle. It was in her walk, slower and belaboured. It was certainly in her hair, or lack of it. It was in her voice, her skin, her smell, her mood. Her sense of identity, both real and perceived, was saturated with the stuff. We tried not to fear it, speaking of it only in terms of what we were going to do with our lives once it was gone, or how we could make her more comfortable. Otherwise it was just a wicked trespasser nobody was sure how to approach.

Then she was gone but the cancer remained. It floated around me like steam from a boiling kettle. It nosed its way between the pages of my book and under my pillow. It hid between the floorboards or behind my cereal bowl. Sometimes it hung from the wall like a giant tapestry, and sometimes it sat in the teaspoon jar. It never taunted or pointed its ugly finger. It didn't have to.

Cancer was the smoking gun.

The disease spread throughout all of us who knew Sue. Some people kept it like a forbidden secret and some people ignored it altogether. Some tried to acknowledge it but always ended up fumbling over their tongues. Usually their words, spoken in hushed tones, thoughtful though they might have been, fell on my deaf ears.

"You know, I feel the loss too," one friend told me.

"I know," I said. But then I wondered why he said that. Was it to show me that Sue had touched so many lives and that her death left more than one hole? Was I so miserable and self-pitying, insisting I was the saddest person in the world, that he thought I needed to snap out of it and see the bigger picture? Or is cancer simply ubiquitous?

"How do you feel the loss?" I wanted to ask, but never did — because actually I didn't care. It was all about me.

Through it all I was manning the toll booth at the edge of the cancer highway. Everything had to get through me first: the flowers in a beautiful garden were muted, greyer as seen through my eyes; the conversation that made me laugh was not quite as funny after I hung up the phone; good news was soured, bad news inconsequential. The world was cancer-coloured.

Including parenthood. My sister, Lainie, three years older than I and an experienced parent to my two nieces, gave me the phrase "extended vulnerability": the need to broaden your own boundaries to protect your child. But my sense of vulnerability had extended so far I couldn't even recognize it. If Myles were to climb the two branches of his family tree, he'd discover signs of cancer before he reached the first bifurcation.

At thirteen months, he got his first cold. With that and every subsequent cold, cough, stomach ache, or indistinct physical nuisance, I was convinced it was an indication of some larger illness. The whispers of cancer. How could it not be? It's bad enough that he has cancer in his genes, but he had also been exposed to cancer treatment, the anti-cancer: a devil in its own right.

Cancer even tested my usually forgiving sense of humour. Shortly after returning home from the Healing Tour, my friend Andrew invited me out to see comedian George Carlin at Roy Thomson Hall in Toronto. I eagerly accepted, not just because I was a Carlin fan, but also because I recognized my friend's effort to help me forget about life for a while. We both thought I could use a laugh — we shared a Monty Pythonesque sense of humour — and we were both right. Sadly nothing was funny as seen through my cancer-coloured glasses. Carlin, whose acerbic, curse-loaded observations usually put me in a state of comedic awe, spent the entire hour and a half talking about fatal diseases, death, war, religion, and other topics I was in no mood to laugh about.

So why did I stay to the end of the show? Why didn't I get up and walk out of the theatre like I wanted to? Was it because I was sitting next to my generous, well-intentioned friend and did not want to appear ungrateful? Did I think it would get funnier? Or was it that omnipresent stalker, cancer, that bound me to my seat, forced me to bear witness, and kept me silent?

In my quest to understand the life I had been given after Sue died, I tried to make sense of how my experiences with cancer might play out in my future. But then I'd turn on the news and just get angry. All news broadcasters seemed to have colluded to ensure that their information would offer me no solace at all. Their segments, with names like "Health Matters" or "Dr. Floyd's Medical Minute," came on about three-quarters of the way through the news — after "Dog Bites Girl" but before sports — and everything seemed to revolve around what caused or prevented cancer. One week a study found that eating too much food from a can will cause cancer. The next week a new study showed that 300 millilitres of Coke per day might actually drive away certain cancer-causing carcinogens. But doesn't Coke come in a can? Finally I just shouted, "Fuck you, Dr. Floyd!" and switched off.

Cancer lingered like the dirt under my fingernails. I started to wonder who the real cancer victim was.

Coming home after nearly seven weeks on the road with Myles was at once comforting and alienating. Even though I was happy that Myles was sleeping in his own bed, that we weren't eating meals in restaurants of questionable reputation, and that the sanctuary of our house had wrapped its warm arms around my weary traveller's bones, I still didn't quite feel at home. The lessons I'd learned on the immortal highway had compelled me to return to Toronto, but being back was merely the beginning of the next step toward my complete healing. Still, I couldn't be sure if I'd ever heal completely or if I would simply "move on," as one does, without completely shedding my layer of old grief.

The revelation I had on top of the treacherous rock back in British Columbia gave me a different perspective: a more honest, perhaps more realistic one. But by acknowledging the tenuousness of our marriage, my sorrow became murky, less defined. The parts of Sue I hated were now as equally memorable as those I loved. That I could miss her and dislike her at the same time made little sense to me. I tried to figure out the role Sue would play in my new life but the memories didn't fit together properly. How could I be optimistic about the future if I still had to sort out the past? My glass-half-full tomorrow was upset by my glass-half-empty yesterday.

If I truly believed that living without her would have been inevitable, regardless of her death, shouldn't it have been easier to accept that she was gone? I still missed her. I still missed the life we were supposed to have together, and I was still no closer to finding out where my new life was going.

If there was one thing from the Healing Tour that I wanted to keep with me, it was the sense of routine. Despite every day being different, Myles and I had kept a relatively steady schedule between driving, seeing things, eating, and sleeping. If I could maintain a schedule that worked in the home environment, then I figured I would continue to make progress in my efforts to sort out my life. I'd become very confident looking after Myles. I had few worries about him or about my ability to parent. But increasingly I was becoming doubtful about my own well-being.

I didn't wake up one morning and say, "Okay, I'm going to heal myself. Starting today I'm going to get over this grief." It doesn't work that way. There are no instructions by which you can determine if you're doing it right or not. You simply must live your life and absorb everything that each day throws at you.

You must rise early or sleep late. You must go for long walks or sit statue-still for hours. You must listen to music, watch TV, and go to movies, or you must have complete silence. You must talk endlessly to your friends, or you must keep them far away from you. You must think constantly of your lost loved one, or you must put them out of your mind entirely. What you need today, you may not need tomorrow.

This was why I needed a new routine.

Myles usually woke me up with a murmur. I'd hear him in his room next door to mine speaking to himself barely above a whisper. His chatter, muffled through the thin plasterboard, sounded like he was telling me about his dreams: mysterious but pleasant reveries that had swept through his baby head all night, telling him the world was an exciting, complex place to wake up in. His monologue proceeded calmly for several minutes unless I took too long to get out from under the refuge of my duvet. Fighting my aversion to mornings, I would wrench myself out of bed, stumble into his room, and grab him from his crib with a smile and a kiss. Still clinging to Doggy Dog, he'd wrap an arm around my neck, and we'd start our day together with a quick diaper change.

His breakfast during the months approaching his first birthday consisted of whichever organic, jarred, prepared baby food he was partial to. It was often something labelled "chicken" that smelled more like old eggs. This would be followed by any apple-based fruit treat: apple-strawberry, apple-plum, apple-banana… Myles could eat a full jar of each in one sitting, which gave him just enough energy to roll around in his ExerSaucer while I sought out some breakfast of my own, usually cereal. Myles's willingness to play on his own allowed me to take care of necessary household chores, typically no more complicated than laundry or dishwashing, that I had ignored the night before when Myles was conveniently asleep.

By the time nine o'clock came around, I'd have gotten us both dressed and strapped Myles into his buggy, a bag full of baby necessities tucked into the hold under his seat. With Mika the dog in tow, we left Humberside Avenue and walked down the hill toward High Park, our family now somehow whole. It would take about a half hour to complete the circuit of the park, not including the time it took to lure Mika back from her squirrel-hounding missions. She was a rescued dog, two years old when we adopted her and already embedded with bad habits; she rarely came when she was called.

On these walks, passing centuries-old oak trees that rose into a dappled canopy above the footpath, I inevitably thought about walking with Sue, always hand in hand. We'd chosen this neighbourhood together, largely due to its proximity to the park.

If Myles hadn't fallen asleep by the time we'd reached the playground, I pushed him on the swings for as long as he liked, which could be indefinitely. Other parents, mostly moms, rarely said hello. Occasionally another dad would try to strike up a conversation in an effort to find someone to commiserate with. I didn't have time for those dads telling me how they were sleepy but happy to be giving their wives a few hours' break from child duty. Our parenting experiences were too unlike. It wasn't simply that they couldn't relate to my intricate, sad story; it was mostly that I had no interest in relating to theirs. So I ignored the people who ignored me.

Then there were the dog walkers. This group of plastic bag–carrying, rubber boot–wearing, going-out-before-they-shower people believe it's their canine-given prerogative to speak to anyone about any topic as long as that person also has a dog. There is an unspoken fraternity among dog owners who meet regularly at the park, knowing they've been annexed to a particular, occasionally fenced-in area. This micro-society gathers twice daily to discuss the weather, real estate, and the most fashionable doggy hardware. I tried to be nice.

"What kind of dog is that?" the woman with the terrier asked me one morning. I didn't even know her dog's name, let alone hers. She always wore a skirt over her designer, calf-high rubber boots, and the same jacket whatever the weather. Her drugstore-brand ginger hair was usually as bedraggled as the jacket.

"Border collie cross," I said. "I'm not sure what she's crossed with."

"He's gorgeous. Had him for long?"

"Since she was two. She was from the pound."

"Oh," she cooed. It came out like "Aww."

"That's nice. I'm sure your boy loves having the dog around."

"Yes, he does. And we've got two cats too." I guess it didn't hurt to share.

"Oh, I love animals. Well, obviously, otherwise you wouldn't see me here every morning with that dog." She pointed at a scruffy thing running around, as unchecked as Mika.

"Obviously."

"How old is your son then?"

"Myles. He's 11 months."

"Oh, he's gorgeous. I love children. My boys, the twins, you know, are ten and I just miss these younger years so much. Not that it doesn't get better but, you know, new challenges and all that." She waited for me to acknowledge

I knew what "all that" was. "What do you do when you're not walking the dog or looking after Myles?"

"Actually that's kind of all I do." Sometimes I was brave enough to give this answer. Mostly I did my best to steer the conversation away from this line of inquiry.

"That's interesting. What does your wife do then?"

After "what do you do?" this was the question I dreaded the most. Aside from the fact that it dripped with assumptions, any question about Sue would start my heart beating faster and my mind spinning. How much of the story do I tell? What is this person capable of hearing? Could I just run away? I took a deep breath.

"My wife died about six months ago," I said.

"You're single?"

Wrong answer. Sure, it was news to her but not what she'd expected — as if her macho son just told her he was gay. In a split second she'd processed the information, wondered what it meant to her, and decided she was okay with it. She practically smiled.

"Yeah. I'm single."

"I never would have guessed. I just always thought, 'Hmm, I've never seen his wife.'"

I shrugged. *Really don't want to talk about it. Just walking the dog.*

"And you're raising your son all by yourself?"

"Yes."

"Oh." She gave a contented sort of sigh. "Good for you. That is so brave."

Brave? He's my son. What should I have done, given him away?

"I don't really have much choice," I said.

"I know but, I mean, you see so many single moms all over the place but not many single dads. It must be so hard for you."

"I have help."

"Of course you do." She started to stumble over her words.

I stared her down, challenging her to put her foot deeper into her big mouth, wondering what was going through her mind before reminding myself that I didn't care.

"Well, I'm just so impressed. You're so brave."

"This is my life," I said.

"Of course it is. Well, I just wanted to say, good for you."

"Thanks." *Good for me. What a triumph.*

We both looked away and watched the dogs sniffing each other's butts.

"So," she said. "He's a border collie, is he?"

I was single. This detail hadn't escaped me, but it certainly hadn't stood out like a Broadway marquee for me the way it did for Terrier Woman. I still felt married. Sue was still my wife, and I had the marriage certificate to prove it. She was just dead, a fact suitably verified by another document.

But I couldn't blame this woman for her reaction, because nobody really knows what to say when they're with someone who has experienced great loss. Everyone's world is blinkered in some way so that anything outside of a narrow scope is inconsequential. To those of us on the receiving end, any sentiments they might offer just sound like awkward babble. That includes words of empathy, warm wishes, or snippets of evocative poetry. Even compliments on your bravery.

I wasn't excluded from this. Having been on both sides, I thought I'd be better at empathy than they were. But I've since been faced with offering words of solace to other men who have lost their wives, the mothers of their small children. My expressions of compassion came off just as flippant and shallow as Terrier

Woman's. I couldn't fault them for reacting, as I did, with such indifference.

Nearly every time I was at the supermarket, the lady at the checkout (it was always a lady) would look at Myles sitting in the shopping cart and say, "Giving Mom a break today?" or some comment that suggested it wasn't normal for me — or any father — to be out with his son, to be parenting. If they saw a woman alone with a child, they'd never assume she were giving the father a break. In fact, they might just as quickly imagine that she's a single mother. I couldn't bear the double standard. Yet more than anything, I just wanted to remain anonymous, to be left alone.

Perhaps I should have expected it. People have funny ways of overcompensating for their discomfort. Most people must have realized they couldn't possibly know what I was feeling or what I needed to hear, but I was the only one who knew they couldn't win against me. My expectations were too high. I insisted on the permission to behave any way I wanted and on having everyone's complete sympathy in the process. I demanded people have a level of understanding I knew I'd never have the capacity for. They had to do everything "right," but I had no idea what "right" was. I should have granted everyone the latitude to fail. But nobody could satisfy the opposing armies in my battle. You can't attack and retreat at the same time.

So there I was, the single dad with the assorted pets, standing in the park talking to Terrier Woman about being a single dad with assorted pets. As far as we both could see, my life came down to little more than that. I had no wife, no job, no ambition, and nothing in the foreseeable future that seemed to differ from the current scenario.

Worse still, at the park at least, I wasn't even anonymous anymore.

* * *

With Myles back in the buggy we'd head for home. Somewhere along the twenty-minute walk, Myles would fall asleep for his first nap of the day. I'd carefully lift the buggy, with him in it, up the stairs onto our front porch, sit down next to him, put my feet up on the bannister, and fall asleep myself. The porch, which I'd finished rebuilding only three months earlier, was a sheltered refuge from the outside world of dog walkers and well-intentioned dads, a safe harbour in which I felt invisible, as though there were a force field over the house. I could've sat there forever.

When Myles was done napping, he'd wake me up by telling me about his dreams again, and we'd go inside for lunch.

Our afternoons were improvised: the occasional play date with a friend; maybe a trip down to the lakeshore. Often, like I'd explained to Dr. Grief, we ended up at the mall to wander in anonymity, and Myles would have his afternoon nap there. Each of his naps lasted one and a half to two hours, so in addition to his twelve hours at night, Myles was only awake for about eight hours a day.

On Wednesdays after our walk, Mom came to pick Myles up. She'd keep him overnight and return him about twenty-four hours later. On those afternoons when he was gone, I'd go for a run. The rhythmic metre of my steps and forward momentum gave me the same feeling as when I had driven five or six hundred kilometres a day on the Healing Tour, but on a smaller, sweatier scale. I'd return home, make myself a healthy fruit smoothie, with a handful of that green powder made from kale and alfalfa and wheatgrass, and take a shower. Then I'd see what movies were playing at the local SilverCity. Going to a film on my own always used to be a pleasure. I enjoyed the whole solo cinematic experience with no distractions. Without Sue, it continued to be one of the best ways to pass the time: in the dark, anonymous, and for two hours living another life. Before the movie I usually went to the generic roadhouse across the parking lot for a steak and a pint of beer. With any luck the television above the bar would be showing sports.

After the movie it was back to the empty house. I avoided watching any television programs filled with information I was expected to know (Dr. Floyd) or shows that were too insipid to entertain me — ruling out most sitcoms and dramas. That left sports, the odd reality show — I often imagined Myles and me being awarded an *Extreme Makeover: Home Edition* out of pity — Letterman, and whatever followed. Mindless distraction. If I went to bed at a sensible time, I'd lie awake with lonely thoughts preventing me from drifting off. So I stayed up as late as I could, Mika the dog at my hip, until my eyes were drooping at the television. That way I'd be sleeping soon after the lights went out.

On Friday afternoons, my sister Lainie watched Myles while I went to see my new counsellor, Jan. Shortly after returning from the road trip, I had my last meeting with Dr. Grief. She asked about the road trip and about how it felt being home.

"I still feel the need to talk to someone regularly," I said, "but I think I'm ready for some other kind of counselling."

"So do I," she said quickly.

I don't think there was very much discussion of the road trip. There wouldn't have been too many widowers in Dr.

Grief's grieving constituency at the Baycrest Centre who could have gone on a similar adventure.

Jan and I spoke in her house surrounded by books and spider plants, quite unlike the atmosphere of Dr. Grief's sterile, steel-grey purgatory. She sat cross-legged in her brown velvet chair across from me as I sprawled on her futon recounting the previous week. Those one-hour meetings sped by due to my endless talking. I was piecing it together, one week at a time.

After my session, I returned to Lainie's house, where Myles and I stayed for Shabbat dinner with my sister, her partner, Adira, and my nieces. I came to love those Friday nights. My sister's family reminded me that my world was bigger than it sometimes seemed.

On Sunday mornings I drove to Burlington, forty minutes with no traffic, to leave Myles with Sue's parents. Occasionally I stayed for lunch before leaving Myles to spend the night with his grandparents. But usually I just dropped him off and went home. In the afternoon I played softball with a bunch of strangers who met every Sunday in Stanley Park (not nearly as grand as Vancouver's park of the same name). I never felt obliged to go for a beer with them after the game, as was the tradition. Instead I went back home, showered, and then returned to the SilverCity for another dinner-and-a-movie date with myself. Seeing two films a week ensured I saw just about everything released during this time, not necessarily a blessing. I'm fairly confident, for instance, that I'm the only person in Toronto who saw the movie *Envy*, starring Jack Black and Ben Stiller.

George and Joyce brought Myles home on Monday evenings. They delivered him already dressed in his pyjamas so that I could put him right to bed, but I'd wait an hour or so first. Even though I made use of my flexible time when Myles was away, having him come home made everything normal again. I was still his dad first, everything else second. When I finally put Myles to bed, he fell asleep immediately. I stayed up with the late-night television pablum waiting for my eyes to droop again.

So another day ended just like the last one did. I didn't accomplish much, unless just-making-it-through-the-day can be considered an accomplishment. I'd done my job. I'd met my responsibilities. I may have interacted with some people that day and the world hadn't exploded because of it. There would have been some tears. I was still sad. I was still lonely. The next day it would all be the same. Or, with any luck, maybe not.

17

It still felt strange being there without Sue and not just because her parents' house was nothing like the one I'd grown up in. It had, among other things, frilly curtains, full sets of matching towels, and an actual dining room. The art on the walls had been chosen to match the decor. The house was always clean. It was like entering a private club into which my relationship with Sue had entitled me entry. But it simply had no appeal without her in it. There had always been a tangible heat that radiated throughout the car as we drove down to the end of the cul-de-sac to the 1960s ranch-style structure. For Sue it was the anticipation of walking back into the cosy clutches of her family home. For me it was never quite knowing what to anticipate. That much, at least, hadn't changed.

I parked the car in my usual spot on the driveway as big as an ice rink, unleashed Myles from his car seat, and carried him up the steps to the front door. I took a deep breath and rang the bell.

"Hi, Myles! Hi, Jon."

"Hello."

"There's our little boy. How's our boy? Let Gramma take those boots off. Yes. Gramma loves you, yes, she does."

"Traffic okay, Jon?"

"Not bad, thanks."

"That's good."

"Have you got a runny little nose? Let Gramma clean that up for you. Gramma has to keep her boy looking handsome."

"Thanks, Joyce."

"You're welcome."

The good china and crystal were set at the dining room table, marking the three places, but there was no high chair. Candles were already lit, and there was a centrepiece of red, orange, and yellow leaves George had retrieved from the oaks and maples in the backyard. I was offered a drink, which I eagerly accepted. The slow-roasting turkey imparted its familiar aroma throughout the house; vegetables were overcooking. I thought I knew what to expect. But this being the first Thanksgiving without Sue, I should have known not to rely on expectations.

Sue and I had been accustomed to the routine of her family's dinners and always looked forward to the lazy, waistband-stretching meals. We ate way too much of the Norman Rockwell feast and washed it down with cheap wine or home-brewed beer. Conversations were light, lively, and frequently sentimental. It was all perfectly familial and familiar.

We knew dinner was officially over when George gently pushed his chair back, wiped his mouth with his napkin, folded it neatly, put it down on the table, and said, while looking adoringly at his wife, "It doesn't get any better than this."

It didn't often get better than that. We were a family, cohesive and complete. I had embraced the symmetry of our intergenerational couplehood and was content in the knowledge that our eternity included all of us. But after Sue died, the closed circle ruptured. Dead air infiltrated conversations that were now sprinkled with formalities. I couldn't communicate with George and Joyce in the shorthand they'd had with their daughter. Nor could I ignore the pall of the suffocating shroud that was draped over us. They made cheerful suggestions, but I didn't think a game of three-handed euchre was going to make me feel better. I wanted to talk about Sue, but my confessions were too often met with uncomfortable silence.

I shouldn't have been surprised. I had to remind myself that they, too, were grieving. But they had each other to talk to. Maybe they didn't need me as much as I needed them. Maybe the only thing we had in common was pinning all of our hopes for the future onto the front of Myles's little "B is for Bananas" bib. Whatever the reasons, the discomfort triggered by what I wanted to talk about was not nearly as great as the discomfort embedded in what they didn't want to talk about.

A part of me admired their stoicism. Sometimes they made it look so easy. I knew we all grieved differently. As much as I wanted to tell them that my sorrow was deeper than theirs, I couldn't know what it was like to lose a child. It became clear to me early on that sharing my sadness with them would be a frustrating and debilitating exercise.

During the first week after Sue died, while Myles and I were still living in my in-laws' house, I stuttered through each day with helpless single-mindedness like someone learning to walk: one foot, then the next, repeat. Dress Myles. Dress myself. Wash. Cry. Feed Myles. Feed myself. Cry. On and on until something made me fall down again. Spending a few more days with Sue's family would, I'd hoped, make things a bit easier. Together we could organize the memorial — Sue's big party. We had purpose and the collective might of a grieving gang. Still, the walking lessons continued in that quiet house.

One afternoon, as Myles was being fussed over by his grandparents, I took an armful of his clean clothes up to the room he slept in. I sat down on the spare bed and found Sue's wool, cable-knit sweater. I picked it up, hugged it, and caught wind of her. I collapsed on the bed, inhaling her, as the sweater sopped up the liquid coming out of my face. I was holding Sue again. She was stroking the back of my neck. Our ten years together flooded over me with the fresh perfume of her skin that was infused in her clothing.

I didn't hear Joyce come in. Through the fog I saw her round figure, her blue eyes looking down at me with something like humility. I wasn't embarrassed to cry in front of her, but I'd felt this was a private moment.

"It smells like her," I sputtered.

"I know," Joyce said, plainly. "That's why I kept it."

I sat up, put the sweater down, and wiped my eyes with my bare hand. I still have a closet full of Sue's clothes at home, I thought. I stood up and left the room.

It was the last time I cried in front of my in-laws. But that didn't dismiss the differences in our grief.

"George, get the baby. He needs to be changed," Joyce said before Thanksgiving dinner was served. It was always "the baby," never the name Sue and I had so carefully chosen for him.

"His name is Myles," I wanted to say. "Myles with a Y because that's his name, and we thought it would look much cooler when it's written down with a Y. Just call him by his name. And by the way, I'm quite capable of knowing when he needs to be changed." But what came out was, "Thanks, Joyce. Thanks for your help."

"You're welcome."

The turkey dinner, with all of the usual fixings, was brought to the table. Hardly any of the white tablecloth showed. Everything around the table was missing some of its usual seasoning that night. Conversations stalled. Eye contact was minimal. I wondered if this was going to be the norm for the rest of our lives: taciturn exchanges, never acknowledging the un-said, being together because we should, not because we wanted to. Maybe someday we'd get over Sue's death, but I questioned whether we'd ever mend the fissure her death had carved into us.

"Lovely meal, dear."

"Yes. Terrific, Joyce."

"All day to make and only five minutes to eat," George said, and we all chuckled as if it was the first time we'd heard it.

Across the table from me in his high chair Myles gobbled down the yams and mashed-up vegetables fed lovingly to him by his grandmother, who sat to his left. To his right was an empty chair.

This would have been the part of the meal when Sue talked about which interesting stories she'd been reporting on recently and the remarkable people she'd met in the process. The joy she got from her still-nascent career was palpable. Then she'd bring her parents up to date on what her friends were doing: this one was still trying to get acting jobs; that one was going back to school. Afterwards there'd be discussion about plans for the house; she was ready to remodel our kitchen. Her parents would listen and nod and add to the conversation by relating some obliquely relevant story. If only Sue had been there on this Thanksgiving to make up for the uncooperative silences. Sue was the glue that held the family together — she was mediator, instigator, cruise director, TV channel changer, restaurant picker, conversation leader, and family guru. With Sue at the helm, our family was like a well-balanced decorative mobile hanging in perfect equilibrium from the ceiling, bobbing in symbiotic rhythm with one another in a snug, familial dance. After she was gone, we were all just dangling helplessly from independent lengths of cable, our legs akimbo and flailing in an effort find a foothold.

I wanted to open up the well inside me and spew the morass of melancholic bile out all over the oak and maple leaves at the centre of the table. *This is all wrong. Can't we just agree that this is a wretched place to be without Sue? She was the only reason the four of us got along. This doesn't work as a trio.* But I remained silent.

At the end of the meal, George gently pushed his chair back, wiped his mouth with his napkin, folded it neatly, put it down on the table, and said, while looking adoringly at his wife, "It doesn't get any better than this."

Dinner was officially over.

* * *

Less than a week later, on October 16th, Myles turned one year old. It had been nearly six months since Sue died. Half of Myles's life. And it felt like half of mine.

I marked his birthday by planting a tree for Sue, a sugar maple: resilient, profoundly Canadian, and filled with sweetness. I'd meant for the tree to stand not only as a flourishing memorial to Sue but also as a reminder of my own growth since her death. In the present it would breathe life into the part of me that was suffocating. In the future it would fortify my past, having long been usurped by a more buoyant, formidable new me. I hoped.

After my application to the City of Toronto Department of Parks and Recreation was accepted — you can't plant a tree just anywhere — I chose a location in the Beaches just down the road from the apartment where Sue and I lived when we were first married. The Beaches is sustained by two distinct and broad shoulders on which the community leans: the sandy shore of Lake Ontario with the hectic traffic of its winding boardwalk; and, a stone's throw away and parallel to the beach, the vibrant marketplace of Queen Street East. Sue's tree was planted near the iconic Leuty Lifeguard Station (it's on all the postcards), and would be visible from both the shore and the road, directly below one of the street lamps lighting up the boardwalk. The tree's trunk, thin and vulnerable, had a gentle bend about a half a metre off the ground that reminded me of Sue's bent fingers. At the base of the tree, facing the lake, a discreet round plaque kept her name. She would have approved, I thought: public, quiet but not isolated, and sufficiently lit at night to acknowledge her minor but genuine fear of the dark.

Because there was no grave to visit, Sue's tree was the only public permanent marker. Moreover, with its regular greenery, shade, and oxygen production, it would give back to the world.

Sue's parents invited everyone to their house in Burlington on a Saturday afternoon for Myles's birthday celebration. Myles and I drove with my mother; my sister and her family arrived a short time later. We all sat in the family room overlooking the stream at the back of the house with drinks in our hands. The uninhibited sun shone in at all angles through the floor-to-ceiling sliding glass doors as Myles demonstrated his new trick: pulling himself up to a standing position with the help of a chair. We cheered and cooed and shared in his joy amid the otherwise vague conversation. There was lunch, gift-giving, and, at least from me, a subdued appreciation of the day.

I excused myself to use the bathroom. As I walked down the hall I instinctively turned left instead of right and went into the guest room — the room in which I last shared a bed with Sue; the same room in which I had awakened alone the morning after she died. The room had been stripped of most comforts aside from the bed. The closet was empty, and all signs of expectant visitors removed, as if the room had died. In one dark corner there was a highboy dresser, the top of which was bare except for a plain brown ceramic cylinder standing forlorn and ghostly. Inside the surprisingly small container were Sue's ashes. I had come in to visit her.

It wasn't the first time I had done this. Just a couple of weeks after she died, I discovered the lidded canister (it was too primitive to be called an urn like they have in the movies, all elaborately decorated porcelain, white and sacred). It had been delivered to her parents' house by the funeral home. Though we had carried out Sue's wishes, it hadn't occurred to me that her remains would actually be returned to us. When she died, she was gone, as far as I was concerned. Seeing Sue bottled inside the cold and solitary object on the dresser was, at first sight, a tangible and tearful exclamation point to the finality of her death. This time, however, as I left my year-old son and his loving family in the other room, I simply put my right hand on the lid and held it there lightly as if I was holding Sue's hand. I felt more grounded in that moment of stillness than I had since returning from the road trip. *So much has happened since you've gone. In so little time.*

"Would you mind taking that home with you today?" Joyce asked from the doorway. *Was she following me? I told her I was going to the bathroom.* "We don't feel comfortable keeping it here anymore."

Why would Sue's ashes — <u>it</u> — make them uncomfortable? This was their eldest daughter, a respected radio and television journalist, and the mother of their only grandchild. She was someone whom they'd raised, loved, and encouraged, and in return received the same unconditional support.

"Of course," I said. "I understand."

But I didn't understand. I had no problem with them keeping her there. If they'd insisted on it, I'd have been happy to let them. We were all there when she died. We'd clung to each other in the knowledge that the most difficult part would be living without her. But I should have known her parents might have had their misgivings. After all they'd kept her in a room they no longer used. Besides, I figured Sue belonged home with me. I'd once considered holding onto a loved one's ashes as being a bit creepy. But this was my wife. When I got home that evening, I placed Sue on my dresser atop her favourite dresser scarf, surrounded by photographs, her terracotta-coloured marble jewellery box, and the Angel of Courage. It was — perhaps intentionally, perhaps not — a shrine of sorts.

Beside my bed the familiar container was always the first thing my eyes awakened to, a beacon through the fog. Like the duvet Sue and I used to share, it became a warm and comforting fixture. But her presence, like her memory, became diluted by the passage of time. Her impression embossed in our bed was smoothed over like footprints under a fresh snowfall. My daily acknowledgement of her ashes became less customary. As my mood echoed the lurking short, dark days of autumn, the beacon faded and became like the many other decorations that scattered the house: I still knew it was there, but the novelty had worn off.

It was never my intention to keep Sue's ashes forever. I knew that one day I would have to part with them. But for now, there she stayed.

* * *

With Myles now a year old, I figured it was time for him to start socializing with other children his age and for me to start doing other things with my days. Like looking for a job. When Sue and I had moved back to Toronto from Windsor, I decided not to reopen the upholstery shop, having already moved it twice. I found work as a sales representative for a high-end textiles company selling to the design trade. It was the only "proper job" I'd ever had. As it turned out, it came at an opportune time. I'd spent the last six months finishing off what was left of Sue's maternity leave; for me they called it parental leave. When it came to an end, I decided not to return to the post I'd been fortunate to have but really wasn't very good at. I didn't miss selling carpets and fabrics. So I resolved to find something new to fit the new me.

Myles and I went to meet Sam, a woman who ran a child-care business from her house around the corner from ours. She greeted us at the door — pale skin, shiny red hair, and smiling — a small blond boy clutched in the crook of her right elbow.

"You must be Myles," she said. "This is my son, Owen. He's fourteen months old."

Myles and Owen, both held at hip level, stared at each other suspiciously. Sam led us into her playroom, the floor replete with soft toys, plastic trucks and cars, books, rubber mats with numbers and letters on them, and craft supplies of every colour. On the walls were drawings, scribblings, and fingerpaintings made by the children in her charge. Myles relinquished his initial dubiousness and dove into the pile of fun. Owen was his new best friend.

"I'm just looking for two half-days a week," I said. "Just for Myles to have some social time."

"That sounds like a good place to start."

Sam and I watched the boys hurtle each other's trucks together in demolition derby fashion.

"How many other children do you look after?"

"I have four others at the moment. They all come at different times so I don't usually have more than two together at once. Sometimes three. I think Myles would fit right in."

"Looks that way."

"I try to take them for a walk to the park every day, weather permitting. I have a red wagon that I can comfortably pull two kids in. They really seem to like it."

"Sounds fun," I said, as Owen took off his socks and showed Myles his fascinating toes. I imagined watching Myles being pulled away from me in the red wagon, getting smaller and smaller as he went down the sidewalk. I thought I should be the one pulling the wagon. That was *my* job. I was acting in my son's best interests and neglecting my responsibilities as his parent at the same time.

"I have to ask," Sam said. "Where … um … Is Myles's mother in the picture?"

I knew she had to ask, but the way she did made it seem like she already knew the answer. Was it obvious? Did the look on my face say "dead wife"? Or was it so unusual for a father to investigate child care?

"My wife died six months ago."

I looked down at the floor between my feet then glanced up at Sam, who sat across the room. She didn't look at me with sadness or pity. There were no mirrors in her eyes. She simply understood.

"I'm sorry," she said. Right answer.

We agreed that Myles would be happy there for a few hours each week. Sam suggested leaving him to play with

Owen for the next half hour, just to make sure he didn't have a meltdown without me. I quietly let myself out and walked back home. The autumn sun wrestled with a smattering of clouds. The leaves on the black locust tree in the front yard had turned yellow-brown and were dropping. In a few weeks we'd have the first frost followed closely by the early, grey signs of winter. I stayed outside while the weather allowed it, sitting on my front porch. I looked at my watch. Twenty-five minutes left.

Staring out at the road I caught my breath. I'd just made my first significant solitary decision about Myles's future. I'd seen a need, sought a solution, and found Sam. Job done. But more strikingly, I never once paused to wonder what Sue would have advised. This was my decision and I'd made it on my own. Automatically. *How could I have forgotten to check with Sue?* My instincts had dictated my actions, and I'd acted decisively. I'd already embraced being "Dad," and I'd accepted the obligatory "single" that had been unceremoniously placed before it, but perhaps I'd grown into the role of "sole decision maker" more readily than I'd thought.

It was a new kind of Harmony Moment. Perhaps less obvious than seeing the road lined with black-eyed Susans or hearing our wedding music in a restaurant, it still reminded me I was living in a world without Sue. Only this time it came with an unusual and fleeting sense of satisfaction. I was doing my job after all.

* * *

The season of firsts was nearly over. Only the first Christmas left to get through, which I was not looking forward to. It was already obvious that I couldn't communicate with Sue's parents, and with the added pressure of the holidays, I was certain that trend would be magnified. With Sue's family, Christmases had been enjoyable, but a traditional helping of tension was always served up with the turkey. Particularly after both Sue and her sister moved away. The family seemed to put extra pressure on themselves to have a holly-jolly holiday, compensating for the lack of quality family time the rest of the year. Inevitably none of us could live up to that challenge.

It was obvious we all grieved for Sue in different ways. Her parents must have had unbearable spells of darkness, as I had. Now that I was a parent, I could only imagine the horror of losing a child. I tried to keep this in mind when managing her family, but it was still difficult to empathize with others when all the concern I had was earmarked for Myles and me. At the end of the day, I didn't have any reserve levels of nurturing left.

If Sue had been there to conduct this out-of-tune orchestra as she normally did, being the one person in the family that all the others listened to, then I wouldn't have anticipated the upcoming holiday with such dread. But without her, anything could happen.

18

The last words Sue said to me were, "I love you." I'm fairly certain those were her last words ever. Fitting — expected even — because during ten years together it was our most often-used phrase. There was always time to share a daily "I love you" or two, or more. Even if one of us didn't feel like it. It was an amorous reflex, a craving of words that never languished in silence. That final morning, as the smothering silence hovered over us, was no different. In barely more than a whisper, she exhaled a three-word poem to me, her private audience. She loved me.

It was the kind of Ontario morning where you could feel the winter chill finally stepping aside for the short but glorious spring. Even I, a non-morning person with a dying wife, couldn't help but wake up energized. I hit the ground running, showered, skipped breakfast, and was at Sue's bedside before my pillow was cold. I sat to her left in the sticky vinyl chair. The stale hospital air was roused by the tendrils of the morning sun growing like ivy through the window slats behind me. It made Sue's ashen face glow. I kissed her and grabbed her hand, fragile but warm to my touch. Astonished by her stillness, I couldn't take my eyes off of her. She looked weary but peaceful, lost in a fading reverie.

"Good morning, sweetie," I said.

I felt the slightest pressure on my fingers as she tried to return the greeting. The extreme doses of morphine had cut her off from the rest of us. Though mercifully sedating, it had drained her of all vitality and, even in her most lucid moments, clouded her mind. When she was able to speak, her voice was hollow and her words muddled. I imagined she was dancing inside herself, overjoyed at being pain free, relieved to let the weight of the world drift away. But from the outside she was like a motionless marionette dangling from the strings of some faceless puppeteer who manoeuvred and spoke through her. Somehow she found the strength and clarity to acknowledge me, pushing the wily puppet master away if only for a moment. She slowly turned her head and opened her eyes just a slit, squinting into the sunlight. She found my face and managed a delicate, surreptitious smile.

"I love you."

Instinctive and unpretentious, they were the words of the Sue I knew. The one who kicked down the morphine-mortared barricade so she could look me in the eye and speak. Who told the ruthless, proliferating cancer to back off because she wasn't done yet. Who never let something like death stand in the way of living.

After the words passed her dry lips, her eyes closed and she turned her face back toward the ceiling. The hole Sue had managed to briefly puncture in the barricade had closed again. But I was thankful for the fleeting moment of compassion. Perhaps the malevolent force that kept Sue under its control had been distracted by my buoyant entrance and turned away from her so that she could look at me one last time and speak her final words.

"I love you too," I said.

If her last words had been less coherent or less poignant, if they had been a disjointed murmur of drug-induced nonsense, would I have remembered them so clearly? Would they have enfolded me in their midst with such purity? Perhaps it was just an example of the perfect meeting of words with time and place. Maybe the diffusion of my memory has made it more sublime. Maybe hearing "I love you" is simply more meaningful than saying it.

We'd arrived in the dark and quiet emergency ward in the very early hours of the morning four days before. The white, pleated curtains hung with a mere suggestion of privacy around every bed. From around the room I heard dim, echoing chimes of medical equipment, the gasping bellows of breathing apparatus, and occasional footsteps. The dim glowing light from down the hall seemed like a fading sun.

Not long after we had been ushered into our corner, the physician on duty entered with his regulation clipboard and hastily introduced himself. After a brief examination and some general questions, he spoke to us in a comfortable but typically impartial tone.

"I'd like your consent to refer you to the palliative care unit," he said, looking directly at Sue.

She turned to me and we stared at each other blankly. I nodded and she turned back to the doctor to say, "Okay." Then he administered the first dose of long-awaited morphine.

Sue fell asleep. I watched her lie comfortably for the first time in several months. In the quiet, I replayed the previous few hours in my head — the efforts her parents and I made to move her after she finally agreed to let us take her to the hospital. Then I thought, *palliative care unit. Palliative?* Palliative care is for alleviating severe pain in terminal patients, people who are dying. Could Sue have understood this when the doctor asked for her consent? Because it only just became clear to me.

What is she thinking as she sleeps? Can she appreciate the pain medication? Is she lucid enough to keep track of what is happening? Can she hear me when I speak to her? Is she dreaming?

The next few hours crawled by. I tried to sleep in the stiff chair beside the bed but was distracted by her abnormally raspy breathing and the perpetual ping of the heart monitor, not to mention the new understanding I had about her prognosis. I was numb, exhausted, and oblivious to any other people in the ward. I just wanted comfort. For both of us. My wife was going to die.

We'd both believed we could handle anything life threw at us, as long as we had each other from whom to derive strength. We talked about the great vacation the three of us were going to take after she had licked this ruinous disease. We constantly spoke of how we wanted to better our lives and work for the things we longed for. We had plans and, more significantly, expectations. We were a team. When we got married there was never any alternative to staying together forever. It was simply not an option.

Now, the whole future that I thought had been promised was being deleted. My life as I had come to know it was about to end with hers.

It had been unusually sunny the whole week that Sue was in the hospital, with vivid beams of light coming in through every available opening, warming the normally indifferent chill with their radiance. The bright light made the air thick and hazy. It was persistent but ghostly. The sunlight was welcome, but its allure was lost on me.

I was sitting with Sue in her private room the day after she was admitted when we learned that her sister, Nancy, would be flying in from British Columbia the following morning. Sue looked at me, her face blanched by the lurid sunlight. Or was it the sudden rush of fear?

"Nancy's here?" Then in her half-drugged innocence she said, "Why? Am I dying?"

Bam! Smack! Pow! There it was, the question I had avoided asking myself for the past ten months, pummelling me into oblivion in true comic-book style. The question I was too terrified to even acknowledge because if I had, I would have spent too much effort and energy trying to ignore the truth. I would have spent every moment of every day running from Sue lest her impending death paralyzed me. But how could I have ignored it for so long? Why did I have to face this question now? Now I knew the answer.

I froze, defenceless in my chair. After her question stopped pounding me about the head, it sat on me like a sumo wrestler, leaving me half-squashed and gasping for breath. Then a second wind ... *Am I dying?* The question reared up again, starting at the top of my head and quickly migrating toward my feet until all of me was smothered. *Am I dying? ... Am I dying?* The words echoed at a deafening volume.

Do I tell her the truth? How do I know what she feels or what she wants to hear? Why would she assume that Nancy's arrival would mean she was dying? What could I possibly say to her that I would be able to live with for the rest of my life?

"No. No, goddammit, you are not dying no matter what anyone else says. Don't you believe it. This wasn't written in the stars for us — you know, the stars that you've followed so closely your whole life. We're supposed to stay together forever. And besides if anyone's going to die first, it's going to be me. This is just wrong. So keep fighting, you. Keep that bastard predator away because I'm not ready for this. You are not going to die. You are not."

But how could I tell her this when the scenario that Sue's cancer was temporary dangled by one feeble finger from the precipice of truth. It was this cliff, this mountain that loomed over me. I had been trying to accept the truth about her, and I wondered if she was trying to accept it too. Somewhere along the line during our tolerant handling of her cancer, the truth — even the possibility of the truth — became locked in a box and thrown into Lake Ontario. Instead denial disguised as positive thinking, management disguised as hope reigned. I desperately wanted Sue to believe that the truth was okay to acknowledge. And that our love alone, intense, broad, persistent, and genuine, would make her death bearable.

The truth made me want to look her straight in the eye and say definitively but calmly, "Yes. Yes, my love, you are going to die. And it's not fair. I'm so sorry but it's true. You are going to die, and I'm going to miss you so, so much. I'm going to feel dreadfully alone without you, but I'm so grateful for our time together. I couldn't have asked for more love in my life than I got from you. The pain of losing you will be soothed only the slightest amount by the merciful knowledge that you have been relieved of your own pain."

I wanted to hold her with my weary arms, tender but firm, and say, "You are dying. And even though it makes no sense, even though it belies every expectation we've held for ourselves, even though it is unstoppable, it's okay. Because I love you now more than I thought I was ever capable of, and if you should die today, you will always remain the object of my love. And it's okay because I know you love me too, and nothing, not even your death, not even the memories that will blur or splinter after you've gone and will continue to do so until I die, nothing will ever change that about you."

Am I dying? ... Am I dying?

I looked at her stone-faced, giving serious consideration to her question, and I wanted to say, "Yes, dammit, yes. It's horrible but it's true. You are going to die. So let's talk about it. What shall we do? How do you want to be remembered? What do you want for Myles? Are you scared? You don't have to be scared. Are our finances in order? Where shall I place your ashes? Is there someone you'd like to give all your favourite books to? Let me tell you all the things I'm going to miss about you."

I looked into her agate eyes of golden brown, fading more to grey by the day, and realized I was unprepared to say any of these things. The great cliff on the mountain of truth towered over me. I couldn't have scaled it if I wanted to. Fear. *Who am I to tell her that she is going to die? I have no divine connection giving me license to prescribe death. People have been known to heal themselves even when it has been deemed impossible. Similarly, if someone is told they are going to die they may believe it strongly enough for it to come true. I don't want it to be true.*

At that moment there was nothing other than Sue's death in my line of sight. It started an inch from my nose and stood thick and flat-footed blocking my view all the way to the horizon. I saw the horror and the sadness; the monstrous arms of death enveloping me and clinging tightly no matter which direction I turned. I saw her death as one of the greatest injustices of our time; a transgression the likes of which human history had never had the misfortune of witnessing before now. A travesty beyond moral and legal boundaries. Certainly nothing any god would allow.

As these vast thoughts swept through my mind during those few seconds after her question, I realized that beyond anything I could have said it was up to Sue to decide if and when she was going to die. That, as far as I was concerned, was the complete truth.

"No, sweetie," I said, trying to appear unruffled. "Nancy just wanted to come see you because she loves you and misses you."

I took a deep breath, satisfied that I had kept the illusion going. I hated her for asking me the question, and I loved her too much to answer it.

The following day I woke up with "Complicated" by Avril Lavigne as an unfortunate earworm; it was all over the radio in the winter and spring of 2003. As I stared at Sue in her drug-induced stillness, held her hand, listened to the sounds of her breathing and my heart beating, my ears rang with Avril's angst-ridden ode to teenage relationships.

"Not now," I said to myself. "Get out. Get out of my head, you stupid, stupid song!" But it was no use. Avril was there for the duration, and trying to keep her quiet was like reading Shakespeare with the radio on. Then I realized that things were in fact complicated, not that it was Sue's fault. Avril had warned me that life was like this. I don't normally take lessons from adolescent pop singers, but she was right. Life is complicated; that was becoming increasingly clear. All I wanted was simplicity in my life, the things clichés are made of: the love of my family and a place to call home. Surely there was a different song about that.

Myles had been with my mother all week, but on Saturday, Sue's third day in the hospital, Mom brought Myles to see us. I met them at the front door of the hospital, picked Myles up, kissed him, and carried him to the elevator up to Sue's room. It had been five days since

I'd seen him, but it felt like weeks. I brought Myles into the room and he smiled when he saw his mom lying in the hospital bed. She was awake, and she lit up when she saw him as if she had just been given a shot of caffeine. She reached out her hand to his.

"My baby," she said excitedly but in a near whisper. Myles focused on her and smiled.

Sue smiled back her typically beaming smile. Only this time there was something missing. Her distinctive twinkle was fading. The smile quickly receded and was replaced by a distant, disconnected gaze. Her eyes, normally bright and solar-powered, were half shut and blank. Soon she had forgotten that her son was there — that anyone was there — and melted back into her desolate cocoon. She lay still while Myles continued to speak to her in his six-month-old language. His cooing interrupted the humming grey silence of the hospital while Sue slept, oblivious and slipping farther and farther away. I looked at my son and my wife. Inside me smiles mingled absurdly with tears. Complicated indeed.

By the next morning, she had just enough lucidity to whisper her final words to me. Late into that evening, Sue had been asleep (I might have said unconscious, but she just appeared to be sleeping) for over twelve hours. The room was half lit with mellow incandescent light, the hospital-grey walls soaking up whatever colour was left. There was no noise coming in from the hallway, and the only sound in the room was a soft but persistent moan that seeped from Sue's exhales. I held her hand, my thoughts brittle like old film. It was clear, though I tried to deny it, that she might never wake up again. I leaned in close, our cheeks touching, and whispered one last plea.

"Sue. Please don't leave me. I need you very much. I can't do this alone. Please. I love you."

We were silent for who knows how long, holding hands in our own private prayer. I cried. We were connected; we had been since the night of our first date. Since our first kiss on the stairs, now ten years in the past.

Sue's parents and her sister came in quietly and joined me at Sue's bedside, each of us dreading what our lives were about to become. Joyce's big-circle eyes already looked empty, as if she had known this day would come. George held Joyce's hand, his muscular arm stopping her from drowning. Nancy, her face already as serene as stone, had told me she knew Sue would be in a peaceful place. I was glad Sue's family was there. We were complete with Sue. As we sat around her, we knew we were a family held together by our collective love for our daughter-sister-wife. We were absolute — a closed circle.

I swallowed my sorrow. If we, while begging for her to get better, could only wait for her to die, then I wanted that time to be as short as possible. I wondered if she, too, was waiting. Sue's own grandmother waited until her loved ones were away on vacation — determined, it seemed, not to burden them — before she passed away alone in her nursing-home bed. There was precedence in the family.

"Sue," I began slowly, "you have the power to free yourself from the pain you are in ... You can let go. Nobody here will think you're a quitter. We love you... You have the power."

Hearing my tearful words was a crippling reminder that I had given myself permission to let go of her just as I was giving her the permission to let go. I hoped she heard me. I think she did.

I was tired of waiting for the cancer shroud that hovered over us for the past ten months to be folded up and put away. How, I thought, did we prepare for the thrilling arrival of our son while still coping with his mother's merciless disease? How many waiting-room magazines did we read during countless visits to doctors of various specialities? I'm still not sure how we resolved the threats of risk during Sue's pregnancy. Everything took patience and trust. Everything took time.

Just after midnight, fifteen hours since I'd last heard Sue speak to me, I noticed that her laboured breathing was changing its pattern. The steady moan had weakened but her inhaled breath was sounding raspy and thick, as if her windpipe were filling with molasses. Her face remained expressionless but her throat quivered under the uncomfortable and ominous strain of breathing.

From the foot of the bed, I watched my dying wife, lying suffused in the colourless overhead lamplight. Her parents were on my right; Nancy had left the room. My eyes, sore from crying, were glued to Sue's face. She was already eerily pale, wraithlike, her head slightly tilted back, and her mouth wide open as if she were drowning and struggling for every bit of air. I was at once terrified and spellbound, knowing that at any moment I would witness the end.

It was as if I were swallowing each of her painful breaths as she exhaled and storing them inside me so that they wouldn't go to waste, so that she would find life in me. Each of her laborious and agonizing breaths rang in my ears like distant bells. With every breath, each chapter of our life together closed, one by one, until at last the final page was written and read.

Shortly after one o'clock in the morning, things got very quiet. It seemed as though Sue was holding her breath.

As she did, so did I. Then a quick inhale and again silence. Inhale. Silence. Then again. This went on for ten minutes. Each quiet gasp weaker than the previous one. Finally, from deep within her throat a quiet crackling sound sputtered and faded. She offered one final gentle exhale. Then complete silence.

In the sudden stillness, the universe distorted in the watercolour periphery of my vision. My eyes still glued to Sue's face, I willed her to breathe. After a few more seconds I realized I wasn't breathing either. I saw Sue's body relax, liberated from the weight of extreme pain. A strange and unexpected wave of relief washed over me. At last Sue's pain was gone.

I asked if I could have a moment alone with Sue and my wish was granted. I gave her one last hug and kiss. Her grey skin was rubbery and already cool against my cheek. In our last embrace I knew that I was making some sounds but I couldn't hear myself. The intangible borders signifying my place on the earth closed in around me as Sue drifted farther away. My life, once full and complex, wrung out everything suddenly deemed extraneous: work, money, home, friends, news, possessions, and on and on. In that moment, I began travelling down a tunnel toward becoming a single, elemental being with little room for excess.

Only six months earlier I had witnessed the beginning of a life. The moment our son emerged into the world forever rests at the top of my memory pyramid. Now the end of a life had chiselled itself into my brain like a name into stone. The two images balanced like a ghostly see-saw.

We left the hospital. Unceremonious and directionless. Out into the warm, dark calm of early morning spring, my body heavy, my thoughts undefined. It seemed strange leaving Sue in that building while the rest of us moved on

to begin living our lives without her. At the end of a life —
unique, inspired, filled with love, and tragically short — is
this all that happens? Do you simply stand up and go?
There should have been more. More time with Sue. More
ceremony. More love. But there wasn't.

As I walked through the dimly lit parking lot, the aloof
but sadly appropriate phrase "Life goes on" flashed
through my head like a newspaper headline. My wife had
just died and, knowing I would never again hold her hand
or talk with her, the only thing I wanted to do was to go
home. I wanted to be alone with my memories and our son.

Having returned to Sue's parents' house, I went into
the bedroom that Sue and I shared there and closed the
door. I put my head down on the pillow in the big empty
bed, tears still trickling. In a sudden rush, thick with the
desire to cling to Sue, I remembered her last words to
me nearly twenty-four hours earlier. "I love you," I
heard her whisper. My heart leapt. How perfect, I
thought. Our time together ended while we were still in
love, and Sue will forever remain constant there. No
matter what happens for the rest of my life, regardless of
whether or not I'm able to forge a new life without her, I
will always hear those words. Her death was as lovely an
ending as I could have wished.

* * *

It was an uneventful Christmas Eve. George, Joyce, and
Nancy seemed happy just to be together as the evening went
along without incident. We didn't talk about Sue much;
although, I did excuse myself a few times to hide in my
room and cry as I became obsessed with the notion that we
might always have ended apart. This may have been the last
Christmas with her family regardless. But I was pleased that

the supply of Christmas cheer was doing its job, making the evening at least bearable. We said good night and quietly drifted into our own quarters in the large, split-level house: George and Joyce upstairs in their room, Myles in the crib in his own room next to his grandparents', Nancy in her basement suite, and me, alone in the guest room — that same room furnished only with the sensations of waking up without Sue the morning after she died.

I didn't stay up late waiting for fatigue to set in as I would have at home, so I lay awake with my thoughts. My sleep, when it finally came, was restless.

I was at my lowest ebb, the apogee of my grief. Winter's deprecating darkness punctuated my mood and the looming threat of Christmas day didn't help. It had been over three months since Myles and I returned from our cross-continental adventure, and in those three months, I had only sunk deeper into that thick mire of grief.

The morning sun elbowed its way into my room, all wintery-grey and a poor excuse for holiday light when compared to its summery cousin. I wrenched myself out of bed and stumbled into the living room, knowing I'd be the last one out there. Even Myles was up, his grandmother already having changed him into his Christmas-morning outfit. Typical of the annual marathon session, presents were handed out, and everyone oohed and aahed like it was the happiest day of their lives. After Myles opened more gifts than I could count — George and Joyce had always gone over-the-top with their kids; now they continued the tradition with Myles, each gift as exciting to him as the last — George made his traditional Christmas morning breakfast of fried eggs, sausages, bacon, hash browns, and toast. It was all so familiar but eerily different.

I grew up in a Jewish house, convinced the only reason I got presents every December was to stay shoulder to shoulder with my Christian friends. Chanukah is not a major holiday in the Jewish calendar if you take away the season in which it falls. Although I'd shared Christmases with other families before, Sue and her family had been my only regular acquaintance with the holiday. They introduced me to indoor trees and decorations, specially knitted sweaters, and an entirely new set of traditions. So when, at only my tenth Christmas, the normal spirit appeared distorted, I not only missed Sue but I missed the best times with her family too.

My lack of sleep didn't help matters. I tried to enjoy myself like my in-laws seemed to be doing on this first Christmas without Sue, but her absence was glaringly obvious to me. In years past she relished the joy of being with her family, buffering the simmering tension when it arose and wrapping the whole holiday season up in a neat little bow. Even the previous Christmas when she was fresh from her mastectomy, her smile lit up the photographs of her son's first holiday.

It felt less like Christmas and more like a bad movie about Christmas. The leading lady, who dies in the opening scene, leaves the leading man to cope with a group of characters he has little in common with besides missing the leading lady. The family knows everything's different but nobody acknowledges that anything has changed. The leading man is left to improvise while a cute baby smiles obliviously at everyone. Nobody listens, they all say the wrong things, and this becomes the new Christmas normal. It's a Hollywood recipe for comedy mayhem that ends with a heartwarming happy ending. Cue music swell.

In addition to absorbing my new feelings about Sue and wondering if our separation would have been inevitable, I now found a reason to be angry with her. How could she have left me here to "celebrate" with these people? She was my partner, and at times like this, though she wished otherwise, I could defer to her skill at leading us through the landmines. I still felt like part of their family — and they were a part of mine — but the tangible shift in our dynamic was starting to look as though it might never equalize. Every effort I'd made to improve my communication skills, to connect with them the way their daughter could, had fallen short. Where it had always been "our family," it looked increasingly again like "her family." Things would never be the same, I thought.

That evening, the traditional feast was being prepared as we awaited the arrival of the Vaskos, a family they'd spent nearly every Christmas with for thirty years. Like George and Joyce, John and Rita Vasko also had two daughters, Linda and Stacy, who were the same ages as Sue and Nancy. The Vasko girls didn't look like sisters any more than Sue and Nancy had; they might just as well have come from different sets of parents. Stacy had a spirit and vivaciousness I'd always found alluring. She was a former model who had also once trained with the Canadian speed-skating team. When she spoke, it was with sincerity and conviction. And she'd proven to Sue and me that she knew how to be a friend.

The mood around that night's turkey dinner benefited from the new blood. Much of the pressure to make conversation was lifted from me, and whatever discomfort I had anticipated was avoided. The Vaskos brought genuine joy for Christmas, a gift I actually needed.

After dinner the generations split and retired to separate rooms. Even though we were all in our thirties, Stacy,

Linda, Nancy, and I (and Sue, when she was around) ended up in the "kids' room" as usual. While the "grown-ups" were next door sipping port and sherry, we joked around the beer-and-wine-sodden Monopoly board as it lit up with little green houses and red hotels to match the Christmas decorations. The frivolous conversation was just what I needed. As the night went on, I led the parade of intoxicated one-liners.

"It's okay to pass Go, just don't pass wind."

"You don't strike me as an orange-property kind of gal."

"Hey, your car just ran over my dog."

With each of these, Stacy, sitting to my right, giggled and slapped my knee.

I like that. I like her touching me. It's electric.

"Virginia Avenue is yours? I didn't know you were a Virginia."

"Time for another peek at Community's Chest."

More knee slapping. The others rightly groaned. I looked at Stacy, trying to get some eye contact, which she returned with a cunning but genuine smile. *What's going on? This is fun and it feels good. Am I ... am I flirting? Is she?* I drew a sharp but silent breath and tried to figure out how it started. Certainly Stacy couldn't have felt comfortable flirting with her dead friend's husband. Could she? Maybe I made the first move and didn't realize it. We were friends after all, so maybe I didn't recognize what I was doing. I thought I was damaged goods when it came to relating to women — I didn't think I had it in me, nor did I think anybody would see me as a prospective suitor — but perhaps she saw beyond that.

I was getting ahead of myself. Still focused on the game, I moved my cowboy around the Monopoly board gobbling up properties and brokering deals. I always was a tad competitive when it came to this game. But I was more focused than normal on the woman with the blonde-streaked, wavy hair.

"I'll trade you this light blue one for your two railroads," I negotiated with Stacy.

"Deal," she said. Her sister tried to talk her out of it, correctly suggesting that it was not a fair trade. But Stacy didn't mind and I had the set of four railroads.

Is the smile on my face as geeky as I think it is?

By the time our game was finished, Stacy and Linda's parents had gone home, so I offered my car to them. I'd had too much to drink to drive them home myself, and I insisted it was the best option. Besides, Stacy promised to return the car the next morning.

"I can't believe you loaned your car to them," Nancy said as they drove away, the RAV4's tail lights still visible up the road.

"I couldn't drive them. Could you?"

Nancy was silent. We stood face to face on the driveway, our breath in the crisp Christmas night clouding up the cold air between us. I put my hands in my pockets and turned to walk back into the house.

"Jon, do you like Stacy?"

What are we, twelve years old? I stopped and turned back to her. "What?"

"You were flirting with her all night."

"I was not."

"Yes, you were," Nancy said, part embarrassed, part missing her sister.

"Don't even go there," I said and I went inside. But I was already going there, ebullient in a dizzying, unexpected crush. And Nancy proved that it wasn't my imagination. I was lifted by the sudden recognition that I felt an attraction to someone other than Sue, and even more amazed that that person had been compelled to flirt back. I wasn't falling in love, this I knew. But the last thing I expected from Christmas was this impulse to connect with someone. With a woman.

But is it too soon to feel this way? Does this mean I'm over Sue? Is it disrespectful? Should I act on my feelings?

The fact that I'd resolved missing Sue while still disliking some of my memories of her meant that I'd made some progress. In recognizing that progress, I must have left myself open to both exhibit and receive whatever vibrations had passed between me and Stacy. It had been eight months of daily crying, learning how to grieve, and figuring out how to parent. Eight months thinking I might be alone for the rest of my life. Some people never get another chance to find love. So why shouldn't I welcome this opportunity, whatever it is?

As the night ended I remembered a brief conversation that Sue initiated late one evening in the depths of her last Toronto winter. She rarely spoke after we'd said good night. But on this night she sat up and turned the light on as if what she was about to say must be seen and not just heard. Four-month-old Myles slept soundly in the next room, but she spoke softly so only I could hear.

"Jon."

"I'm here," I said, making my voice sound as awake as possible. It wasn't unusual for her to need something in the night: a new dressing on her mastectomy wound, a pair of socks, a glass of water.

"I need to tell you something."

"Yes?" I put my glasses on and sat up with her.

She paused. "If something should happen to me..." She'd never started a sentence with those words before.

It was akin to her starting a conversation about hockey or rutabagas.

"Nothing's going to happen, sweetie."

"Let me finish. If something happens, I want you to promise me you'll find someone else to be with."

Someone to be with? This is what she's concerned about? She could have raised concerns about how Myles would be raised, about our finances or where we'd live. But the only time she openly dared to imagine the scenario of her own death, however obliquely, it regarded my future happiness. At least that's how I interpreted it. This was strangely comforting at a time when the last thing on my mind was alternative companionship. The notion of finding a new mate had never crossed my mind. She wasn't going to die. But what was stranger was the sudden change in the script. When I committed myself to Sue for the rest of my life, it had never occurred to me that it might only be for the rest of her life.

"Promise me," she said.

I put my arm around her and pulled her close. She rested her cheek on my chest and brushed a tear away from her face.

"I promise," I said. "But it's not an issue. Okay?"

"Okay," she said weakly. She turned out the light and we lay down, still clinging to each other. I stroked her back until she fell asleep.

"Sweet dreams," I said. They were the last two words I said to her every night. The subject — either of her death or of what I was to do afterward — was never raised again.

I went to bed that Christmas night with Sue's words playing in a loop and my thoughts swirling in the kind of delirium I hadn't felt for over ten years. The buzz from the proceedings around the Monopoly board filtered its way into my dreams. I didn't envision passion or sex or even companionship. It was simply that, after all this time, a tiny gap had opened up to show me the possibility of a rich future. An optimistic future. A normal future.

19

I awoke on Boxing Day at Sue's parents' house without that heavy feeling that usually comes after a night of serious eating and drinking. Instead I was buoyant as if somewhere in my dreams I'd broken through the thick walls that had confined me the past eight months. The pain behind my eyes was gone, and my teeth didn't hurt from grinding them in my sleep. It was no doubt partly due to the flirting — the curative powers of unmapped affection.

Overnight it became clear that the worst was behind me. In the eight months since Sue died, I'd felt like I was on a constant downward slope, sliding deeper and deeper into a murky, contorted adaptation of my life. I had worked diligently after Sue's death at trying to manufacture a new life for me and Myles. I still wasn't certain I'd found my footing but when I woke up that morning, I realized that the downward slope had plateaued. If I'd been on skis, I'd be gliding aimlessly along the flatland after barely making a successful descent down the precarious mountain. I knew that with hard work and the help of my son, I would, from this point on, somehow start heading in a positive direction.

But mostly, perhaps inspired by the night before, my delight that morning was due to the recognition of what I had to do. This was going to be the day I buried Sue's ashes. That would appropriately mark this occasion, I decided. If only symbolically.

At breakfast I asked Nancy, George, and Joyce if they would come with me that evening to bury the ashes at the roots of her tree.

"I think it has to be today," I said. "I've held on to them long enough."

They looked at each other as if I'd just suggested robbing a bank.

"I don't know," George said, looking at his wife. "What do you think, dear?"

"I think we'll let you do that on your own," she said. "I think that's more *your* thing."

My *thing*? I didn't think this could be branded a *thing*, let alone *mine*. Wearing jeans and a t-shirt is my *thing*. Pizza and beer is my *thing*. The music of Joe Jackson is definitely my *thing*. But burying Sue's ashes for all eternity was an undertaking I thought we all could have shared in as a family, to honour this moment in post-Sue time and to unite us in our memories. It could, at the very least, be *our* thing.

"What about you, Nance?" I said.

Nancy sat casually against the back of the chair and looked up from her breakfast. Her eyes were sad but not sentimental as she took in an audible breath.

"Yeah, I agree. I think it's your thing. I'll pass, thanks."

I appreciated their honesty, and though I'd sincerely hoped they'd all join me, secretly I was relieved. Since shortly after Sue's tree was planted, my plan had been that her ashes would ultimately rest there, so I was grateful to be allowed to inter Sue on my own. Perhaps it was my thing after all.

Later that morning, Stacy returned with my car. She stayed long enough to chat with Sue's parents about Christmas dinner and thank them again for their hospitality. In the meantime, I packed my bag and sorted out Myles's things before leaving him with his grandparents. I drove Stacy back to her house, recognizing along the way that what had passed between us the night before might actually have been more than just a shadowy reflection in a Christmas hangover. Then I drove back to Toronto to bury my wife.

* * *

At ten o'clock that night, well after dark, I scanned the collection of tools I'd stowed in my backpack to see if I was prepared for my mission: garden spade, claw hammer, flathead screwdriver, keyhole saw, chisel, and anything else I thought might help whittle away at the hard soil. If I'd owned an ice pick, I'm sure I would have packed one. I went back upstairs and changed my clothes, convinced my outfit for this operation should be head-to-toe black. I couldn't be sure if what I was about to do was illegal, immoral, or simply frowned upon. Still, I thought I should try and blend into the shadows, if only for discretion. On the way downstairs, I grabbed Sue from the dresser. I put on my black wool jacket, threw the backpack over my shoulder, and quietly went out the back door to my car. I tossed in the backpack and then carefully strapped Sue into Myles's car seat. Should I encounter a sudden jolt during the ride, I didn't want ashes embedded forever in the loosely woven Toyota upholstery.

I pulled out of my parking spot and into the lane that fed the back of the house. Slowly I drove out to the road, careful to avoid the potholes and the remaining piles of snow, checking to see that my passenger was securely belted in. I turned left onto Keele Street, the main road that headed down toward the lake. Only when I stopped at the first red light did I realize that I hadn't turned my headlights on. My stealth-like preparation and focus on my objective had made me forget the first rule of motoring: safety first.

Having taken the usual west-to-east route along the lakeshore, I arrived fifteen minutes later on Lee Avenue in the Beaches and parked the car halfway between our old apartment and the new tree. I shut off the engine and sat in the dark stillness of the night. On hot summer days, the lakeside boardwalk was the most popular pedestrian thoroughfare in Toronto, and up on Queen Street, one block north, you often could hardly move for all the people. When I got out of the car on this night, the neighbourhood was ghostly quiet. All I could hear were the sleepy Lake Ontario waves treading up the shore and my breath in the icy December air. I unfastened Sue from Myles's seat, pulled out my backpack, and closed the car door. I walked with purpose toward the lake, cradling the container in my left arm, until we reached the young sugar maple, proud and lustrous under the nearby street lamp. Its thin, crooked trunk posed resolutely in the frozen earth like a heroic statue bent only slightly at the knees, its thin arms raised in triumph.

Standing on the boardwalk in front of the tree, I momentarily considered changing my mind. The wall of frozen mist suspended over the shore bore down on me. I looked east into the wind and then west toward the lights of downtown to see if any people were out for a late walk. The coast was clear.

I knelt down, placed the canister on the ground, and removed the small spade from my backpack. One last look around before I plunged the spade into the dirt about twenty centimetres from the tree trunk. The ground was harder than I'd expected; the spade barely made a dent.

There was a *tink-tink* sound like metal on stone. I reached for the hammer instead and tried loosening the dense earth with the claw end. This proved to be more effective. I scooped out the free soil with my other hand. Clawing and scooping like this for two or three minutes, I went down maybe ten centimetres. My heart pounded in anticipation like I was panning for gold. Then I heard voices. I stood up and saw two people and a dog heading my way from the west. I quickly covered the partially dug hole with my backpack and took my cell phone out of my jacket pocket. Pacing slowly in front of the tree, I pretended to be just another late-night Beacher hanging around the boardwalk having a private conversation.

"Yes… Uh-huh. No, no, everything's fine," I said as the people drew even with me, their dog obediently heeling. "I'll be home soon. I just have one more thing to do."

Finally the interlopers passed by and I was left to resume my campaign of digging. But I wondered if I had the fortitude to continue. All of a sudden this seemed like a larger task than I was capable of finishing. Watching the hole in the ground take shape, I saw it as more of a grave than I'd originally considered. Graves are so final, irrevocable. Within them, I had imagined, people disintegrate. They disappear forever. I'd admitted that the worst was behind me and that Sue and I may not have made it, but I didn't want her to vanish.

Switching to autopilot, I picked up the hammer again. Claw. Scoop. Claw. Scoop. I worked quickly, nervously. The ground still resisted like frozen rubber. I had nearly reached what I thought was an acceptable depth when I heard more people coming from the other direction. Backpack over the hole, I stood up and resumed my pantomime with the cellphone.

"Hi, it's me," I said. And suddenly Sue was listening on the other end of the phone. "I'm here now, sweetie … I'm at the tree right now. And you're here with me."

Sue was sitting comfortably in a quiet, warm, white, dare-I-say "heavenly" place, cordless phone in her hand, listening peacefully to my supplication. She wasn't smiling as I'd typically imagined her, but rather she had that serious, stern look she'd get when she was fixed on something critical, something she wasn't quite sure how to manage.

"I need you to steady my hands or whatever it is I need steadying." I wasn't sure what I meant by that. But I'd been diluted. "We can do this together. Can't we? You and me forever … And after we do this, I might be able to move forward, little by little." This was more of a question than a prediction. I'd been so determined to bury her ashes today, but I had no idea what that would mean for tomorrow.

The people passed by, completely ignoring me. I wiped my eyes and looked at the container of ashes sitting at the foot of the tree. Sue told me to keep talking.

"There's so much I want to tell you," I said. "But I'm not sure how. I got confused when Myles and I were on the road because … because … loving you and hating you at the same time is confusing. All of my memories have changed colour. Without you things are … blurry."

I looked toward the lake, the frothy white waves fading to distant black. The cold night burrowed into me under my wool coat, but I'd stopped noticing. I thought of the seven weeks on the road with Myles and the revelations that I wished I'd been able to share with Sue. I wondered if I should confess.

"Everything I've discovered since you left is pulling me in a different direction," I said. "I could have spent the rest

of my life with you, and that would have been fantastic …
but, you know, we might not have made it. We weren't
perfect. I've accepted that. Because that was us."

That was us: imperfectly in love.

"Up on that rock in BC, by Nancy's place…" I didn't
need to fill Sue in on what happened. For the purposes of
this conversation, she knew. "You had a lot of anger when
I nearly fell off the cliff with Myles on my back. And that
really mattered because it wasn't out of character.
Sometimes I deserved your anger but mostly … I think you
just didn't get me."

Where was I going with this? It was one thing to talk to
Jan or Dr. Grief or my sister about what I'd discovered.
But telling Sue directly was a completely different
confession. Because she might have felt the same way.

"I know you still loved me. But I lost pieces of myself
in my effort to please you. I think fighting defined us more
than either of us were prepared to admit. We got it wrong a
lot of the time." I swallowed and took a cleansing breath.
"If you hadn't died … we may still have ended up apart."

Telling Sue how I felt was proof that the thick, aching
emptiness was starting to lift. If she had really been there,
she may have protested as she usually did, but I was in
control of this conversation. She couldn't have changed
my mind this time. I looked up the road toward the
building we lived in a lifetime ago — before we'd moved
away so Sue could chase down her journalism career,
before Myles, before cancer.

"The more I think about it," I said, "the more I believe
you would have found some reason to leave me … and I
wouldn't have had the strength to fight you."

I didn't want to say goodbye. It felt good talking to her
again despite the confession. Eight months earlier as Sue

lay in that hospital bed, I'd said goodbye to her and felt the relief of seeing her out of pain. But now my own pain was lifting without aid, without wondering what she'd think. I'd once tried with all my strength to hang on to every sense of her — to remember her completely. But the complete memory of her now included things I didn't want to hang on to. I'd awoken that morning knowing I'd been holding on to the past for fear of the future. If this telephone conversation was any proof, Sue was giving me her consent to let go.

"Myles reminds me of you," I told her, changing the subject. "He has your smile ... the perfectly formed pointy corners, the same shaped lips ... I can see your happiness in him. He has your beauty."

Sometimes I forgot that we made him, that Sue could be just as proud of him as I was. But then I'd just look at him and inevitably there she was.

"Whatever happens to me from now on, good or bad, it will be because of you. You got me here ... and without you, I'll simply go down some other path than the one you and I would have travelled."

Instead of dreading a future without Sue, I realized I could choose to welcome the opportunities that came my way because of her absence. Some good things could still happen to me. I was thirty-five years old; I still had a lot of life left. Accepting the possibility of a happy future wouldn't mean I'd forgotten the life I'd had with Sue. The good wouldn't negate the bad. They would simply be the two sides of one life.

"I have to do this now. It's time."

Maybe this is what Sue meant by life after death. I might have taken her too literally when she spoke of her beliefs. Because I knew she would always live — in a non-physical sense — within me. My life evolved with her. Before she came along I was an immature, lazy idealist looking for a mate. Sue gave me perspective, energy, wisdom, and love. She forced me to grow up. She gave me a son.

"I am so thankful for having been able to spend this part of my life with you. And wherever you are right now, wherever it is that you believed you would end up, I know you are happy and pain free."

I moved over to the hole completely oblivious to whether or not people were walking by. The cold beach had grown peaceful, composed. I could no longer hear the whispering waves.

"This tree will be here forever and so will you."

I knelt at the hole, the cellphone still at my ear with Sue breathing on the other end. "Okay, I'm going to hang up now ... Here I go."

The calm of night wrapped me in its dark cloak. I looked down at the shadowy hollow I'd mined, pausing in a moment of pseudo-prayer. *There's nothing to fear. Everything's going to be all right.*

"I love you ... Sweet dreams ... Bye."

I put the phone in my jacket pocket, removed the lid from the container, and lifted out the clear plastic bag holding the ashes. I'd never taken it out before. The amount of ashes seemed curiously small, and it weighed less than I'd imagined. A bag of sand the same size would have weighed more. I wondered if all of Sue was in there. My cold hands shook as I fumbled with the knot in the plastic bag. For fear of lingering too long I tore the bag open and tipped it toward the hole in one motion. The little bits of black, grey, and white filled it up like water flowing into a bowl. In the heavy, frozen air no residual ash dust came off the empty bag. She was all out. Without pausing, I put the bag into the empty container that once held Sue and then ladled the cold dirt back over the ashes with my hands. I stood up and packed it down with my feet, firm enough to level the soil but not so firm as to feel I was stomping on her. I surveyed the area, making sure it didn't look like someone had just buried his wife in the roots of the tree dedicated to her.

But it wasn't Sue I buried that night. The Sue I loved was gone the moment she died. What filled that icy hole was a piece of the past I no longer hung on to. Not ignored, just set aside. A past, I'd figured out, that could stay in the past without fear of it extinguishing my future. Eight months of grieving, sadness, hard work, confusion, personal challenges, epiphanies, and loneliness were buried. The tree that sprouted from that struggle stood as a marker in time, resting between what was and what will be.

I packed up my tools and walked back to the car. The icy air filled my lungs and cleared my head. I was certain I was breathing easier than I had been an hour earlier. Before I stepped onto the sidewalk, I passed a Department of Parks regulation garbage can chained to a lamppost. The generic canister that Sue had rested in for the past several months had no more symbolic meaning than anything else she touched. Sue was worth more than what housed her. What had true meaning for me had been left at the roots of the sugar maple next to the boardwalk. The cheap ceramic container landed at the bottom of the garbage can with a thud.

* * *

The next morning I woke up. Because that's what you do. Without ceremony. I lay on my back and looked up at the ceiling. The winter sun pushed through the soft threads of the curtains. My breathing was strangely audible, a faint breeze blowing through my distant thoughts. Back on the beach, I was still kneeling at the foot of Sue's tree, the crisp sound of the lapping waves piercing the still night. I recalled a different shore a few months earlier: the California shore with its ragged cliffs standing at attention. There, as I faced the vast, arching horizon, the lonely sea lion sat larger in its domain than I did in mine. But now my vision was clearer, my heavy heart a bit lighter. I was big again. Inflated by the rushing wind of time. With Sue now permanently and peacefully shaded by her tree, I was assured that the worst was definitely behind me. In my sanctuary-house I mingled with the old and the new. I was the walls, ceiling, and floor; I was the furniture and the doors, comfortable in a shelter of my own design. And I knew that one day I might lift the roof off and fly out to soar above my world, liberated, celebrating all that is good within it.

Everything can change overnight.

I didn't cry that morning. Or the rest of the day either. I've hardly cried at all since the night I spoke with Sue on the phone while kneeling at her tree. My sadness had kept me in tears, and weeping had become a way of keeping me in my sadness. Crying was a welcome and necessary tool in ensuring all of the grief was forced out of me. Eventually, every other sadness would be merely a feeble irritation relative to the sorrow I carried for the first eight months after Sue died.

Only a few days earlier I didn't think this day would ever come. So with my head still on my pillow, I recognized that morning as the beginning of the first day toward finding, what I thought I'd call "the new me." I smiled.

The dark memories that had coloured all the good ones began to fade. We fought; most married couples do. Maybe we would have ended up apart anyway. Maybe not. That mattered less this morning because the only truth I could be obliged to hang on to was the actual truth: Sue was gone. We had ten years and a son together. What if she had never stopped me on the stairs and kissed me at the end of our first date? What if I'd never gone back to our house in Windsor after driving away from that senseless fight? What if she'd lived and my revelation of splitting up had come to pass? Had we gotten divorced, Myles would have had to split his time between his parents. I'd have been only a part-time single dad.

I considered phoning Stacy, not knowing what I'd say or where it might lead, if anywhere. But it didn't matter. My unsure footing was firmer this morning than it was the day before. And tomorrow, with any luck, firmer still. If there were any risk in taking this next step, it would be far less dangerous than running out of gas in Kansas or being chased by a bear in New Mexico or falling off a cliff in British Columbia. Or watching my wife die. I had lived through those things. I could face making a phone call.

Maybe Sue was right. Maybe we were meant to be together. Her steadfast belief in destiny was certainly contagious enough for me to believe it while she was alive. But even if it had been preordained, maybe it was only meant to be for a limited time. She couldn't have predicted her death, but maybe she knew something I didn't.

Sue loved to remind me that "what doesn't kill you makes you stronger." I believe that, but I would add: what kills other people can make you stronger too. In time I'll be stronger. I'll be better. I'll be more attuned to my feelings and more honest with myself about them. I just wish Sue didn't have to die for that to happen. In order to find your equilibrium, sometimes you must first be knocked off balance. Maybe years from now when happiness has completely supplanted grief and I can look back at my life with Sue through the prism of age and perspective, a part of me might actually believe that in a very specific way this was all of some merit. By then, perhaps I'll be able to reflect on the long, dark months of my grief with a sense of satisfaction in having overcome it, my contentment all the greater for having endured the sorrow.

Soon I would get out of bed, eat breakfast, get dressed, and drive to Burlington to collect my son from his grandparents. On the way back we'd ride together in our family vehicle as we did during our seven-week road trip, the three of us. Myles would squint out his window at the still-rising sun, his world passing by him in a dependable rhythm and, like me, he would recognize the light that signifies going home.

Epilogue

What our thoughts have made us

On a midnight ride in the back of a Land Rover bounding over a pothole-infested road somewhere in Nicaragua, I couldn't see anything through the windows except for occasional oncoming headlights. As I tried to prevent my head from hitting the roof of the vehicle, I wondered if this was what it was like being kidnapped. But the tropical temperature felt good on my skin as it melted the sub-freezing Toronto residue. It was two days before Christmas, the year after I buried Sue's ashes.

Through my travel-weary daze, I reached forward to the passenger seat, grabbed Deborah's hand, and stroked her arm. As we neared our destination in the town of Grenada, our driver told us all about what I couldn't see outside, but I wasn't listening. Deborah squeezed my hand in return. The electricity ran up my arm and jolted me into the realization that I was far from home. Far from the treacherous daily routine of single fatherhood. Away from the reminders of my loneliness. I hadn't been kidnapped, of course, but I had been taken away. I was living for the moment. That moment.

Only two weeks earlier I'd been unloading to Deborah in an email. She'd just left her home in London for a three-month sabbatical in Latin America. After Sue died, my old friend from high school got back in touch with me, and we began chatting online. For the past few months we'd been getting closer — if that's the right word to describe a friendship between people who live eight thousand kilometres apart and only communicate in cyberspace — our emails and e-messaging becoming daily practice. After barely negotiating the first Christmas without Sue, the anticipation of another one was becoming too much to consider. I moaned to Deborah:

> *I'm not looking forward to it. It's not even the reminders of Sue — I can handle those. It's having to be with her family and pretending that I'm having a good time. I can't talk about my feelings with them, especially at Christmas. It's not comfortable at all. I guess I'll just have to take the dog out for a walk several times a day.*

I received a short reply:

> *Say "fuck it" to the snow. Say "fuck it" to spooning the dog. Buy a ticket to Nicaragua and come to the sun.*

I stared at her words on my computer screen. Until that moment I'd been feeling like I was wearing clothes that were too small for me. I'd been lost and lonely in a cold, claustrophobic Canadian city. Then suddenly, with her invitation, my world expanded. I could see myself actually tearing off my constricting outer layer and embracing the kind of freedom I had long forgotten existed. All I had to do was buy a plane ticket to Nicaragua and go to the sun. The same sun in whose shadows I had been cloaked over the past twenty months.

I wrote Deborah back right away:

I'm looking into it.

The next day I wrote her again:

I'll arrive on the 23rd.

We shared a bed on the floor of a room overlooking an open-air courtyard. On the wall above us was a window with no glass, out of which we could see the stars. On the other side of the room was an electric fan working hard to keep our sweaty bodies cool. I lay on my back with Deborah to my right.

"I can't believe I'm here," I said.

"Neither can I," she replied.

I had been uncharacteristically impulsive, picking myself up out of the shadows and going into the sun. We thought it was a bubble, a fleeting moment to share, both of us relying on our friendship to see us through some trying times. I still didn't have my feet firmly on the ground, and Deborah had been singing the singles' blues. But the bubble never burst. Before I knew it, I was falling in love with my old friend, and so was she.

When she finished her sabbatical in Brazil, Deborah came through Toronto on her way home to see if what we felt in Nicaragua was still there. Were we excited by the novel and impetuous intimacy, or could our love for each other as friends truly translate into being lovers? I took her for dinner at an Italian eatery near my house. I paid.

"I've missed you," I said, staring into her deep brown eyes.

She smiled. "Are you sure?" She sat with her elbows on the table, her arms visible through the sheer black sleeves of her blouse. She stared back at me, her challenge unwavering.

"You don't believe me?"

"I mean, this was supposed to be a bubble. I just want to be sure … did you miss me? Or did you miss … it?"

With Deborah there was no need to negotiate the awkward months of getting to know each other because we'd been friends since we were fifteen. She didn't see me as damaged goods. Communication flowed with the natural shorthand of shared experiences. In Deborah I saw a woman of intelligence, sincerity, passion, lucidity, and decency. None of that had changed just because we'd slept together. Moreover, I'd promised myself after Sue died that if I were ever to get into another relationship, I would be completely honest from the outset. Honest to her and honest to myself. I didn't want to start the same pattern of behaviour that I'd started with Sue.

"It was you," I said. "I missed you."

She smiled again and gently took my hand across the table. "I missed you too," she said.

That was the exact moment I knew for sure that I'd fallen in love again.

We soon found ourselves talking about a future that included each other. Somehow, somewhere, we would be together.

The next April I left Myles with my mother and took my first trip to Britain to spend a week with Deborah. Three months later, Myles and I spent most of the summer in London, learning what it might be like for the three of us to live together. One mid-July afternoon I stood on Clapham Common in south London under a clear blue sky, the rare English sun hitting me with its spotlight. I'd been playing soccer — footy, as the lads call it — with some of Deborah's friends while she spent the day with Myles, and I knew that this was where I needed to be. Looking around at this welcoming sight, the liberation that I'd been seeking finally revealed itself to me fully. This was where my new life would start.

By the next Christmas, Myles and I had moved to London. Deborah and I were married the following February — Myles wore his Spider-Man costume to our pub reception — and soon after Deborah adopted Myles.

I've often wondered if anyone thought that getting married again within three years of Sue's death was too fast. I certainly don't; those three years felt like ten to me. But I prefer to embrace my good fortune. How many people are lucky enough to say they've genuinely fallen in love twice in their lives? How many children can say they've had two mothers who loved them? Still, I can't help but acknowledge, somewhat deferentially, that my current fortune is only due to having endured the misfortune of Sue's death.

While Deborah ticks some of the same wifely boxes that Sue did — smart, driven, confident, funny, wise — my relationship with her is completely different. I can trust myself to be honest with her because she's known me long enough to recognize who the "honest me" is. I don't fear the instability and volatility Sue and I suffered because I've learned how to be truthful to myself. Most importantly, I don't feel as though I've given up a part of myself to be with her. I've been liberated into being me.

I like to remind myself that this new life — living in London, exciting travel opportunities nearby, and love — would not have been possible without Sue. Her life brought to mine, among other things, wisdom, maturity, and fatherhood. Her death brought me here.

The bond I'd forged with Myles during our road trip and for the first three years of his life has also endured. Even with Deborah, whom Myles calls "Mum," I'm still the primary caregiver and Myles's default parent for school runs, doctors' visits, and soccer practices. He still holds my hand when we walk down the street, and there remains an unspoken understanding between us: with every smile and hug a cryptic nod to what we underwent together. But he no longer depends exclusively on me, and I am not solely responsible for his welfare. For that I am truly thankful.

We are a family again, whole and complete. I'm confident that Myles's future is full of promise for growing up in a house full of love. And so is mine.

SECTION HEADINGS ARE SOURCED FROM THE
FOLLOWING QUOTES:

PROLOGUE:

Though we travel the world over **to find the
beautiful**, we must carry it with us or we find it not.

- Ralph Waldo Emerson

PART I:

Fort my part, I travel not to go anywhere, but to go. I
travel for the travel's sake. **The great affair** is to
move.

- Robert Louis Stevenson

PART II:

The traveler sees what he sees, the tourist sees what
he has come to see.

- Gilbert K. Chesterton

PART III:

The real voyage of discovery consists not in seeking
new landscapes, but in **having new eyes**.

- Marcel Proust

EPILOGUE:

We are **what our thoughts have made us**; so take
care about what you think. Words are secondary.
Thoughts live; they travel far.

- Swami Vivekananda

Songs from the Healing Tour

"Wild West" - Joe Jackson
"Two of Us" - The Beatles
"If I Have to Be Alone" - Todd Rundgren
"Waiting for You" - Seal
"Still Haven't Found What I'm Looking For" - U2
"Hearts and Bones" - Paul Simon
"Waiting for My Real Life to Begin" - Colin Hay
"Dreamline" - Rush
"Come Back to Bed" - John Mayer
"Every Little Thing About You" - Raul Malo
"Next to You" - The Police
"Better Be Home Soon" - Crowded House
"Will You Remember Me?" - Jann Arden
"Darling Lorraine" - Paul Simon
"Alone" - Jacques Brel
"I Think I See the Light" - Cat Stevens
"And So It Goes" - Billy Joel
"Salvation" - Elton John

Acknowledgements

I'm immeasurably grateful to all those who have read all or parts of *Immortal Highway* in its various stages and incarnations. Particularly Maria Black, who illuminated for me the framework in which this narrative should be written. Also Mollie Jeffery, Shannon Fowler, Judith Barrington, and Horatio Clare from the Arvon group at Totleigh Barton. To my colleagues at City University, especially Naturi Thomas, Carol Greenway, Leisha Fullick, Nigel Pickford, Kelly Hearn, Alice Sherwood, and Anne Vaughan, whose insight and empathy all helped shape this memoir. Julie Wheelwright and Sarah Bakewell, who steered me in the right direction. Jeremy Harding, who treated me as a fellow writer and without whose generosity of experience, time, and genuine concern, this project would never have evolved.

To my family, Lainie and Adira Magidsohn, Kristine Magidsohn, Adriane Chalastra, and Selene Chalastra, whose influence on the telling of this story cannot be underestimated. Everyone who hosted Myles and me on our journey: Amy, Jason and Joelle Jackson, Jack Jackson and Kathleen Sullivan, Rob Levine and Hilary Robison, Nancy Westmoreland, and the late Melba Weiner. My sincere appreciation for you all being a part of this crazy adventure called Life.

I'm indebted to all those who contributed to the *Immortal Highway* crowdfunding campaign, with particular mention to Lawrence Aronovitch, Luke Venables, Tara Rao, Jim Hines, Richard Golden, Mik Connolly, Vanessa Cohen,

Shanan Spencer Brown, Lisa Miller, and Anria Loubser for their generosity and support. To Pubslush for granting me the platform to make this book a publishing reality.

Profound thanks to Léonie Cronin for her time and talent, her vision and care during the process of designing the cover image.

Thanks to my editor, Kate Unrau, who simply made this book better. Greg Ioannou and everyone at Iguana Books in Toronto for helping to finally bring this lengthy project to fruition.

Unfathomable love and gratitude to the brilliant, insightful and sometimes patient Deborah Doane, in whose secure embrace I was able to become a writer and complete this memoir. And to Myles for giving me the reason to write this story.

Some edited sections of *Immortal Highway* have been featured in the following online journals and printed publications:

dadzclub.com

Full Grown People, and published in *Full Grown People's Greatest Hits, Volume 1*

Gutsy Living, and published in *My Gutsy Story Anthology, Volume 2*

Mojave River Review

What's Your Story?: 2013 Memoir Anthology (Lifetales Book

Lightning Source UK Ltd.
Milton Keynes UK
UKHW010748260121
377695UK00003B/391

9 781771 801423